re-readings

interior architecture and
the design principles
of remodelling existing buildings

© Graeme Brooker and Sally Stone, 2004

Published by RIBA Enterprises Ltd,
15 Bonhill Street, London EC2P 2EA

ISBN 1 85946 132 8

Product Code 31996

The rights of Graeme Brooker and Sally
Stone to be identified as the Authors of
this Work have been asserted in
accordance with the Copyright, Design
and Patents Act 1988.

British Library Cataloguing in
Publications Data
A catalogue record for this book is
available from the British Library.

Publisher: Steven Cross
Commissioning Editor: Matthew Thompson
Project Editor: Anna Walters
Designed by: Brighten the Corners
Printed and bound by Cambridge Printing,
Cambridge

While every effort has been made to check
the accuracy of the information given in
this book, readers should always make
their own checks. Neither the Authors nor
the Publisher accept any responsibility for
misstatements made in it or
misunderstandings arising from it.

Front cover: Küppersmühle Museum,
Duisburg, Germany
Photographer: Graeme Brooker

Back cover: Museum for Pre- and Early
History, Frankfurt, Germany
Photographer: Graeme Brooker

Contents page: The Baltic Art Factory,
Gateshead, UK
Photographer: Paul Ring

Graeme Brooker and Sally Stone

interior architecture and
the design principles
of remodelling existing buildings

rereadings

RIBA Enterprises

Acknowledgements

Graeme Brooker would like to thank the UWIC Interior Architecture team for their help and insight, to acknowledge the generous contributions made by the UWIC research fund and also to thank the Interior Design team at the Manchester Metropolitan University. In addition, Graeme would like to thank the Haas family for their kind hospitality, in particular Holger for his good company and safe driving while conducting research across Europe and especially to express gratitude to Claire Miles for her help and understanding throughout the project.

Sally Stone would like to acknowledge the contribution made by the Manchester School of Architecture, to thank Jo and Peter Stone, Becky Watson and Yvonne Roberts for their benevolent child care, to Reuben, Ivan and Agnes for being quiet and to Dominic for staying calm.

Both Graeme Brooker and Sally Stone would like to thank Wen-Wei Chen, Dominic Roberts, Siv Senneset, Peter Brough and Paul Ring for various drawings and photographs and Matthew Thompson and Anna Walters for their dedication to the project.

About the authors

Graeme Brooker MA, is a senior lecturer in Interior Design at Manchester Metropolitan University and was until recently a senior lecturer at University of Wales Institute Cardiff.

Sally Stone MA, is a practising designer and a senior lecturer at the Manchester School of Architecture. She teaches a studio course concerned with building re-use and the relationship between interior architecture and installation art.

The Baltic Art Factory,
Gateshead. Ellis
Williams Architects,
2002

Contents

Fig. 1. American Bar
by Adolf Loos,
Vienna, 1907

Fig. 2. The Querini
Stampalia Foundation,
Venice. Carlo Scarpa
1961-63

History of remodelling

Buildings outlast civilisations, they evolve and they are changed, but their reuse emphasises continuity. A building can retain a remembrance of the former function and value; it has a memory of its previous purpose engrained within its very structure. The exploitation and development of this can create a composite of meaning and consequence. The inherent qualities of the place and its surroundings, combined with the anticipation of the future use, produce a multi-layered complexity impossible to replicate in a new building. Louis Kahn once asked: 'What does it want to be?' and it is the purpose of this book to show that the unique answer is hidden within the profundity of the existing building.

Throughout history, buildings have been adapted for new uses; there is really nothing new about the remodelling of a structure to contain a new function. The Roman Arena in Nîmes, France, became a small fortified town in the Middle Ages; the inhabitants resided within the massive arches of the structure and built houses in the open performance space. The Baths of Diocletian in Rome were converted into a church by Michelangelo (Santa Maria degli Angeli) and the Great Mosque in Cordova was remodelled by inserting a new church directly into the middle of its structure. Sir John Soane, who remodelled a pair of town houses in London at the start of the 19th century to house both his family and his extensive collection of art and artefacts, created an extremely dexterous sequence of spaces and environments within a surprisingly small building.

It appeared that the art of remodelling was lost to the dogma of modernism, but this is patently untrue. It has not always been the case that the modernists overlooked the existing. The work of the great architects such as Le Corbusier, Adolf Loos, Ludwig Mies Van De Rohe, Alvar Aalto and Frank Lloyd Wright often made reference to the past without ever reworking existing buildings (with a few notable exceptions such as Le Corbusier's Beistegui apartment in Paris, 1931 and the American Bar by Adolf Loos). Many examples of modern architecture were the product of a formal system that was essentially self-sufficient. Yet this denies the fact that much of its qualities were based on an interpretation of the city, through technology, nature and function, locating modernity as a product of its cultural context. Nevertheless, modern architecture is characterised essentially by the image of the crisp white villa situated in the landscape unfettered by its surroundings (Villa Savoye by Le Corbusier). The emphasis on the development of contextualist and continuous approaches to buildings and urbanism is characterised by later modernists such as Eric Gunnar Asplund, Aldo Rossi, Giancarlo de Carlo, Carlo Scarpa and Giorgio Grassi. Scarpa, who practised almost exclusively in and around the Veneto, is recognised as having developed a constant dialogue with history in his work. This is particularly conspicuous in the designs for the Querini Stampalia Foundation in Venice and the building that is considered to be his masterpiece, the Castelvecchio Museum in Verona. The contribution of these architects to the development of the city and its buildings is based upon the notion that they are objects and places that are to be analysed and then reworked according to their latent

Fig. 3. King Street,
Manchester, by
Holford Associates.
The bank was
retained to become
the foyer for
the new office block
towering behind it

characteristics. This idea is personified by de Carlo who, when reflecting on his career in an interview in 1990, stated;

> I believe a lot in the revelatory capacity of reading...if one is able to interpret the meaning of what has remained engraved, not only does one come to understand when this mark was made and what the motivation behind it was, but one also becomes conscious of how the various events that have left their mark have become layered, how they relate to one another and how, through time, they have set off other events and have woven together our history.[1]

The rise in the number of buildings being remodelled and the gradual acceptance and respectability of the practice is based upon the reaction to what is perceived as the detrimental erosion of the city and its contents by modern architecture. The development of conservation and preservation laws, in America the 1966 Historic Preservation Act and in Britain the Civic Amenities Act of 1967, encouraged authorities to designate conservation areas in cities and towns. The lobbying by many major modernist architects, such as the Smithsons, against the demolition of Euston Arch in London did much to promote the cause of condemned worthy buildings. Today, with the planning authorities desperate to preserve the cultural heritage of a place and avoid the wholesale demolition prevalent in the modernist age, any building over a certain age, however dubious its quality, is considered worthy of conservation and the result is the stultification and overburdening of towns and cities with old buildings, which are retained solely because they are old. Also damaging is the remodelling of a building in such a way as to be a copy or pastiche of the existing in order to fit in or blend in with the context. Another process of doubtful value is the practice of retaining just the façade of a building and constructing behind it a sometimes huge and frequently unsympathetic structure. This gives no dignity to the retained façade and compromises the new building. The city is in danger of becoming little more than a theatre, the real buildings hidden behind the stage sets of the retained façades. Nevertheless, society, especially in the UK, values the old and the picturesque; the ideal of the garden village and the utopian vision of the days long past is still prevalent. This means that the backlash against modernism is the predominant attitude. Just as in the mid-20th century, when Victorian buildings were seen as having little worth, so those constructed during that period of demolition in the 20th century are now being demolished themselves, without consideration for their quality or the possibilities of adaptation. The bus station in Preston, northwest England, is a fine example of a heroic concrete structure built by the BDP Partnership in 1969. The whole area needed re-ordering, but the 2001 masterplan by Terry Farrell Architects proposed demolition, the possibilities of reuse not even being considered by the council. It will be a great loss that will be regretted in the future.

Clarification of the different methods of building conservation

There are a number of different approaches to the problem of the particular attitude to take to the existing building and it is important to distinguish between the different methods used in the conservation of a structure.

Preservation maintains the building in the found state, whether ruinous or not. The building is made safe and any further decay prevented; the ruined condition is important to the historical understanding of the place.

Restoration is the process of returning the condition of the building to its original state and this often involves using materials and techniques of the original period to ensure that the building appears as though it has just been constructed.

Renovation is the process of renewing and updating a building; a palace or large mansion might be adapted for 21st century living but not substantially changed.

Remodelling is the process of wholeheartedly altering a building. The function is the most obvious change, but other alterations may be made to the building itself such as the circulation route, the orientation, the relationships between spaces; additions may be built and other areas may be demolished. This process is sometimes referred to as adaptive reuse, especially in the USA, or as reworking, adaptation, interior architecture or even interior design.

Sometimes two of the methods may be employed in unison; for example, when designing the Sackler Galleries at the Royal Academy in London, Foster Associates ensured that the façades of the original buildings were completely restored before embarking on the remodelling of the space.

The value of remodelling

The reshaping of the city and its contents poses difficult questions of how to re-address the meaning and the value of the existing built fabric. The relationship between the existing and a new remodelling is dependent upon the cultural values attributed to an existing building, by the economics of the project and by the approach of the designer of the new addition. Of the three, the economic factor is the easiest to discern, and it is the most straightforward to establish. Remodelling existing buildings is labour intensive whereas new build tends to be capital expensive. Remodelling is energy saving whereas new build often consumes enormous amounts of energy and resources. Financial incentives and tax breaks are offered for the restoration and adaptation of old buildings.

The cultural value of ordinary buildings can change considerably; for example, until the last decade of the 20th century, city centre buildings in provincial cities in England were considered quite undesirable, businesses preferred to be located out of town, huge shopping centres were constructed on the motorway at the edge of the city and people wanted to live in the suburbs. This position has now virtually reversed, especially in places like Manchester and Leeds, where loft living in the city centre is the height of sophistication, and shops are moving back and so attracting a lot of businesses.

Fig. 4. Preston
Bus Station, NW England.
BDP Partnership, 1969

Fig. 5. The glass staircase leading to the Sackler Galleries, at the Royal Academy, London. Julian Harrap Architects restored the original building before the remodelling by Foster Associates.

In Europe over the last few years, the architectural and the national press have devoted huge amounts of coverage to a series of massive new remodelling projects. In the UK, the Tate Modern in London, a gallery housed in the comprehensively reworked massive Bankside Power Station designed by Sir Giles Gilbert Scott, was extensively described. The Baltic Art Factory, situated within a disused flour mill in Gateshead, Newcastle, was also very well reported, as was the re-roofing of the great court in the British Museum in London, to create an enormous new gallery space and circulation route around Sydney Smirke's magnificent British Library building. These three massive projects demonstrate that the remodelling of the existing is of great cultural value; the adaptation of a building can contribute to the regeneration of an area. In Europe in the 1980s and 1990s, three of President Mitterrand's nine *Grands Projects* involved the remodelling of existing buildings: the Musée d'Orsay, a museum placed within a disused train station, the Grand Louvre pyramid and courtyard, and the reworking of the old abattoirs and gardens to become the Parc de la Villette. The politically loaded gesture that involved relocating the German Parliament back into Berlin, from its pre-unified home in Bonn, significantly rehoused the government in the remodelled Reichstag building. An iconic glass dome signalled the residency. In the last twenty years all of these projects have been undertaken by large and famous architectural practices and so have received massive amounts of coverage in newspapers, journals and books. Has remodelling become so respectable that these prestigious architects are prepared to practise it or have the architects raised its profile?

As well as the perceived value of remodelling significant buildings, the reuse of the insignificant and overlooked is also becoming common practice. The reworking of the odd and strange buildings of the city, often changing their function to something completely different, can now be discerned as a viable architectural consideration. Larger-scale and more unusual projects are being reworked to contain cultural and leisure activities. A flak tower in Vienna, one of a series built to defend the city from Allied bombers during the Second World War and with walls that are between two and seven metres thick, is in the process of becoming a new gallery for the MAK Museum of Modern Art in Vienna, Austria. The Thyssen steelwork plant in Duisburg, Germany is now the host to many groups and clubs using the open-air cinema, the diving club in the old water cooler towers and the park created out of the contaminated land. Ramblers roam between the massive blast furnace towers and over the surrounding industrial landscape of slag heaps, coke and ore storage bunkers. The old pump house in Wapping, London, has become an elegant restaurant and art-space among the hydraulics and pumps that previously served London's buildings with power and heat.

As people become more interested in the value and culture of living in the city centre, so warehouses, offices and department stores are being converted. The Smithfield Building, a magnificent Edwardian structure in the Northern Quarter, just off the centre of Manchester, was originally constructed to hold the Affleck and Brown store. During the 20th century, it underwent a number of transformations from the British Home Stores to the Affleck's Palace. Stephenson Bell Architects converted the whole building, in the year 2000, into 80 loft apartments with very swanky shops on the ground floor. It would appear that among many of the major projects featured in the pages of architectural press, remodelling is an ever more meaningful way of making new space in our increasingly congested cities.

The book

Re-readings is based not upon the proposed or consequential function of a remodelled building, but upon an understanding of the theoretical method of the interpretation and adaptation employed by the architect or designer. The book proposes an analysis and, from that, a catalogue of the relationship between the existing building and the new elements of the remodelling. The premise is that to establish a satisfactory symbiotic association between the new and the old, the factors influencing the condition of the existing need to be comprehended and an appreciation of why a particular approach was taken has to be established. As one might expect, because the architect or designer is not dealing with a greenfield site, indeed not even considering a cleared site, the existing building in whatever form influences the outcome of the final design. This appreciation will inevitably affect the approach taken by the architect or designer and ultimately the look of the ensuing building. The form of the existing building and the form of the resultant are inexorably linked.

This process can be broken down into a number of different stages, although in practice the separate factors inevitably merge. The formal act of designing is not necessarily a smooth procession of independent considerations. Precedent is used as the basis of the investigation. Each chapter discusses a particular aspect of the process and the argument is reinforced by illustrated case studies. The chapters are subdivided to provide greater clarity of argument.

Fig. 7. The British Museum, London. Remodelled 2000, Foster Associates.

Analysis

As Christine Boyer observes:

The name of a city's streets and squares, the gaps in its very plan and physical form, its local monuments and celebrations, remain as traces and ruins of their former selves. They are tokens or hieroglyphs from the past to be literally re-read, re-analysed, and reworked over time.[2]

The form of the adaptation must be based on the form of the original building. Without an in-depth understanding of the unique qualities of the existing situation, it is impossible to create a coherent and comfortable remodelling. The analysis is divided into four sections; each approaches the existing building differently and discusses a particular yet influential aspect. The Form and Structure of the existing building are often the easiest aspects to understand: how the building stands up, whether it has a distinct rhythm or order and what the relationships between the rooms and spaces are like. The Historical and Functional factors can sometimes be more elusive. The previous use of the building and what has happened to it are very important, but how can that influence the outcome of the redesign? The analysis of the Context and Environment of the existing building establishes relationships between the site, its neighbours and occasionally things further away, and also discusses the influence that climate can have upon the adaptation. Without an understanding of the requirements of the Proposed Function, it is difficult to appreciate whether a relationship with the original building can be established.

Strategy

This chapter examines the specific strategies employed in the reuse of buildings. The approach or the plan for the building is influenced or based upon the factors discovered within the analysis of the place. The three types of strategy are classified according to the intimacy of the relationship between the old and the new. If the existing building is so transformed that it can no longer viably exist independently and the nature of the remodelling is such that the old and new are completely intertwined, then the category is intervention. If a new autonomous element, the dimensions of which are completely dictated by those of the existing, that is, it is built to fit, is placed within the confines of the existing, then the category is insertion. The final classification, that of installation, includes examples in which the old and the new exist independently. The new elements are placed within the boundaries of the building. The design or the grouping of these elements may be influenced by the existing, but the fit is not exact and should the elements be removed then the building would revert to its original state.

Tactics

This chapter could be subtitled 'the detail' or even 'the elements'. It takes a closer look at the methods by which strategies are realised. The tactics express the very qualities of the building, what it looks like, how it sounds, what it feels like. For example, a strategically placed wall can manifest itself in many different ways; the materials that it is made from depend upon its situation, the expectations of the client and the whim of the architect. There are six categories of tactics introduced in this chapter and each section discusses a different type of tactical element and how it has been deployed.

Planes are normally either horizontal or vertical and can be used to organise and separate space. The category is sub-divided into the wall, the floor, the façade and the soffit. Object discusses elements such as furniture or larger-scale things that can provide a focus or a rhythm to a space. The articulation of light and the effect of both natural and artificial light can radically transform a building. Surface is the use of specific materials to confer identity and meaning. Movement refers to circulation and Opening describes how physical and visual relationships can be established between places and things.

Case Studies

The final chapter is dedicated to the in-depth analysis of six significant examples of remodelled buildings. The principles discussed within the earlier chapters are applied to each of them and the analysis and explanation will confirm the reputation of both the building and the architects.

Today, remodelling represents a sizeable market that cannot be ignored. The evidence of big name architectural firms involved in reworking buildings is testimony to the fact that it is a sector of design and architecture that is no longer seen as insignificant. It is important to establish the principles of working with the existing in order to define this field of practice, to demonstrate that this area of work is rich in creative inspiration and packed with some of the best design work of recent years. *Re-readings* is an attempt to prove that the remodelling and adaptation of building can be based upon a sound analysis and a theoretical approach.

Chapter One
Analysis

Introduction

**Previous pages:
Cathedral Museum,
Lucca, Italy. Pietro
Carlo Pellegrini**

Analysis
Introduction

Buildings are remodelled,
reused, rethought
and yet a suggestion
of the former meaning
disturbs and inspires
the subsequent design.

The reading or re-reading of a building provides the principles or basis of the argument for the remodelling of a specific place. This understanding can generate the strategy and tactics of the redesign.

Rodolfo Machado uses the palimpsest or overwriting as a metaphor for building reuse; the text of the manuscript has been scraped off and the canvas or parchment used again, but inevitably a trace of the original text remains, a shadow that haunts and influences the author of the succeeding inscription. And so with buildings: they are remodelled, reused, rethought and yet a suggestion of the former meaning disturbs and inspires the subsequent design and it is this search for meaning that is the basis of the analytical chapter. As Rodolfo Machado describes it:

Remodelling is a process of providing a balance between the past and the future. In the process of remodelling the past takes on a greater significance because it, itself, is the material to be altered and reshaped. The past provides the already written, the marked 'canvas' on which each successive remodelling will find its own place. Thus the past becomes a 'package of sense', of built up meaning to be accepted (maintained), transformed or suppressed (refused).[1]

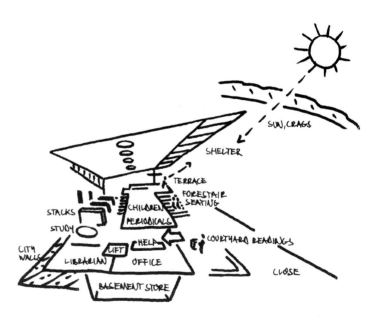

Fig.1. Malcolm Fraser
Architects subjected
the site to a thorough
analysis before
embarking upon the
design of the Scottish
Poetry Library

The most successful building reuse projects are produced when a firm understanding of the original building is combined with a sympathetic remodelling. The existing context, structure, spaces, function and history can offer many significant conceptual opportunities and an appreciation and interpretation of these can provide the inspiration for the redesign. The uncovering of the meaning in the precondition of the building determines the rules or strategies for the subsequent redesign.

The analysis may be as simple as an awareness of the orientation of the building, so that sunlight can be admitted into a particular area of a building or a relationship established with a landmark or entrance. Or perhaps the complexities and the history of the existing building need to be explored to unravel and uncover its intricacies and depth.

An understanding of the site provided much of the stimulation for the design of the Scottish Poetry Library in Edinburgh. It is situated next to the city walls in an area that is a real historical composite, incorporating a 16th century gable end, a fragment of the 17th century city wall and the end of a 19th century warehouse. Malcolm Fraser Architects' small insertion snuggles gently against this amalgamation of history; it is almost buried within parts of the old city walls, the existing eyelets actually lighting the bookshelves, and yet the topography of the site allows the library to open out and provides views of distant hills. A book is selected within the dark depths of the building and is taken into the light to be read. These strong heavy city walls also support the structural steel frame of the

Fig. 2. The form and orientation of the Scottish Poetry Library in Edinburgh reflect its context

new building. The architects have simultaneously created
a relationship between the history, the structure and the landscape.
There is an ability for the building to nestle up to history on one side
and to open up to the crags and the sun on the other.[2]

This chapter is divided into four sections, each discussing
a particular aspect of building analysis; inevitably in reality these
analyses all combine to provide a rich context for the remodelling.
Without an appreciation of the basic structural system employed
to construct the building it is, of course, impossible to be confident
that any alterations will stand up! This knowledge will allow the
architect to make alterations to the original building and ensure that
any new constructions are adequately supported. The mass, the size,
the rhythm and the form of the building all provide opportunities
for balance or for counterpoint.

The memory of the building can be written on its walls, its history
pathetically exposed or deeply suppressed. The original function
for which the building was designed may have dictated a ridiculous
and particular organisation of quality of spaces or forms.
A building may have been used and reused a number of times.
There are many interesting and valuable inspirational factors that
make up the history of a site.

A building occupies a specific place. It has its own identity and
a distinct relationship with its surroundings, involving not just its
immediate neighbours but also things more remote. The perception,
the character and scale of a particular building or place can be
influenced by its context. It is just a small element within a huge
collage of different points and references.

The successful marriage of old and new, of past and future is
dependent upon a thorough knowledge or anticipation of what is
expected. The nature of the proposed function for the building
inevitably has a massive influence upon the final design.

Analysis
Form and Structure

The mass, the size, the rhythm and the form of the building all provide opportunities for balance or counter points.

The house is a question of materials. Its walls, floors and roof are questions of suitability, which part supports, which is supported, which does neither one nor the other. [3]

Traditionally there are two basic types of structure, load-bearing and framed, and these produce distinctly different types of space. Masonry walls are thick heavy structures with a limited span that tend to close space down and create smallish rooms, while frames can allow an enormous span and create free space. (There are of course other methods of construction; the 21st century has brought Liebeskind's fractals and Gehry's computer-generated building of the model and Future Systems' monocoque constructions, all of which have renounced the traditional walls and roof architecture.)

The frame or column allows an uninterrupted floor plane and thus a free plan. This frame, whether steel, concrete or timber, is usually based upon the Cartesian model, the same series of repeated elements in a grid formation. Once the walls and the floors are separated from the structure and they have only themselves to support, the choice of their position and materials is almost unlimited. Consequently, the extent of any remodelling is restricted only by the respect for the frame. The construction of the exterior walls is usually limited by concerns of environmental control, admission of light and weathering ability; the interior divisions have even fewer restrictions. The most appropriate materials in the circumstances can be used and these can be almost anything in any combination, glass, metal panels, timber, plastic, stone, water or even steam.

Fig.1. The bomb damaged Altes Pinakothek was reconstructed using the proportion and rhythm of the original and yet still provides a clear contrast

Load-bearing masonry structures are quite the opposite. The walls are built up layer by layer from the ground and as they are raised they support themselves and other elements, such as floors, staircases and roofs. The length of the element that spans across these walls limits the size of the spaces that these constructions create.

The choice of constructional materials is inevitably restricted, stone, brick and concrete blocks generally being used, as these are able to withstand the enormous compacting pressure. Changes that are made to these types of constructions again have to respect the integrity of the structure, and any sculpting or reordering of the spaces or structure has to be compensated for.

Whatever the structural system, a rhythm of repeated elements to the form of the building is often created. This rhythm may be related to the position of the windows, the change in cladding material or the proportions of the spaces. It was an appreciation of this that led Hans Dollgast to the sensitive interpretation and reconstruction of the bombed Altes Pinakothek museum in Munich after the Second World War. It was considered to be 'one of the most valuable examples of the modern museum type that had been established in 19th century Europe' and was designed by Leo von Klenze in the Roman High Renaissance style.[4] Dollgast based the remodelling on a contemporary interpretation of the classical façade, the rhythm and proportions were respected and the scarring of the bomb was visible but there is no doubt about the difference between the old and the new.

**Fig. 2. The scar where
the new meets the old
can be clearly seen**

Fig.1. The rational
structure of the Kodak
Factory was very
obvious before
remodelling

Fig. 2. The 'new office'
organisation of the
advertising studio is
informed by the
original Kodak Building

CAWLEY NEA \ TBWA Advertising Agency Offices

Location: **Dublin**
Previous Function: **Kodak Factory**
Remodelled: **1998**
Architect: **Paul Keogh Architects**

Paul Keogh Architects have a reputation for the sensitive approach that they take to architecture, for both new building and remodelling. They were key members of Group 91, the collaboration of architects responsible for the successful regeneration of the Temple Bar area of Dublin. Although not part of that project, the remodelling of the Kodak Factory underlined their perceptive attitude of thoroughly reading and understanding the building before embarking upon any changes.

The listed Kodak factory building was constructed from a riveted steel frame clad in a rendered block skin. The frame created great order within the building and this formed the basis of the redesign. The grid system occupied three bays across the width of the building; this enabled the architects to raise a half-curved roof over the central section. The non-curving north face of the roof was glazed to allow not just ample natural light to penetrate into the building, but also views across the rooftops of south Dublin. A mezzanine was slipped in under this higher level thus creating a number of different atmospheres within the ostensibly open plan office.

The austere and mechanical qualities of the original Kodak building suggested that the remodelling should also contain those simple and industrial characteristics. At the front of the remodelled building are private meeting rooms and at the back are the kitchen and toilets, the rest of the office being organised according to the three-part system of the building. The north side provides individual workstations, the desks laid out in rows and set at a diagonal to provide more space. This formation deters a lot of personal interaction because the workers need relative privacy to concentrate, but conversation, especially on the telephone, gives this area a quiet buzz. On the south side of the building there is a much more creative atmosphere. The desks are situated around the edge of the bright crimson space. The large open area in the centre encourages interaction and thus creativity. Below the mezzanine are individual rooms to accommodate noisy activities such as the photocopiers, the back-up for the computers and the table football machine, or activities that require quiet and concentration, such as the library and the very silent still room. The mezzanine is a different type of space altogether. The raising up, the high levels of natural light and the view give the serene feeling of being apart from the general bustle of the main office and up here are settees and coffee tables, the informal atmosphere encouraging other types of interaction.

The advertising designer clients are very receptive to the notion of the 'new office', the idea that rather than sit in a particular place within the office building, a person might occupy the specific space most suitable for the individual activity that they are completing. The principle of the 'new office' is well applied; creativity is not an individual activity and interaction is, indeed, very valuable and necessary. Within the strict order of the existing building, a variety of working spaces are created, whether across the football table, over coffee on the relaxing chairs on the mezzanine level, within the crimson creative space or the intense privacy of the library.

The gridded order behind the white art deco façade of the original building provided a framework that encourages great freedom and creativity.

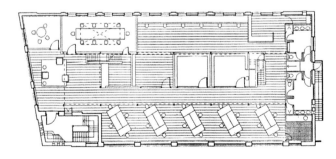

Fig. 3. Plan of the building. The new elements fit very closely to the pattern of the original

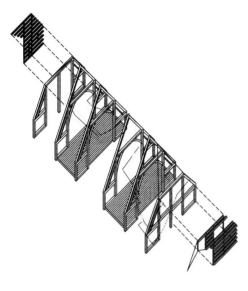

Fig.1. The barn is ordered by timber trusses with the new elements slipped between them

Fig. 2. The ground floor is relatively free, the balconies defining the position of the activities

Pheasant Barn

Location: **Faversham, Kent**
Previous Function: **Threshing Barn**
Remodelled: **2000**
Architect: **Circus**

A large pheasant barn nestling in the Kent landscape was converted into a family home. The clients found the derelict barn and were enchanted by its qualities.

A dark cavernous space with occasional openings to the fabric, giving surprise glimpse views and stark shafts of light.[5]

The 17th century, Grade II-listed building was constructed as an aisled barn with open trusses. The exterior was clad with horizontal weatherboarding and on the interior walls, the infill panels between the exposed structure were painted white. The timber trusses divided the inside into five equal bays and supported a huge tiled roof. The admission of natural light was severely limited and the building contained the unusual feature of a pit.

The listing requirements of the building meant that the exterior had to retain the appearance of a 17th century barn, so the architects concentrated on creating a radical juxtaposing interior. To achieve this they inserted two enormous organic floating balcony structures into the interior space. These elements control the position of the various activities on the ground floor and enclose the private spaces on the upper mezzanine level. As designer Nigel Hetherington states:

New elements are inserted – aligned to the various functions of a dwelling that hug, warp and fold around the constricting timber structure, bringing alive the strong geometry and encouraging movement through the space …The mezzanines come somewhere in-between: gravitating around the main timber aisle posts, their more free form composition aims to create localised intimacy within the larger free flowing space and articulate a visual interplay between line, plane and texture.[6]

In the remodelled form the whole of the ground floor is open: the kitchen, dining area, lounge and bedroom sit relatively freely in the space. The existing pit is reused as a sunken seating area using the only natural opening in the building to give spectacular and specific views of the countryside.

The soffits of the mezzanine elements dictate the positions of the various zones downstairs; at the upper level they contain the bedrooms, dressing area, bathrooms and a study. These white organically shaped floating rooms take most of their support from columns hidden within the structure of the existing building. To avoid any movement of the balcony edges, supplementary support is supplied by a series of stainless steel rods that transfer weight to the existing timber structure. This complex system avoids placing any new load on the open trusses.

Removing the wattle and daub infill from the sidewalls and glazing the timber frame solved the problem of the lack of natural light. This creates a dynamic space with extremely atmospheric lighting, which contains two huge, slightly ephemeral forms. All these are juxtaposed against the order, age and rhythm of the timber structure of the existing barn.

The new form of the interior of the barn is indirectly influenced by the existing form and structure of the old. The rigid timber frame acts as counterpoint to the fluidity of the new elements, even lending some structural support. The undersides of the mezzanines enclose space and offer a startling sequence of experiences, from intimacy to the openness of the full height of the barn.

Fig.1. The Netherlands Pavilion, showing each floor treated differently

Netherlands Pavilion, Expo 2000

Location: **Hanover, Germany**
Date: **2000**
Architect: **MVRDV**

The pavilion was the Dutch contribution to the Expo 2000 in Hanover. The building, as designed, had an extremely limited lifespan, just the duration of the exhibition. The structure, however, was destined to be reused; the whole site was designed to be converted into a business park upon the completion of the Exposition.

'Holland Creates Space' was the theme of the pavilion; the concept was to show the ability of the Dutch to make optimum use of their limited available space. It was literally a series of different landscapes stacked one upon another; this was intended to symbolise the close connection between the Dutch landscape and its architecture.

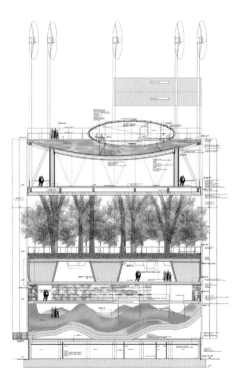

Fig. 2. Section showing the layers of Dutch landscape inserted between the structural supports

The structure was nearly 40 m high and contained six exhibition levels, each over 1000 sq m of floor space. About 90 per cent of this floor space was available for exhibition use, the rest being necessary for circulation and other services. The architects intended the visitor to take the lift to the very top of the building, then perambulate down through the various levels and landscapes to exit at the ground floor.

Each of the floors represented a different aspect of the Dutch landscape. At the top was a floor of windmills, pools and grasses; the floor below contained a theatre and below that was a forest of oak trees, planted in a thick layer of soil. A waterfall linked these floors. The first floor level featured a field of flowers divided by plasma screens decorated with oversized bumble bees. The ground level was a cave of shops and information and the basement contained the café and other services.

The 'free plan' provided the architects with an opportunity to insert almost anything they wanted into each level. The structural elements were relatively unobtrusive apart from those in the forested area, where the angled columns were literally huge tree trunks. The objects placed into the building were autonomous; they were not restricted by anything other than the absolute proportions of the building. The concept of placing a living landscape within a tiered structure had been proposed by the radical American architects SITE in the early 1980s with a series of projects called Highrise of Homes. This project was a response to unimaginative design of many blocks of flats and the idea was for a collage of architectural elements to be inserted, by individuals, into a structural matrix. Each family group could choose not only the space, but also the type of building and plants that represented their personality.

This pavilion may at first seem an odd inclusion in a book about building reuse, but its relevance is not in the remodelling of the simple framed structure but in the use of the frame as a blank canvas in which to impose the concept of the architects and the country.

Fig.1. Basement gallery.
The arches inform the
position of the
exhibition display

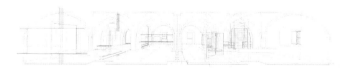

Fig. 2. Section
perspective
through the
basement gallery

Museum of Fine Arts

Location: **Caceres, Spain**
Previous Function: **Castle, Houses**
Remodelled: **1988-1993**
Architect: **Maria Jose Aranguren, Jose Gonzalez Gallegos**

The Museum is located in three small converted buildings, La Casa De Las Veletas, La Casa de Caballos, and a small restoration workshop. The origins of the two main museum buildings are not exactly known but in a chequered history they formed part of the defences of Caceres and in Moorish times they held the water supply for the town. This was contained in impressive vaulted basement space that can still be viewed today.

Although the main buildings were converted in the late 1980s, the remodelling of the restoration workshop, which was sunk into the ground behind the retaining wall of the façade of the Casa de Caballos building, was made much later.

La Casa De Las Veletas building was left unaltered and was subjected to only minor restoration. However, the Casa De Caballos building, a three-storey masonry construction located to the south of the site, was extensively remodelled to contain the service areas on the ground floor and two exhibition spaces on the floors below and above. The sloping position meant that the outer wall required three large masonry buttresses to support and brace it. These buttresses exposed the rhythm of the interior space, which was divided into vaults supported by extremely thick brick columns.

The original structural system divides the basement and ground floor into a system of four by three bays. Because the building is partially underground, the access of natural light into these areas is restricted. The first floor, at the top of the building, is much more open. The masonry columns are more slender and natural light enters this level from all four sides. The lowest basement is very shallow, the rock that the building sits on prevents it from being the full width at this point.

The heaviness of the masonry construction and its dominant scale and proportions determined the way in which the building was remodelled. The architect's strategy was to counterpoint the dominance of the masonry structure with a series of ephemeral installations.

A lightweight steel, glass and panel exhibition system, highlighted by spotlights attached to catenary wires, displays the works of art; the curve of the arch of each vault is carefully followed by the new display system. The exhibition panels become lighter and freer as they rise through the building, and so on the first floor, where the system is constructed from slender steel rods and fine mesh. The staircase, carved from the innermost space of the building, occupies the enclosed area between the edge of the building and the site itself. A lightweight staircase inserted within the space rises up towards the light, linking all three floors.

The structural integrity of the masonry building severely restricted the possibilities of reuse, but these limitations led to a creative and subtle response.

Fig. 3. The new steel and timber stair inserted into just one bay of the Museum of Fine Arts, contrasts with the rough masonry of the original building

Fig.1. The enigmatic
brushed aluminium
elements, which
appear to have been
extruded from the
floor, glow from within

Fig. 2. The juxtaposition
of new curves against
the old rectilinear
structure engenders
interest and delight

Restaurant

Location: **Pompidou Centre, Paris, France**
Previous Function: **Cafeteria**
Remodelled: **1997**
Architect: **Dominique Jakob and Brendan Macfarlane**

The renovation of the sixth floor Pompidou cafeteria formed part of the two-year renovation of the Piano and Rogers' ground-breaking building of 1977. The daunting task of creating a dining space for over 200 people in one of the most famous and arguably radical structures of the 20th century led the architects to develop an unusual strategy.

When we first visited the site we were completely scared, we had two reactions – to search for something we could work with, or freak out and not do the project.[7]

The architect's analysis of the structure revealed that the whole building was based upon a 800 mm x 800 mm grid. Every element within it conformed to this fundamental pattern right up to the primary structure, which was spaced at centres of 12.80 m. Another important and influential factor was the thinness of the floor slabs, a mere 140 mm, hardly sufficient to support anything substantial, and therefore any proposed structural loads had to be lightweight and evenly distributed. The building was covered by a number of preservation orders; the distinctive trademark red, blue and green colours of the HVAC ducts in the ceiling could not be touched, and neither could the two glass screens at the front and side of the space, nor the only solid walls in the room.

From this analysis of the structure and other constraints, the architects concluded that the only possible strategy was to distribute a series of lightweight structures across the floor.

A brushed aluminium, floating floor informed by the grid was laid over the existing slab and then four huge elements were installed that appeared to grow from the new floor. In the remodelling, these large elements, completely out of proportion with the space and the grid, hold the key service spaces for the restaurant. They are large, moulded, stretched, computer-modelled objects and the exterior of each pod is clad in panels of brushed aluminium, the same material as the floor. The inside of each, however, appropriates the multi-coloured character of the Centre and is lined with a distinct coloured rubber floor and wall: red for dining, yellow for the bar, grey for the kitchen and green for the cloakroom and toilets. Around the elements, a landscape of seats and tables provides accommodation for the diners and affords views out over Paris.

The architects appreciated from the start that if they were not to be overawed, they had to design something radical. The new floor uses the nature of the grid but distorts it to create something completely contradictory to the original intention of the existing building; the design of the organic forms contrasts with the rigidity of the unrelenting structural logic of the Pompidou Centre.

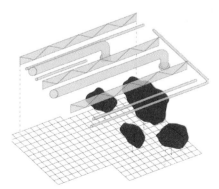

Fig. 3. The four organic elements deliberately counterpoint the rigid grid of the original building

**Fig.1. The Gothenburg
Law Courts' exterior
interprets the
proportions and
rhythm of the original
building**

Gothenburg Law Courts

Location: **Gothenburg, Sweden**
Previous Function: **Law Courts**
Remodelled: **1934-37**
Architect: **Erik Gunnar Asplund**

The conversion and extension of Gothenburg Law Courts is regarded as one of Asplund's masterpieces. The reinterpretation of the neo-classical building is considered to be a key point in the evolution of modernism and is especially relevant at the beginning of the 21st century when modernism is now considered to be part of a continuum rather than a completely new style.

The law courts are located in the centre of old Gothenburg, its principal elevation facing onto Gustaf Adolf Square. The building had already undergone a number of alterations and extensions before Asplund won the competition to extend it. Nicodemus Tessin constructed a neo-classical stone building in 1672 to replace the timber law courts of 1624. The building was substantially rebuilt in 1732 after a fire and B. W. Carlberg added an upper storey between 1814 and 1817.

Although Asplund won the competition in 1913, the construction work was delayed until the mid-1930s – which was just about the same amount of time that the committee for rebuilding, which was formed in 1886, needed to announce the competition. Asplund used the time productively and his design for the building changed considerably. The initial design was in a National Romantic style that transformed the existing building completely. This was followed by a succession of schemes that slowly accepted the classicism of the old building while expressing the new addition in a rigorous yet sensitively modernist style.

The rhythm and complexity of the new façade are drawn from the form of the existing building. The height of the building, its formal proportions, floor levels, and scale, are all taken from this analysis and understanding. The new façade shows deference to the original; a recess separates the two and the windows are all positioned to the left-hand side of the grid and thus appear to look towards the main entrance, which is in the centre of the original building. The colour scheme of the original building is replicated, white for structure and yellow for infill, and the important rooms on the first floor have enlarged windows with decorated reliefs above. Asplund contained the courtyard within the building, thus completing the great composition. He concerned himself with the detailed design of every aspect of the building, right down to the furniture, carpets and lighting.

The new building could not exist independently and while there are many differences between the old and the new in style, method of construction and distribution of space, Asplund's extension makes and interprets many references from the existing. The form of the new is based upon the form of the old. As Peter Blundell Jones comments:

At Gothenburg, Asplund tied together old and new in such a subtle way that each profits from the other: the old building is actually better for the experience and the new one cannot live without it.[8]

MPV (Multi Purpose Venue)

Location: **Leeds, England**
Previous Function: **Railway Viaduct**
Remodelled: **2001**
Architect: **Union North**

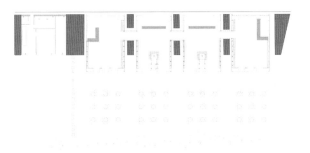

Fig.1. Units are linked through an existing jack-arch in the viaduct piers

Underneath the arches of the main trans-Pennine railway are four extraordinary bright red structures. Just a kilometre from the city centre the unusually shaped steel boxes have transported the nightlife of Leeds into the 21st century.

Lance Routh, architect, Union North, explains:

> We aimed for a response which would achieve maximum contrast between the existing structure, which we weren't allowed to alter, and the new intervention.[9]

The four interlinked huge steel boxes form a nightclub venue and hold bars, dance floors and supporting activities. The boxes were prefabricated off-site by Merseyside shipbuilders, and were constructed like boats. A series of rolled steel sections were clad with steel plates and then transported to the site on a convoy of huge lorries escorted along the motorway by a fleet of police.

The dimensions of the masonry viaduct with the connecting jack-arches in each pier determined the precise size and form of the club structures. They were built to fit exactly into the voids. The pods are linked through arched openings built into each pier of the viaduct, making four spaces in one venue. The pods protrude slightly from their solid homes and the fronts rise up like garage doors, exposing the interior to the outside. Inside, each box is lined with timber and the seating and the bars are richly detailed in oak and upholstered with black leather.

The form of the original structure led to a particularly individual and extreme response. The possible problems of water ingress and sound transfer are solved by the construction of the self-sufficient pods, which, although they express the language of the present day, are built to a similar robustness as the original structure.

Fig. 2. The MPV sits within the arches of the masonry viaduct

Fig. 3. Each element opens up to reveal the bar and club inside

Alexander McQueen

Location: **Conduit Street, London**
Built: **Early 18th century**
Remodelled: **1999**
Architect: **Azman Owens Architects**

The fashion designer Alexander McQueen is renowned for his extraordinarily sculptural clothes and the inventive cutting techniques that he uses to realise them. It was important that his shop portrayed these two vital aspects of his work and communicated his intrinsic creativity.

The shop was carved from a late 17th century Grade II-listed building with a modern extension. It was inserted into the odd, very long thin space, some 32 m in length. The entrance was shared with access to the accommodation above, thus reducing the window area to about 4 m, while the rest of the shop opened up to a still narrow 6 m.

The form of the original building influenced the form of the new interior. The direction pursued by the designers was to accentuate the length of the space, then to break it up with a series of long thin installed elements.

A glass display protrudes from the shop window like a translucent catwalk, presenting a line of mannequins to the street. At the front of the shop a long steel counter slides through the space linking front and back. This contains an indented glass display case for jewellery and other accessories. The next architectural event is the bulk of the changing rooms and staff facilities attached to the side wall. Finally, a centrally placed display system dominates the rear of the shop. It consists of a steel frame that supports a collection of large-scale photographic images. The panels can rotate or slide across the frame, thus reducing or further extending the length of the space.

The form of the existing space provided the direction for the remodelling. The reading of the slender space encouraged the architects to accentuate and exaggerate it. The series of elements installed throughout the length ensures that the journey is delightful. Form follows form.

Fig.1. View from the counter into the shop

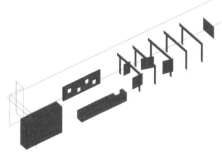

Fig. 2. The long thin space populated by long thin forms. The reception, window display case and side wall all link the excessive space together

History and Function

'To live is to leave traces.'

– Walter Benjamin [10]

Buildings change over time; they can evolve, grow or be reduced in size. Their function can alter, as can the prevailing attitude towards them. This narrative of change is sometimes hidden, and sometimes it is written upon the very walls of the building itself. When remodelling the Reichstag in Berlin, Foster Associates, in an attempt to come to terms with the history and nature of the building, preserved the shell and bullet marks on the walls made by the Russian soldiers during the Second World War.

Carlo Scarpa really is the grand master of the historical reading of a site. The understanding and interpretation exhibited in the remodelling of the Castelvecchio in Verona set a benchmark for all future building reuse. As Sergio Los comments:

With selective digs and creative demolitions, Scarpa attempted to isolate and uncover the various historical strata of the complex. He attempted to untangle the intricate remains of the various eras of construction so as to make the building itself one giant artefact or find, whose various phases of expansion and structural modifications were revealed by the various phases of restoration. More than a theory of restoration, he was interested in historic clarity, so that history might become recognisable through the orderly coexistence of the various fragments. [11]

The previous function of the building will of course have had an enormous influence upon its redesign, whether a factory with huge open spaces and even natural north light, or a house with domestic-scale rooms and windows. The building's function will have dictated many factors in the building: the quality of the light, the ceiling height, the size of the rooms and the windows and, of course, the relationships between the internal spaces. These factors pre-exist within the site and inevitably influence the remodelling, although Paul Robbrecht of Robbrecht and Daem Architects believes that the conversion process is so harsh and it is so difficult to balance the reality of the space as found against the project dynamics that he advocates a process of 'denial of the purpose for which the building was originally conceived, of the life that formerly went on inside it'. [12]

Redundant elements or structures are valuable reminders of the previous activities. Architects Wilkinson Eyre transformed the disused Templeborough Steelworks in Rotherham, England, into a science adventure centre. The Magna Centre, winner of the 2001 Stirling Prize, is littered with relics of its former use. Steel-making plant was treated like industrial archaeology, enormous gantry cranes, hoppers and smelting cauldrons became museum exhibits and among all this detritus the architects installed four immaculate pavilions to house the ancillary activities.

Fig.1. Scarpa's approach to the Castelvecchio set the benchmark for all future building reuse

A considerably less extreme example is the quite simple changes made to the windows of the Church of St Peter in Prague. As the acceptable style of the era changed, so the original Gothic windows were altered. New windows were imposed over the old, the stone mullions still visible beneath the new cill. The layers of reuse and thus the history of the building are clear to see.

The process of weathering marks a building. The rain, the sun, the wind will all contribute to the staining, the erosion, the attrition that a building receives. 'Buildings are single substantial structures that can be demolished by men or nature or both in time. In architecture the gradual destruction of buildings by nature in time is weathering'.[13] But these corrosive factors equally can improve a place; they can be seen as romantic. The value that is attributed to the old or ancient is actually enhanced by signs of wear. An architect may regard the rustic qualities as a charming counterpoint to any new additions, the stained weathering balancing the pristine newness. Many architects control the manner in which the building ages; some of the later work of Le Corbusier for example was deliberately given a very rough finish both to hide and to incorporate the anticipated staining. Weathering is a reminder that a building is ever-changing and that time is passing.

The visible presence of the past is a valuable tool in the transformation of a building and rather than acting as a constraining factor, it can be an instrument of liberation.

Fig. 2. Remnants of the Gothic church are exposed underneath the later Renaissance windows

Museum of Contemporary Art

Location: **Rivoli, Turin, Italy**
Previous Function: **Picture Gallery, Chateau de Rivoli**
Remodelled: **1978-1998**
Architect: **Andrea Bruno**

To the west of Turin lies the town of Rivoli, the home of the Savoy family who built an elegant chateau there in the 18th century. This was one of a series of palaces planned around the city to demonstrate their wealth and power. The hilltop site chosen for the chateau had been occupied many times before. The architect Fillipo Juvarra built the chateau on top of the ruins of a 17th century palace that had been constructed over the remains of a 16th century castle, which, in turn, had been built upon the existing medieval fortifications. The layered site read like a palimpsest, a compaction of the layers of history, with building built on top of building.

Juvarra abruptly stopped work in 1727, leaving only one half of the building complete. The massive chateau lay half-finished, the arches of the planned great hall only partially built. Rather than completely clearing the site prior to the start of construction, Juvarra had demolished the 17th century palace as and when necessary, with the consequence that when the work stopped, a number of the existing buildings were still standing. Therefore, half of the site consisted of Juvarra's palace for the Savoys and the other half, the previous building. This was a long,

thin picture gallery built for Charles Emmanuel I, the previous occupant, who had a vast collection of paintings. This unusual volume of space – 140 m long by only 7m wide and four storeys high – had provided Charles with an environment in which he could gaze at his paintings and survey the surrounding landscape.

In the early 1970s the Turin based architect, Andrea Bruno, was commissioned to transform the building into the Museum of Contemporary Art. Bruno's immediate response was to piece together meticulously the convoluted history and layers of the site. For many years the buildings had been neglected; they had been used as a barracks and as a car mechanics' garage and had also suffered many unsympathetic additions.

From an analysis of the existing, Bruno formulated an approach based upon the distinction between the disparate layers of history. He selectively demolished insensitive additions and accretions, in particular a bridge that had been added to span the junction between the two buildings, and then proposed a strategy of restoration and minimal intervention. The history of the building was so unusual that it stood as

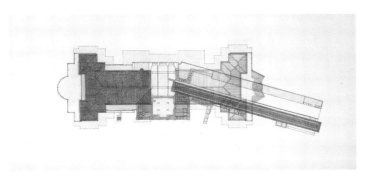

Fig.1. Bruno's drawing shows the layers of the history of the site

Fig. 2. Aerial view of the museum clearly showing the difference between the chateau and long picture gallery

Fig. 3. The steel and glass stair installed into the position of the original grand staircase

a monument to itself: a half-completed building. Bruno overlaid a drawing of the Juvarra building as it would have been when completed on top of a plan of the still intact long gallery. The drawing reveals the site's layers of the history and the completely disparate nature of the two buildings.

Bruno made careful interventions in order to facilitate new functions. The older long thin building was used to house the temporary exhibitions and the half-finished chateau, the permanent collection. A modern steel vault was constructed over the long wing. This roof emphasises and exaggerates the linear nature of the building and echoes the qualities of the original element.

Movement through the chateau and the long wing was particularly inadequate. Juvarra's plans for a grand stair that ascended into the great hall were never realised. The long thin wing was not intended to be a public building and therefore the vertical circulation through it was wholly insufficient for an art gallery. In the event Bruno placed a staircase on the outside so as not to compromise the interior space. The contemporary design of the steel and glass cubes that contain the staircase expressed another layer of history on the site. Within the void left by the original staircase in the chateau, an equally uncompromising element of vertical circulation was placed. The original incomplete staircase by Juvarra was discovered and exposed in order to contrast with the new steel and glass intervention. The rooms of the residence had been extensively decorated by contemporaries of Juvarra such as Somasso, Randoni, Minei and Van Loo. Bruno researched the richness and extent of the decoration and wherever possible it was left intact to act as a powerful backdrop to the pieces of modern art. Bruno resisted any temptation to join the wing and the unfinished chateau and instead celebrated the difference. Bruno built a small viewing platform high up on the façade of the chateau that cantilevers out into the space. It affords visitors a view across the site, allowing them to make their own connection between the different buildings.

**Fig.1. The new and old
simply co-exist**

**Fig. 2. Main gallery
space showing
the sunken display
'trenches'**

Museum of the First World War

Location: **Peronne, France**
Previous Function: **Castle**
Remodelled: **1992**
Architect: **Henri Ciriani**

The northern French town of Peronne is situated at the edge of the Somme, one of the most evocatively tragic places connected with World War One. It formed one end of the 30 km long front line where for five months in 1916 over a million soldiers lost their lives. There are many deeply moving cemeteries and memorials in this area, but this is the first museum dedicated to the First World War, specifically concentrating upon the Battle of the Somme. The intention of the museum was to develop a narrative based upon the five major periods of the War; the build-up to war, the first two years, the Somme, the Armistice, and the aftermath.

The Musée de la Grande Guerre was built in and around the ruins of the stronghold of the 13th century Castle of Peronne. The castle was always strategically important and was subject to many attacks since its construction. Indeed, the mass of the low-set round-towered castle was progressively reinforced, especially in the 16th and 17th centuries, to become a thick-set robust fortification.

The newly created museum is divided into two parts; the first reuses the 13th century castle with its massively thick rampart walls and moat, and connected to it is the other part, a new building next to the river Somme.

Ciriani uses the unaltered ruins of the castle as an entrance to the museum, with a footbridge laid across the now dry moat and leading directly to the heart of the castle, the inner courtyard. From here, the visitor gets the first glimpses of the main parts of the museum in the new extension. The new concrete elements simply stand next to the castle ruins. The visitor passes through the courtyard, ascends a ramp and enters through the mass of the thick walls into the new building.

Everything began with the site ... We wanted to develop the contact between the castle and our new building neither by contrast nor by integration, but simply by allowing the two architectures to coexist – the castle by its physical presence, with its hill-like weight and mass, with our light and almost fragile building beside it, playing on the notion of transition from one to the other.[14]

The extension, which is linked to the castle by a partially glazed bridge, is a horizontally emphasised series of top-lit volumes raised on pilotis and clad in fair-faced concrete. The procession of the interior is organised around the five themes of the exhibition. There are four distinct rooms and an auditorium space, which shows film footage of 'The Battle of the Somme'. The clever exhibition displays are placed in cabinets lining the walls of the gallery spaces. Other exhibits such as guns and uniforms are placed chillingly in recesses in the floor, evoking trenches and graves, and disturbingly remind the visitor of the scale of the tragic loss of life in the War.

The existing building provides the architect with an evocative symbol to open the exhibition and from which to counterpoint the tranquillity of the new building. The intrusion of the museum and the awful memory of the place now provides a balance with the 13th century castle.

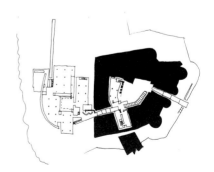

**Fig. 3. The thick walls
of the fort
contrast with the
slender structure
of the museum**

**Fig.1. The new addition
has been slotted
into the centre
of the old flour mill**

The Baltic Art Factory

Location: **Gateshead, England**
Previous Function: **Flour Mill**
Remodelled: **2002**
Architect: **Ellis Williams Architects**

The Baltic Flour Mill is a magnificent building on the south bank of the river Tyne in Gateshead. It is symbolic of the area's industrial heritage and cultural future. A new gallery was slotted into the existing mill and the facilities distributed among seven new floor levels (including mezzanines) to provide accommodation for exhibitions, artists' studios, restaurants, bookshops, rehearsal spaces, auditoria and all administration requirements.

The local council and the architect were anxious that the exterior view of the building should not be compromised by the new gallery. The majestic presence should be retained; both the form of the building and the huge lettering high up on the side walls were an explicit indication of its previous function. Even the new name, 'Baltic Art Factory', refers to its former function.

The original function of the building had dictated its design and, even though holding and distributing flour presented a very different set of requirements to that of holding and displaying art, the building proved to be very suitable for converting into an art gallery. The mill was constructed as a series of concrete shafts or silos, which,

with the four towers, one on each corner, provided the structural stability of the building. Ellis Williams intended that new floors would brace the building, but the silos had to be demolished first, ironically rendering the building unstable. The architects, in collaboration with the structural engineers Atelier One, came up with an ingenious solution. A temporary space frame was wrapped around the building to stabilise and support it while the interior structure was removed.

There were three months between the completion of this process and the commencement of the new construction. During this time Anish Kapoor, one of the foremost British contemporary artists, built a huge tensile art installation, a bright red fabric horizontal hourglass-like structure that stretched through the whole of the interior void.

The corner towers were retained for vertical circulation and columns were inset from the perimeter walls to provide unbroken interior space. New beams were then slung across the space to support the floors.

The architects made a number of other massive interventions. The two short ends of the building were glazed to provide natural light and a view; a huge movable Teflon sail was attached to the eastern elevation to block the direct sunlight when necessary; a floating box was positioned on the roof to hold the restaurant and throw light into the gallery below; and a single-storey wave-like curving structure was constructed immediately in front of the building to provide an entrance area. The massive and quite brutal form of the existing building called for an equally brave approach from the architects. Dominic Williams explained this position:

The main aim of the project is to allow contemporary art to happen in whatever form it takes …The original function of the building was to collect, contain and distribute flour through the unseen workings of the silos. In a similar way the artworks will come, be created and move on, the functionless secret between its sheer walls.[15]

Fig. 2. The glass and steel insertion is a counterpoint to the masonry flanks of the host building

**Fig.1. The entrance
to the archive bursts
out of the corner
of the building**

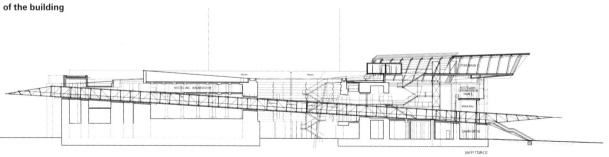

**Fig. 2. Long section of
remodelled building
showing new
circulation cutting
through it**

Centre for the Documentation of the Third Reich

Location: **Nuremberg, Germany**
Previous Function: **Kongresshalle**
Remodelled: **2002**
Architect: **Günther Domenig**

Nuremburg has confronted the uncomfortable nature of its recent history by the remodelling of the Nazi Kongresshalle. Some 80 per cent of the city was destroyed by Allied bombing during the Second World War and nearly all of it was quickly reconstructed after the War, much of it using the original bricks. But it took fifty years for a solution to be found to the problem of what to do with the massive Kongresshalle.

By virtue of its position in the German psyche as a city of great tradition, Nuremberg was in 1933 officially designated the 'City of Congresses', a privilege that entitled it to host the greatest gatherings of the Nazi Party. The great Nazi architect Albert Speer was responsible for the planning and development of a stadium for 400,000 spectators, parade grounds, Zeppelin fields, halls, barracks and other structures to house these spectacular shows. The site was linked to the centre of the town by a two kilometre long avenue. The centrepiece of the master plan was the Kongresshalle, designed by Ludwig Ruff, with his son Franz. It was a massive horseshoe-shaped auditorium intended to house 50,000 party officials. It was more than 275 m wide by 265 m deep, the colossal size and shape being an appropriately monumental backdrop for the huge rallies held there. The hall suffered from structural problems caused by the marshy ground that it was built upon, the heaviness of the granite cladding and the sheer weight and size of the roof. It was never completed.

The building had been vacant since 1945. A number of different uses were considered, some more ludicrous than others; a sports stadium, rehearsal rooms for the Nuremburg Orchestra, an exhibition and trade fair site and even a shopping centre. It was declared a national monument in 1973. Günther Domenig won the competition to remodel the Kongresshalle to accommodate the Documentation Centre in 1998. The building is so huge that this project only occupies a small proportion of it, the rectangular court-yarded hall to the north of the main semi-circular buildings. The Centre was designed to contain exhibitions, lecture rooms, film studios and workshops, the purpose of which was to provide a documentation of the events that took place in the city specifically focusing upon the Party Rally Grounds.

Domenig made a direct statement of intent which symbolised the new use. He inserted a dynamic diagonal element directly against the grain of the original orthogonal building, beginning as an entrance in the most northerly corner of the structure, brutally cutting through the rooms and the courtyard to emerge into the massive open space in the centre of the horseshoe building. This blade-like element lacerates the space to create a circulation route through the building.

The remodelling is deliberately uncompromising as this was not the time or the place for sensitive reappraisals and careful installations. The form of the new directly counterpoints the old, making a bold proclamation about the history of the building and its relationship with the new function. The heavy masonry of the fabric of the Kongresshalle is literally cut away to accommodate the insertion. The end of the shard opens out to form an entrance for the museum. Inside it links a series of rooms, which were originally intended as the meeting chambers and offices of the party and now form the exhibition spaces and the documentation archive. The 130 m by 1.8 m wide corridor is inclined, rising through the space until it shoots into the main central arena of the hall. Here the objective of the original architects becomes shockingly apparent as the enormity of the hall impresses itself upon the viewer. Domenig's intentions are to counteract, heighten and expose the existing building:

I used oblique lines against the existing symmetry and its ideological significance. To contrast the heaviness of the concrete, brick and granite I turned to lighter materials: glass, steel and aluminium. The historic walls are left in their original state without ever being touched by the new work.[16]

Domenig has undermined the potent symbolism of the scale and orthogonal geometry of the existing building with a savage slice through it, making a powerful statement that is at once honest and unambiguous.

**Fig.1. Yellow Verner
Panton chairs contrast
with the raw backdrop**

The Wapping Project

Location: **Wapping, London**
Previous Function: **Hydraulic Power station**
Remodelled: **2000**
Architect: **Shed 54**

The Wapping Project is a gallery and restaurant that was installed into a disused hydraulic power station in East London. The existing building consisted of a main turbine hall and boiler house. The turbine hall is Grade II listed and still contains the original pumps, turbines and piping from the 1890s. This meant that any changes had to preserve the qualities and elements of the original building, even the 186 miles of pipes used to pump water to the parts of the city that required hydraulic power had to be left in situ. The boiler house was a large empty space. Joshua Wright of Shed 54 explains:

> The Building had a life of its own, it had been added to, chopped about and changed throughout its history. We picked up on that idea. I'm just making another small input into the life of a building, which will be around long, long after I am gone. I was not trying to match what was already there, I just wanted to make sympathetic intrusions into the existing spaces.[17]

The unusual qualities of the existing building ensured that the remodelling of the space derived its dominant characteristics from its past use. The designers realised that the best strategy was to do very little with the actual building, to leave the raw and industrial character intact. The turbine hall was retained in its rough and ready state with the turbines, pumps, dials and switches kept in place. Around these the restaurant was installed with bright yellow Verner Panton chairs that complement the olive green engines. The kitchen is housed behind a sleek stainless steel screen, which contrasts with the rusted steel of the environment. Graphic artists Frost Design appropriated the typeface and design of the machine labels and instructions and printed them onto glass display screens, which were then positioned around the room. In the boiler house the clear space was used as a gallery. A new staircase, which drops into the room from the adjoining turbine hall corridor, is finished in steel and is hung from the roof.

In its remodelled form the space of the new gallery shares close links with the past, a continuity that creates an intense dialogue between old and new. The retained objects of the power station and the installed elements of the restaurant quite simply exist side-by-side.

Fig. 2. The restaurant is placed among the relics of the former pumping station

Fig.1. Interior with
Sleeping Maid
and her Mistress
('The Idle Servant'),
Nicolaes Maes, 1655.
National Gallery,
London

Analysis
Context and Environment

A building occupies
a specific space.
It is but a small element
within a huge collage
of different points and
references.

Gordon Cullen in *Townscape* describes the drama that is created by the rapport and the weaving together of the elements that make up the city as the 'art of relationship'.[18] The individual buildings in cities are not regarded as isolated figures but as small elements within a constantly evolving state, a complex situation that is affected by many factors including cultural systems, context, history and time.

The possible impact created by a specific building among a collage or collection of other structures can be far greater than if positioned in isolation. Cullen cites the example of the impact that a large building can have within a built-up area. The qualities of a big building standing on its own can be assessed in terms of size, colour and intricacy, but if that big building is placed in among smaller buildings the scale becomes apparent. The sheer size of the building is made obvious by the relationship and comparison between the two scales. Instead of just being a tower, it actually towers. Cullen regards the city as much more than the sum of its parts; the intricate interrelation of the disparate elements of the city generates a place of stimulation and excitement, 'a city is a dramatic event in the environment'.[19]

There are a number of influential contextual factors that can be investigated and considered, and the uncovered clues can stimulate the design process. The patterns of streets, lanes, roads, intersections and squares around the specific site of a redevelopment may have evolved over thousands of years. The position of the streets may have been dictated by the field patterns and these in turn by even earlier trade routes and paths. The streets may have been built as part of an 18th century grand plan, or emerged amid 19th century industrial squalor or created as part of some modernist 20th century utopian town-planning exercise. The street itself may be a major trunk road or a minor back lane. It may be a principal link between one important edifice and another or a quiet cul-de-sac. It may accommodate a varied collection of different activities, set within a dense culturally diverse area, or perhaps a parade of identical units.

Opportunities for counterpoint or adoration can be provided by an important monument or landmark, a relationship established over great distance, or a dramatic view that can be acknowledged.

The topography can be influential, too. Perhaps a sloping site can provide the opportunity for surprising vistas from the building or the introduction of vertical relationships within it.

If the building is in a temperate northern climate, it may be specifically orientated so that the major areas catch as much sunlight as possible, while in a hotter climate those important spaces need to face away from that direct heat. The consideration of the beauty or the timing of the morning or evening light can influence design decisions.

The quality of light can also differ enormously depending upon the latitude of the site. The very long and narrow domestic spaces so evocatively depicted in the 17th century paintings of the great Dutch artists such as de Hooch or Maes could only have evolved in a northern country. Here, with the winter sun low in the sky, light can penetrate well into the depths of these extraordinary houses. The light quality is quite different in a far northerly or far southerly position to a place closer to the equator, where it is of course stronger, higher and more direct.

The weather can influence the design of a building; it may be necessary to shade areas from direct sunlight perhaps because of too much solar gain or maybe because of delicate objects that need protection. Shelter may be needed from rain or even harsher conditions or perhaps from an unforgiving wind blowing from a particular direction.

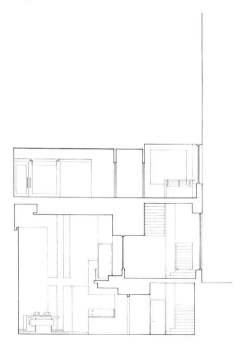

Fig. 2. Section cut through building exposing spaces for contemplation and worship in the Church of Christ Scientist, Manchester, England. OMI Architects.

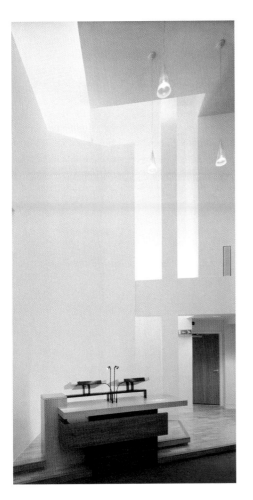

Fig. 3. The light-filled double-height chapel of the Church of Christ Scientist, carved from the formally dark and oppressive office space

The building that is to be remodelled is also part of its own context. The quality of the individual spaces, the relationship of one room with another and of each floor with the one below or above, the positions of the doors, the windows and the circulation areas all contribute to the intricate composition of the existing building. For example, OMI architects carved the Church of Christ Scientist from the innermost spaces of a disused office block in Manchester, England. This atmospheric triple height space is subtly lit from large west-facing windows. The long evening sun glows through the circulation areas to provide the congregation with secondary yet evocative light. This is reinforced by artificial light secreted behind structural openings, and thus the chapel is radiant with hidden luminosity. A tiny reading room was inserted into the barely double height space of the reception area and bookshop. This clever little structure contains bookshelves and a service desk at the lower level and a quiet retreat above. The reading of the interior spaces of the original building provided the catalyst for the organisation of the remodelling.

Colin Rowe and Fred Koetter describe the city as 'a didactic instrument' [20], that is, a place in which a desirable discourse can be formulated, and it is through these investigations that the evidence for the argument of redesign is collected. The reading and understanding of the message of the city or of the individual building provides the basis for the discussion and eventual agreement that is the process of remodelling.

The uncovering and examination of the contextual evidence can reveal and influence the remodelling design direction of the existing spaces and structures, allowing a place to emerge which sits dynamically and appropriately within its environment.

Fig.1. 1° 2° 3° 4°,
Robert Irwin
(1992)

Date: **1985**
Artist: **Robert Irwin**

Mae West, speaking of some small town in the USA, quipped: 'There is no there there!' Many years later Robert Irwin retorted: 'There is no there there until you see there there!'

Robert Irwin is an artist who works with places or environments and from this he has developed a theory of aesthetic perception. In 1985, he produced his seminal discourse, 'Being and Circumstance: Notes Towards a Confidential Art', that defined the relationship of sculpture to its setting. His theory was rooted in the idea that the sheer amount of integration between the work of art and its setting could be quantified and thus classified. He suggested that there were four classifications: site-dominant, site-adjusted, site-specific and site-conditioned/determined. Each category described a greater integration of art and context. Site-dominant discussed works of art conceived and constructed in the studio with absolutely no thought or idea of the final position of the piece, while at the other extreme, site-conditioned/determined examined art that was totally integrated with its site. It was this final category that he advocated and practised in his own work.

Site conditioned/determined. Here the sculptural response draws all its cues (reasons for being) from its surroundings. This requires the process to begin with a intimate, hands on reading of the site...[21]

Irwin divided the examination and analysis of a place into two parts. The first, classified as environmental, was to look at the changes that occurred in the site while the art was being viewed. This took into account things like the changing light, seasons and number of people. The second part, classified as contextual, looked minutely at the place that the art was situated within, that is, other buildings, scale, uses, distance, organisation systems, historical lineage etc. Irwin believes that art is not seen in a vacuum; that the appreciation of the viewer is inevitably influenced by the position that the work of art is placed in. It is comprehended differently depending on its position, whether inside a national gallery or a provincial gallery, within a municipal park or an urban square, inside someone's home or in a scruffy warehouse. It is impossible to divorce the perception and appreciation of a work of art from its context.

Irwin explored the notion of art and place within his own work. In a series of installations he attempted to make the actual site into the work of art, by heightening the viewer's perception of the place. By supplying the viewer with a number of cues to the very nature of a particular place, the viewer would be more acutely aware of its qualities, and appreciate and notice what might very well have been overlooked. The many installations, although they all followed the same intellectual process, were different because they evolved from the character of the space.

1° 2° 3° 4° (1992), an installation at the Pace Gallery in New York, heightened the perception of the space of the gallery with the use of scrim, colour and natural light. Scrim is a gauze-like material that Irwin discovered being used as window coverings in Amsterdam in 1970. In the new installation, stretched screens of it arrested the focal length of the eye and the semi-transparency of the material made it very difficult for the viewer to judge the position of the screen and the location of elements behind it. 1° 2° 3° 4° used several screens of scrim with coloured panels stretched in front of the windows of the gallery. The installation made the actual dimensions of the space seem unclear – it was difficult to determine where the room stopped. The changing quality of light gave the screens an ephemeral quality that is naturally transferred into the space.

As Robert Irwin discussed within the discourse 'Being and Circumstance', '...[he] seeks to discover and value the potential for experiencing beauty in everything'[22]

Fig.1. The openings
cut into the structure
and the intervention
unite the three buildings

Cathedral Museum

Location: **Lucca, Italy**
Previous function: **House, Church, and Storehouse**
Remodelled: **1993**
Architect: **Pietro Carlo Pellegrini**

Lucca is a characteristically dense Italian city, a slowly evolving collection of historical layers and volumes. It is the provincial capital and is set inside a thick swathe of Renaissance walls. The street pattern is almost entirely medieval. To form the Museo Della Cattedrale, three quite different but adjacent buildings were remodelled: a 13th century tower house, a 16th century church and a group of 17th century storehouses with a courtyard garden. The three together formed an L-shaped plot, next to and dominated by the Cathedral of San Martino.

Pellegrini's approach was to retain the integrity of each building, and to preserve its character while imposing a new function upon the series of internal spaces. The exteriors of the buildings were restored, repaired and cleaned, and all were covered with the same off-white render. Although they could still be read as individual buildings, this had the effect of uniting them. Internally, the spaces were restored and the plaster or decoration was removed to reveal the pure surface of the brick walls.

Openings were made between the buildings to create connections but without destroying the nature of each. This generated a number of different types of space; rooms of great intimacy, rooms with open natural light, big bright spaces and dark enclosed ones, not unlike the city itself, which is made up of spaces of diverse and distinct qualities. New elements of steel, glass and timber were placed within the collection of places and these contrasted with the strong solid walls of the existing buildings and served to tie the different spaces together.

The newly created museum is entered through the 13th century town house from the narrow alley next to the Cathedral. The new contrasting elements define the somewhat convoluted circulation route but the contemporary apertures linking the original building provide views of the complete space and allow light to penetrate through the museum.

Pellegrini was determined that the new museum should be part of its developing context, that the remodelling should not stand out or distinctly juxtapose against the existing grain of the city, but should exist as a sympathetic and appropriate late 20th century layer of evolution.

Fig. 2. The three façades of the buildings facing the Piazza Antelminelli

**Fig.1. The library
inhabits the old
courtyard**

The University Library

Location: **Eichstatt, Germany**
Previous function: **Ulmer Hof**
Remodelled: **1990**
Architect: **Karl-Josef Schattner**

Eichstatt is a small town near Munich in southern Germany set in the valley of the river Altmuhl. Since its foundation it had been a Bishopric and was the seat of Bavarian Prince-Bishops. The importance of the town had always been ecclesiastical; hence it suffered greatly in the Thirty Years War. Indeed, two thirds of the town was razed to the ground in 1634. Rebuilding the town was placed under the guidance of three Italian architects, Jakob Engel, Gabriel Gabrieli, and Maurizio Pedetti. They retained the medieval plan but the new buildings were Baroque in style.

Karl-Josef Schattner had lived and worked in Eichstatt for over thirty years. He has been responsible for the repair, reworking and the expansion of the urban fabric of the town and has guided the developments needed for the city to acknowledge the modern way of life in a way that is sensitive to the scale and context of the existing place. Schattner used the existing structures and spaces to anchor new interventions into the fabric of the city. Through the rehabilitation of the existing and the grafting on of new elements, Eichstatt became a city that was reworked to create a close connection between old and new. Gilberto Botti explains:

Unusual and in some ways unique circumstances define the background out of which the work of Karl-Josef Schattner has emerged … Within it, and with admirable constancy and care, a work of slow but continuous mutation … retracing the thread of structure, reinterpreting some outstanding stages in it in terms of new uses and proposing new perceptions.[23]

The recent architectural developments of Eichstatt were centred around the development of the Catholic University. The College of Theology and Pedagogy was expanded in the mid-1970s and transformed into the University, now accommodating over 3000 students – almost a quarter of the population of Eichstatt. The College was neatly inserted into a courtyard between existing buildings. Its orientation and entrance are articulated through the close rapport with the neighbouring Baroque Sommerresidenz (which Schattner also restored and remodelled) and in particular its Hofgarten. While respecting this relationship between the new and the old, the College building is a stark new modern addition that addresses the formal symmetry of the gardens and buildings that it faces.

The new Institutes for Psychology and Journalism are located in Maurizio Pedetti's 1758 Baroque orphanage, a striking building organised as two separate houses each accommodating either the boys or the girls. Schattner's design reworks the gap between the two and stitches the buildings together. The new University Library is housed in the old Ulmer Hof. The main reading room inhabits what was once the central open-air courtyard.

Schattner's work is based on an understanding of the context in which he is working. His circumstances allow him to concentrate on the redevelopment of the whole town. The contextual knowledge and appreciation he has built up gives him an intimate awareness of every aspect of the place, however small, and this appreciation has developed into a simple, appropriate and yet modern interpretation in the new building.

Fig. 2. Ground floor
view through the
arches

Fig.1. The museum
basement. The new
arches rise respectfully
among the ruins
of the old Roman
settlement

Museo Nacional de Arte Romano

Location: **Merida, Spain**
Previous Function: **Roman Town**
Remodelled: **1985**
Architect: **Rafael Moneo**

The Emperor Augustus founded Merida in 25BC and so much attention was bestowed on it that it soon became the capital of Lusitania. The Romans created huge monuments there and these are probably now the best-preserved remains in Spain. The whole town of Merida was built upon these Roman ruins, the ancient buildings lying beneath the foundations of the modern buildings.

A new building, the National Museum of Roman Art, is constructed like the rest of the town directly upon ruins. The basement is so deep that it exposes these ruins, where they have been left in situ, becoming an archaeological investigation, while the modern building climbs carefully over them. The Museum is in the town centre adjacent to the ruins of the great Roman amphitheatre and the outstanding theatre built by Agrippa in 24BC. The majesty of the Roman monuments is balanced by the striking presence of the new museum. This relationship visually connects them while a tunnel physically links them.

This huge and uncompromising museum is constructed from Roman bricks. The rational building is based upon a series of strong parallel walls, all of which contain arched openings. These elements are built as the Romans would have built them; they are of a similar scale and made with similar materials. The walls, a metre thick in the basement and half a metre elsewhere, are built from unreinforced concrete within a brick skin and the openings are of course constructed as Roman arches. The floors are 20th century, made from thin slabs of reinforced concrete edged with a steel balustrade.

In the basement among the uncovered Roman remains, Moneo reduces the impact of the rigid rhythm of the walls by constructing them as a series of arches marching through the underground space. It is extraordinary that, although the grid of the ancient and that of the modern building are actually diametrically opposed to each other, the relationship is remarkably sympathetic. Occasionally the succession of columns and arches breaks or skips with a larger arch to allow a particularly precious relic to be exposed. Peter Buchanan comments:

The logic and virtues of the approach may be debatable but the poetic consequences are powerful. It is made clear that the ruins are not just part of the Museum but continue beneath the earth in all directions.[24]

The important history of the place led Moneo to design a building that not only preserves and exhibits Roman remains, but also expresses the very same qualities of Roman architecture.

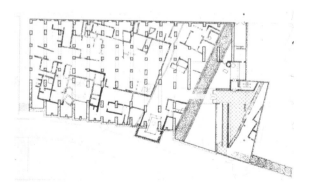

Fig. 3. The structure of the new building steps across the grain of the old Roman town

**Fig.1. The glass and
steel cupola rising
above the Reichstag**

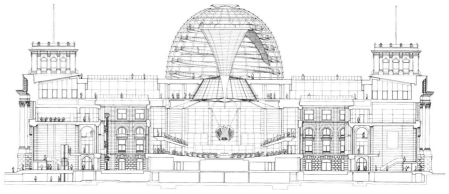

**Fig. 2. Section through
the building showing
the chamber and the
new dome. The movable
screen is to the right
inside the dome**

Reichstag

Location: **Berlin, Germany**
Previous function: **Parliamentary building**
Remodelled: **1999**
Architect: **Foster Associates**

The Reichstag, the building in which the legislative assembly of Germany meets, was built by the Frankfurt architect Paul Wallot between 1884 and 1894. It was constructed in an Italianate or Neo-Renaissance style and the winning competition design showed a cupola over the debating chamber, a design feature which changed dimension over the course of construction but remained – much to the consternation of the Emperor – perched on top of the building when complete.
The building was severely damaged twice during its turbulent history; once by a fire in 1933 and then by the advancing Red Army at the end of the Second World War. In 1954 the damaged cupola was dismantled. In 1961 Paul Baumgarten won the competition to repair and reconstruct the Reichstag. The work finished in 1971 but the building remained obsolete and unusable due to the political climate of the time. After reunification in 1989 an architectural competition was held to remodel the Reichstag in order to house the new German Bundestag. This was won by Foster Associates.

Their proposal for remodelling reinstated the cupola as a symbolic glass dome rising from the ruins of the Reichstag building. It was positioned directly over the debating chamber and contained a spiral ramp that allowed visitors to travel to the top of the dome and see down into the chamber and then to travel back down in a continuous journey, a metaphor for democracy.

Foster Associates, while creating an element of great symbolic quality, had also created a massive environmental problem; the transparency of glass in the new dome would allow the heat of the sun to penetrate into the space, causing it to overheat. The huge glass dome has massive problems of solar gain, yet to cover the glass with louvres or screens would have severely diminished the view out over the city and its emblematic impact. To counteract this, Foster Associates developed a movable louvre screen that attaches to the edge of the ramp and slides around the dome in response to the movement of the sun, thus in effect projecting a shadow of itself into the great chamber. This is supplemented by the stack effect of the natural upward movement of hot air ventilated out of the building at the top of the dome. The environmental problems created by the glass dome were solved in a simple mechanical manner without affecting its symbolic power.

**Fig.1. The ramp
after restoration**

**Fig. 2. Urbino,
the walled city**

Mercatale Ramp

Location: **Urbino, Italy**
Previous Function: **Royal Access Route**
Remodelled: **1983**
Architect: **Giancarlo De Carlo**

The reading of context is central to the thinking of Giancarlo De Carlo. He developed a method of understanding the nature of a place and through that, a method of forming a thoughtful and considerate response. He concerned himself with the problems of scale and context and with preserving urban memory. His response to the topography and urban order of the city of Urbino is one of significant abstraction. He does not work with pastiche, but creates a contemporary interpretation that fits sympathetically into its context.

Although De Carlo does not live in Urbino, he will always be associated with the city; he drew up the master plan and masterminded the restorations. Urbino is a hill town in Italy that occupies an important strategic position between Rome and Rimini. It flourished throughout the Middle Ages and then in particular during the Renaissance, when it was associated with the powerful Montefeltro family. These rich patrons commissioned important architects such as Francesco De Giorgio to design the city. Urbino is renowned for its walled historic core that contains the cultural monuments. The town suffered during the 20th century from the many poorly planned suburbs developed outside the city walls, the emigration of the population to larger cities, and the attraction of Urbino as a popular tourist destination.

De Carlo was first commissioned to work as architect to the university in Urbino. The success of this (still ongoing) project led him to be approached in 1958 to rethink and master plan the future of the whole city. Upon receiving the commission De Carlo wrote:

The master plan does not interpret renewal of the historic centre as mere improvement and modernization of buildings and hygienic conditions but as a radical restructuring of the city in patterns and forms capable of guaranteeing continuity between the existing and new physical frameworks.[25]

De Carlo analysed the existing city by carrying out detailed surveys of the fabric. He commissioned statistical analysis of the population, geography, economics and infrastructure. He also compiled reports on sanitary conditions, ownership and the uses of buildings. His report mapped out landmarks, views, paths, entrances, green spaces, and road surfaces. It described the gradient of Urbino's streets, the architectural quality of the buildings, and their condition.

An important step was an examination of the historical development of the city. Urbino began its life as a trading town orientated toward Rimini and the east. Later, Rome in the southwest grew more important to the city's markets. De Carlo noted how the city's orientation and subsequently its identity had changed quite considerably as the trading influences had shifted. A third and much more recent problem was the significant cultural impact of tourism on the city. The popularity of Urbino promised that it was in danger of becoming nothing more than a 'cultural curiosity' for tourists.

De Carlo's published findings questioned whether the town had lost its identity, whether over time the memory of the city had been eroded and whether the considerable shift of influence from east to west had had a significant impact upon the orientation of the city.

This research formed the basis of De Carlo's transformation of the city, a project that is still continuing over 45 years later. The master plan reconciled the twin objectives of conservation and rehabilitation, and provided the city with a method by which they could embrace the 20th century and beyond without compromising the integrity of the place. As Pierluigi Nicolin observes:

You can't reuse an existing space except by re-designing it and that means going through an operation which 'de-structures' it from its previous context and 're-structures' it in the new one.[26]

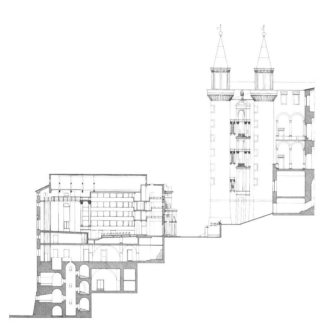

Fig. 3. Section from the Mercatale square up through the Teatro Sanzio and towards the Palace showing the spiralling ramp inside the bastion wall

Among the many interventions made by De Carlo, one of the most important was the Mercatale ramp. In the southwest corner of the historic centre of Urbino is a large square known as the Mercatale, above which sits the Ducal Palace. The square was created to acknowledge the importance of Rome, which became an important trading post under Montefeltro. In the 19th century the view from the Mercatale up to the Ducal Palace was radically compromised by the construction of the Teatro Sanzio on top of a bastion of the old city wall.

In his master plan De Carlo anticipated that the Mercatale had an important role in the future development of the city. He predicted that the centre of the city would become fully pedestrianised and therefore the square would develop into an important connection point between the historic urban centre and the suburbs. The problem was, then, how to reconcile the difference in level between the centre and the square.

Among the historical plans and texts were the designs for a stable block to house the Duke's 300 horses that was set into the bastion walls. Intrigued by the discovery, De Carlo also found information for the design of a spiralling ramp that permitted the Duke to ride his horses from the Mercatale to the Ducal Palace. Upon re-examining the site, De Carlo discovered, sealed into the bastion wall, the entrance to the ramp. Upon subsequent excavation, it was revealed that when the theatre was constructed, the architect Ghinelli filled the ramp with building rubble to consolidate the foundations. The rubble was of course excavated and the ramp reopened, thus recreating the valuable link between the edge and the centre of the city.

The selective archaeology, based upon the intimate examination of the place, generated the discovery of a long discarded, yet important element, which when reinstated, facilitated the continuing revitalisation of the city.

Analysis
Proposed Function

The successful marriage of old and new, of past and future is dependent upon a thorough knowledge or anticipation of what is expected.

The nature of the proposed new use for an existing building is not always the starting point in the design process but unsurprisingly it has an enormous impact on the remodelling. As part of the analytical process, the programmatic requirements of the new function need to be examined to ensure compatibility between the old and new. It is not just a question of size but also of harmony. To understand the exact requirements of those who are to occupy the remodelled building is essential; for example, it may be important that certain areas are shielded from direct sunlight or indeed from any natural light at all and, conversely, some activities might positively benefit from contact with the afternoon sun. Some functions may require small individual rooms and others large open spaces, and the intimate hierarchy of those who are to occupy the spaces needs to be appreciated. Those who occupy the remodelled building generally want to feel that it is theirs, that their functional requirements have been met and yet that the past has not been obliterated but incorporated and embraced as part of the pattern of the present.

The Irish Film Centre in Dublin demanded exacting functional requirements from the remodelling of the Quaker Meeting House by O'Donnell and Tuomey Architects. The architects quickly realised that unless the building could adequately hold the two cinemas required with their shared projection room, the project would not be viable. Their survey revealed that the site was actually composed of no less than nine separate buildings and luckily two of them were sufficiently large to accommodate the cinema spaces. The establishment of the position of these with the shared projection box dictated much: 'everything else really just fell into place'.[27] The specific spaces necessary for the Irish Film Centre to function successfully determined the position of the key elements and spaces in the design.

In his essay 'Old Buildings as Palimpsest', Rodolfo Machado discusses the analogy of the building that is built of layers of writing and rewriting. The remodelling or refunctioning of the building is the formation of another layer of meaning and information. This new layer is as valuable and can contribute to the re-enlivening of the place.

… when the alterations in the building's content are of such a type that the building's original or latest function is changed; then the building is refunctionalized, a different story is born, a new plot is composed out of the old words, a new interpretation has taken place.[28]

There are certain remodelling projects that are almost completely dictated by the needs of the future function. With the high street chain store, the only contextual consideration is how much of the centrally designed image can fit into the retail unit and the shop designers often take little more than the shape and size of the existing space into consideration, the dimension of the space dictating how much or how little of the corporate design is used.

Fig.1. Irish Film Centre. The aperture of the elevated projection room is apparent above the entrance from the Sycamore Street courtyard

4-you Youth Savings Bank

Location: **Krems, Austria**
Previous Function: **Unknown**
Remodelled: **2000**
Architect: **The Unit, (Burgler and Petrovic)**

The '4-you' bank is specifically aimed at the youth market, therefore the identity and imagery of the premises were designed to appeal to this particular group. The traditional banking hall was designed to alleviate the customer's burden of financial worries by expressing solidity and dependability in the building. Today many banks are no longer designed in this way, preferring to portray themselves as just another retail space on the high street. Banks also realised the potential of attracting young people and now invest heavily in developing methods of appealing to the young.

The new 4-you bank represents one such experiment. The bank is a place for savers to 'hang out' and to receive advice from advisers who are of a similar age group. The proposed function allowed the designers free rein to design a space that would appeal directly to the young savers.

The design of the unit deploys a variety of tactics to entice 'the kids', a sloping floor that acts either as seats or a skateboard ramp, M I V videos projected onto the walls, open access to the internet, and on the upper level, a ball court marked out on the floor surface. Customers can surf the net or kick a football at each other, and then make a deposit to the bank.

The space was remodelled to appeal specifically to a young market. It was designed to project a particular image and this was the overriding factor in the design process.

**Fig.1. The main
banking hall**

Baltic Restaurant

Location: **Blackfriars Road, London**
Previous Function: **Georgian terrace and garage for coach builders**
Remodelled: **2001**
Architect: **Seth Stein Architects with Drury Browne Architects**

Baltic is a Polish restaurant that has been neatly inserted into a Georgian terraced house joined to an old mechanics garage. Faced with a tricky problem of differing levels and types of space, the designers remodelled the building to create an atmospheric and delightful place.

The existing building consisted of two main components: a slender shard of space fronting the street and forming the end of the terrace, and the main garage hall, which was linked to the front by a raised tapering corridor. The form of the existing building suggested the organisation of the new space. The bar and front of house facilities were placed behind the terrace façade, while the main dining hall was situated in the old garage space. This has been punctuated by a series of top-lit bays, divided by the timber trusses that have been left exposed to create a light airy space in contrast to the low and darker entrance space at the front bar.

The reorganisation of the building creates a nice simple space, but the real character of the restaurant is derived from the objects placed in it and the colours used to decorate it. Muted greens and grey, like the northern seas, are painted on to the walls which contrast with and highlight the other distinguishing element and colour, amber. Both ends of the bar are filled with chips of the yellowish fossil resin and a light sculpture that exploits the translucent qualities of amber hangs in the dining area.

The identity of the remodelled restaurant is therefore expressed by these imported elements carefully and sparingly used within the space: the colour and the Baltic amber.

**Fig.1. The hanging amber
light sculpture animates
the dining area**

The Kaufmann Apartment

Location: **London**
Previous Function: **Warehouse**
Remodelled: **2001**
Architect: **Simon Conder Architects**

Fig.1. Sculptural translucent glass cylinders house the bathroom and toilet

Loft living uses the big open spaces of converted warehouses. While the multifaceted airy quality of the large space makes very desirable flats or apartments, the problems with open-plan living occur with the service or private spaces, such as the bathroom or shower. The usual solution is to attach these elements to a partition, in effect to thicken the plane out and hide the service spaces within a false wall. Another answer is to avoid the embarrassment of the private space by brazenly placing the usually concealed quite openly within the space.

Simon Conder Architects developed a solution that occupies the middle ground between the two. The idea evolved and progressed through a number of different domestic projects, from a converted terraced house to a remodelled warehouse.

In the new design a bathroom and shower are enclosed within two translucent glass cylinders. The units restrain the damp and smell of the traditional bathroom, but do not afford complete privacy. The diffuse glass unit is lit from within and therefore glows, especially at night, projecting silhouettes of the occupant into the space around it. The private space becomes a sculptural focal point.

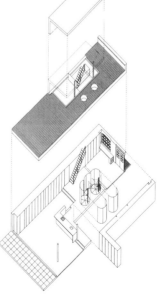

Fig. 2. Axonometric drawing showing how the eloquent glass screens dominate the space

Helmut Lang Perfumery

Location: **Manhattan, New York**
Previous Function: **Retail space**
Remodelled: **2001**
Architect: **Gluckman Mayer**

Fig.1. The imagery
of the perfumery
is crisp and clinical

Fig. 2. The balustrade
displays impertinent
electronic messages
by Jenny Holzer

The Helmut Lang perfumery was designed to embody the distinct identity of the range of sensuous Helmut Lang cosmetics. Sited opposite the Lang flagship store in SoHo, also designed by Gluckman Mayer, the sparse clean retail space was created to complement the clothes store.

In its remodelled form the perfumery expresses itself as a sort of laboratory, the spaces being clean, the objects placed within it pure and the features evocatively scientific.

The perfumery is entered from the street through a long thin space that opens into a main room. The sparse room is populated by a series of minimal elements, a central monolithic black display box, a large cash desk and, at the far end of the room, a tall translucent glass screen. The staircase to the basement level is cut into the side of the room and it is bounded by a long thin white wall. This enamelled steel plane extends from the entrance space to the main room, linking the two. On top of this wall, at balustrade height, is moving electronic text by the artist Jenny Holzer.

The impeccable perfumery space embodies the scientific-style processes happening in the building. Products are developed in the basement. Behind the translucent glass screen, private consultations take place. The showroom has the air of a clinic, or dispensary. The electronic messages add to the technologically advanced feel of the space.

Fig.1. New steel structure and stair framing the hovering exhibition

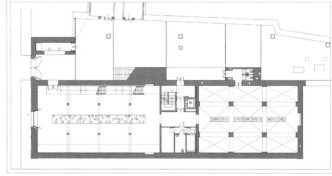

Fig. 2. Ground floor plan showing how the service block divides the space

Tuscolano Museum of Roman Archaeology

Location: **Frascati, Italy**
Previous Function: **Stables**
Remodelled: **2001**
Architect: **Studio Fuksas (Massimiliano Fuksas)**

**Fig. 3. Exhibition case
sitting alone in
the preserved space**

Studio Fuksas converted the 17th century stables of the Villa Aldobrandini to create a cultural centre, consisting of an archaeological exhibit display, auditorium, temporary exhibition space and administration offices. The main hall of the stables now holds the museum display, and a new floor inserted into the building allows a second level for a temporary exhibition space.

In the remodelled building the archaeological museum is positioned on the ground floor. A service block has been introduced into the centre of the space with the effect of cutting it in half. A steel frame supports the new first floor, which has been left a metre clear of the edges of the space. The gap allows for the insertion of a steel and timber stair to link the two levels.

What is particularly interesting is the method the architects used to display the archaeological exhibits. The objects appear to be suspended somewhere between the earth and the sky. Each is individually displayed on a slender bronze stand and illuminated by a tiny hanging spotlight. The exhibits are arranged in a long procession and secured behind transparent sheets of toughened glass over two and a half metres high and set into a recessed channel in the polished concrete floor. The artefacts seem to float through the main gallery, each one picked out by its thin pendant light hung from the soffit, and appear to sail through the red rendered wall of the service block and into the vaulted room beyond. It is an expression of the journey the exhibits have taken from the subterranean depths to the light of the museum space. The exhibits look so natural that it almost seems as if they are still lying in the ground, only the soil and dirt having been removed.

Fig.1. 'Who am I ?'
at the Science Museum

Location: **Science Museum, Kensington, London**
Previous Function: **Gallery**
Remodelled: **2001**
Architect: **Casson Mann**

Casson Mann were approached to design the inaugural exhibition in the Wellcome Wing at the Science Museum. They had little context to work with, for the gallery itself was not completed, so the exhibition was designed with little more information than the sizes of the three floors and the position of the entrances and exits. As Roger Mann explains:

We had to come up with a different way of doing it, so we designed this gallery to be more like a CD-Rom than a book.[29]

The theme of the exhibition was based upon the effect that technology has upon people's lives. Rather than begin with a series of objects, the designers began with a set of assumptions. Three themes were identified and developed: 'Who am I?', 'Digitopolis' and 'The Future'. These themes fitted well with the three levels of the exhibition space.

'Who am I?' explored ideas about what we are. The lowest level of the exhibition was expressed traditionally as a series of glass cases displaying objects based on genetics: DNA, fingerprints, and so on. More unusually, this level also displayed modular aluminium objects called Bloids (Biomedical & Life Science Organic Interactive Structures). Each of these, like the humans that they represented, was similar in construction and surface but never exactly the same.

The next floor was dedicated to digital technology. This comprised a matrix of five ribbon-like structures of steel and glass that created a landscape of lights and objects. The structures were interwoven with panels of glazing that looped up and through the space to create tables for display or even small enclosures. Above this floor, 'The Future' gallery questioned how technology will change us in the future, a relatively bare space in comparison to the density of the lower floors, suggesting the uncertainty of the future. A series of large round tables invited visitors to play the games that were projected onto the surfaces from above and allowed participation in selected topics, such as male pregnancy, genetic modification, cloning and so on.

This exhibition was developed from questions about the implications that science and technology have for human life. Casson Mann knew that each floor of the exhibition would have two entrances/exits and therefore designing an exhibition with a traditional narrative structure would be ineffective. The exhibits and the information were collected and positioned in a much more arbitrary manner, the relationships established were with the other objects rather than with the building or the containing space.

Fig. 2. 'How do you know so much ?'

Chapter Two
Strategy

Previous Pages:
The Tate Modern,
London. Herzog
and de Meuron

Strategy
Introduction

When a building is reused
the most important
and meaningful factor in
the design is the
relationship between
the old and the new.

When designing a new building, whether consciously or not, the architect will employ an architectural strategy, that is, a device that will inform and order the building. This controlling device is often the basis of the theoretical issues that drive the design of the building. This strategy can manifest itself in many different ways, whether it is the controlling grid and ultimate freedom of Le Corbusier's *plan libre* used for example in the Villa Savoye or the spatial qualities of Adolf Loos's *Raumplan* as shown in the Möller or the Moller Houses, the complex contextual issues of Hans Hollein's Gallery in Mönchengladbach or the prominent symbolic imagery of Smirke's British Museum.

These strategic moves are of course supplemented by a complex combination of different factors, such as site conditions, structural systems, programmatic requirements, the era in which the building was constructed or the pursuit of the individual architect. These all combine to produce a building of rich complexity driven by an often simple strategy.

But when a building is reused, the most important and meaningful factor in the design is, of course, the original building, and it is the establishment of a relationship between the old and the new that is the most influential device in the design. The new could not exist without the original. The method by which the relationship is established is the key to the strategic analysis of building reuse. Of course the factors essential for the design of new building play an important part in the redesign of a building, but they are overshadowed by this association of the new programme with the original building.

It is the understanding of how the two fit together, of their affinity or otherwise, of their complete integration or their standing apart, that provides the categories for the analysis of types of building reuse.

Three categories of building reuse have been developed based upon the sheer extent of the integration between the host building and the new elements. If the original building wholeheartedly accepts and establishes an intimate relationship with the new design, that is, the two become one, the category is intervention. When the host building allows and accommodates new elements, which are built to fit the exact dimensions of the existing, to be introduced in or around it yet remains very much unchanged, then the category is insertion; and if the old and the new exist together but very little rapport between them is established, then the category is installation.

**Fig.1. Interior of the
Castlevecchio
Museum, Verona,
Italy. Carlo Scarpa**

Strategy
Intervention

Intervention is a process that transforms a building, the new and the old become interwined and completely dependent upon each other.

Intervention is a procedure that activates the potential or repressed meaning of a specific place. It only truly works when the architectural response of the modifications draw all their cues from the existing building. The architect will regard the building as a narrative, a story to be discovered and retold and, through a process of uncovering, clarification and interpretation will reveal and reactivate the place.

The original building provides the impetus for change; the architect's localised and highly specific reading of the place will dictate the appropriate moves. In order to impose a degree of control or order, the building may need to be simplified, thus producing a new way of looking at or understanding it. The analysis and reading of the original building can often be as destructive as it is constructive; the architect will strip away, remove, clarify, undo in order to reveal new or hidden meanings.

Carlo Scarpa was the architect responsible for the restoration and remodelling of the Castelvecchio Museum in Verona. By the use of creative demolition he uncovered the various historic strata of the building. The castle was a complicated confusion of many eras of construction and Scarpa strove to explore and isolate the various phases of building to reveal the complex and rich beauty of the place. John Kurtich and Garret Eakin describe this:

Scarpa achieved three things with his adaptive reuse project. First, he accepted and presented parts of the building complex as historically pre-existing, therefore maintaining their original integrity. Second, he lay bare through conceptual surgery all the genuine survivals of the Castelvecchio. Finally, he added new parts, which would bind together the entire complex and fill in the gaps without destroying the patina or even the mishaps or wounds of time.[1]

The modifications to the building can interact intrusively, with new elements imposing themselves directly upon the existing structure. The new elements, which are often many small changes, alterations, additions and subtractions, are, of course, related entirely to the original building because they are inspired by it, but the language used is usually completely at odds with the host although the character may be balanced.

When converting Giles Gilbert Scott's Bankside Power Station in London into the Tate Modern, Hertzog and de Meuron strove not to obliterate the qualities of the industrial building but to heighten them. They aimed to integrate the everyday life and the cityscape with the urban fabric of the building. (The transformation of now defunct industrial areas into places of high cultural interest can be found in every western country; the impact that Frank Gehry's Guggenheim Museum in Bilbao has had makes it a fantastic example). The position of the old power station, which was originally designed as a counterpoint to St Paul's Cathedral, directly opposite it on the south bank of the Thames, gave it the prime conditions for regeneration. Herzog and de Meuron describe their strategy as one that unleashes the hidden depths of the building:

Fig.1. The lantern
on top of the
Tate Modern functions
as a beacon at night,
glowing with stored
energy

It is exciting to deal with existing structures, because the
constraints demand a very different kind of creative energy. When
you don't start from scratch you need architectural strategies that
are not primarily motivated by taste or stylistic preferences.
Our strategy was to accept the physical power of Bankside's
massive mountain-like brick building and even to enhance it rather
than breaking it up or trying to diminish it. This is a kind of Aikido
strategy, where you use your enemy's strategy for your own
purposes. Instead of fighting it, you take all the energy and shape it
in an unexpected and new way.[2]

The majority of the spaces in the recent conversion were dictated
by the original building. The huge former turbine hall provides
a massive street or public space, which penetrates the entire length
and height of the building, and from this the galleries and other
activities are accessed. The gallery spaces themselves vary
in proportions, scale and size and their use of natural or artificial
light, all of which is of course dependent on their position within
the building. But the modification that is the most obvious and has
the greatest impact is the creation of the glazed roof, a huge
body of light hovering above the main bulk of the massive brick
structure of the building. This functions as a light well during the day
and as a beacon at night. Most importantly, this intervention has
the symbolic quality of representing the sheer quantity of raw power
once physically generated in the building and it now appears to glow
with the stored latent energy.

Interventions are rarely function-led. The form of the new
building is dictated by the form of the original building. Form follows
form! The building determines how it is to be reused, the position of
the new spaces, how they are to relate to one another and their size
and scale, is already imbued within it. The distinctive qualities of the
building are explored, the story is read, and it is altered, reshaped
and retold and often irretrievably changed. New or hidden meanings
are revealed, the building becomes endowed with significance
often greater than the value of the new use: intervention can be seen
as the activation of the place.

The Naked City

Location: **Paris**
Date: **1957**
Artist: **Guy Debord with Asger Jorn**

The Situationist International was a loose association of European artists and poets who campaigned against the general poverty of intellectual life and for the creation of revolutionary 'Situations'. They published and distributed an essay entitled 'On the Poverty of Student Life' in 1966–7, which is reputed to have influenced the protests at universities and the troubled events of May 1968.

Guy Debord, a founder member of the Situationist movement, fashioned a collage from cut-out pieces of a map of Paris and then rearranged the fragments according to the 'Dérive'. Meaning literally 'drifting', this was a journey taken through a given place and consisted of moving through a series of arbitrarily chosen 'ambiences', using the technique of roaming through the city on randomly selected routes to explore different passages or places. The Naked City, as the resultant map was called, represented a series of centres or 'Plaque Tournants', where important happenings had been established through the Dérive. A 'Plaque Tournant' was a centre of an important 'ambience', and it signified a major place of interaction for the Situationist 'Psycho-

Geographique'. These centres corresponded to important buildings or spaces where human behaviour was perceived as unusual and modified by the environment.

Intervention, a strategy that can activate the potential or repressed meaning of a place, works best when it is used to uncover or reveal new meaning through isolation and exposure. The strategy is equally powerful either when constructing new meanings and connections through addition or when exposing connections through destruction and cutting.

The Naked City therefore maps a new reading of the city, made in reaction to various journeys through its streets. It is a powerful example of the appropriation of the existing by cutting, in order to expose and reconnect, and ultimately to create new meanings. Intervention is used to activate a different meaning in the map of Paris. It takes the existing and re-works it in order to convey another reading of the city. The cutting up of the map of the city is a creative act that uses what is there to establish new relationships, a process in which a deliberate and often robust act provides a new dialogue.

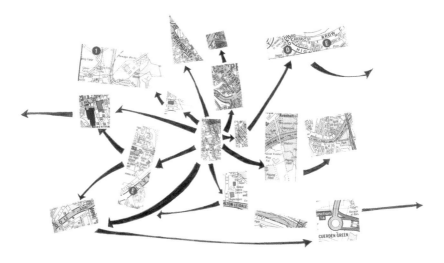

**Fig.1. A study of
Preston according to
the rules of the Dérive**

La Llauna School

Location: **Badalona, Nr Barcelona Spain** Former Function: **Printing Factory**
Built: **Late 19th century** Architect: **Unknown**
New Function: **Secondary School for Boys**
Remodelled: **1984** Architects: **Enric Miralles, Carme Pinós**

The school occupies a redundant printing factory building situated on a narrow road in a densely occupied industrial area on the outskirts of Barcelona. The building is locked into its context, being completely surrounded by other buildings, and the school necessarily occupies all the three floors, that is, every bit of the available space. Given the tightness of the site, the relationship between the context and the building is necessarily strong. The functional requirements of the school were a playground, classrooms, an entrance area and spaces for support activities.

**Fig.1. The ground floor
was completely opened
up to provide a post-
industrial playground**

The interior of the building was dominated by its strong steel frame structure, consisting of columns and latticed steel beams that supported a series of vaults, typical for Spanish factory buildings built at the turn of the century. The structure compartmentalised the building into a series of bays with parallel rows of columns, giving the interior a specific rhythm and proportion and providing the building with its character.

The architects' approach was to selectively demolish parts of the building to open up certain areas and thus to allow light to fall vertically and glow horizontally through the building. Kenneth Powell portrayed this as 'an explosion of the constraining context'.[3] After this opening up, new deliberately contrasting elements were introduced into the building.

Intervention is a strategy closely tied to the characteristics of the original building, any modification being born from an understanding of the host, the unique structure of the building, and its resultant spaces. Intervention is often distinguished by a series of small moves consisting of cuts and additions which are in keeping with the existing building. In La Llauna School, the basic nature of the building is left relatively untouched except for selected subtractions and the addition of carefully detailed and controlled circulation.

The provision of an area for children to expend their energy and play is extremely important for both themselves and for their teachers. To create this the architects removed any unnecessary and non-structural elements from the ground level, allowing it to become completely open, and utilised this as the entrance and recreational area. The children now happily amuse themselves in this shaded post-industrial playground.

In the remodelled design Miralles and Pinos use the spaces afforded by the structure of the building to inform the positions of the other interventions. Cuts made into the space between the columns and the masonry wall furthest from the ground floor entrance open up a space for movement. Vertical circulation, in the form of ramps and stairs, is slotted in this space. On the ground floor the stairs run out into long ramps, playfully animating the ground floor playground, and on the upper floors the stairs are neatly locked into the building and contained within two bays of the structure. The schoolchildren now enter through the ground floor playground and ascend the stairs and ramps in order to reach the various classrooms.

However, at the second floor level of the stairs, the lack of space meant that an intervention had to be made into the fabric of the building. A new landing or balcony was added in to the roof space in order to create a connection to the third floor. This involved cutting back one side of the roof to expose the truss. The roof was then glazed to allow natural light to penetrate into the space. The cutting back of the roof created a mezzanine at the top of the triple flight stair, making a pleasant place from a difficult circulation problem and also establishing a visual connection between this area at the very top of the building and the moment of entrance on the ground floor.

The upper floors now hold the classrooms. These are bounded by the structure of the interior and the position of the walls are placed according to the pattern of the beams and columns. The obvious structure of the factory, its space and proportions allow its easy reuse as classrooms. Intervention is used to create a distinct scale and proportion for the new function, which is derived from the host and creates a dialogue between new and old.

Miralles and Pinós complemented the addition of classrooms and circulation with a

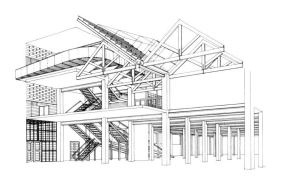

Fig. 2. New elements are placed between the existing structure

robust intervention upon the building façade, to create a new entrance. This involved the cutting and removal of part of the front wall in order to expose the building to its context. It takes its size and proportion from the building and involved the removal of two bays of masonry at ground and first floor levels and one at the upper floor. The upper levels were in-filled with glazing, while at ground level, a large curved sliding steel door was inserted. This served not only as a security seal but also to signal the new occupation.

Intervention is a robust strategy in which a dialogue between the old building and the remodelling is developed; the two do not exist independently but become intertwined. La Llauna derives much of its new character from an understanding of the nature of the old factory; the new school is distinct from the original building yet obviously derives its qualities from the constraints and opportunities provided by the host.

Fig. 3. The wide circulation area links the classrooms and provides an area for interaction

**Fig.1. House, a ghost-like
simulacrum of a former
East End home**

House

Location: **193 Grove Road, London**
Date: **1993**
Artist: **Rachel Whiteread**

Rachel Whiteread is an artist who, through the process of casting, creates meaningful representations of everyday objects that reveal the previously disregarded qualities of the piece. Her simulacra deal with issues such as memories, relationships and death. In late 1993 she made a cast of an entire Edwardian terraced house in East London. The project involved spraying the interior of the house with concrete and then removing the shell of the building itself to leave just a perfect casting of the interior. The sculpture was a positive cast of the previously negative space of the house.

'House' became the centre of a political controversy, instigating a Parliamentary debate about its retention as a monument. Opponents argued that not only was it ugly and a waste of money but also that the sculpture defiled every notion of the 'home' and was disrespectful to those who once lived in the house. The local London authority in which it resided threatened demolition. The dispute raged until 11 January 1994, when House was razed and thus immortalised.

House was a direct cast of an existing space. Its shape and volume were completely dictated by the shape and volume of the original building. Its form followed the exact form of the host, except that it was not an literal copy but a simulacrum or representation. It revealed the previously hidden or unnoticed parts of the house, the space. The volume of air within the rooms was made solid and the exact placc of occupation was exposed, laid open, made naked and it is this uncovering that was so disturbing; the house seemed indecently exposed.

Intervention is a procedure activating the potential or hidden meaning of a specific building or a place. Not only is the form of the new building dictated by the old but its narrative is embedded into its surfaces. In this case the casting of the interior had filled the niches and corners of all of the spaces of the house. The dents, scratches and marks of the inhabitants' lives were embedded in the new concrete skin. The process of 'gunniting' the interior – literally spraying the interior with liquid concrete through a gun – filled every crease and gap of the house. All the pre-existing spaces and marks were concretised without any repair or conservation. The intervention of the cast of House revealed the story of the place without destroying the mishaps or wounds of the patina of time. It is from this that the intervention revealed and reactivated the house.

Küppersmühle Museum, Grothe Collection

Location: **Duisburg, Germany**
Former Function: **Warehouse** Built: **1908-1916**
Architects: **Kiefer Brothers and Joseph Weiss**
New Function: **Gallery for German art**
Remodelled: **1999** Architects: **Herzog and de Meuron**

Fig.1. Glazed strips simply interrupt the rhythm of the bricked-up openings, emphasising the building's monolithic quality

Herzog and de Meuron have a reputation for creating beautifully executed, extremely logical buildings. Although their work does not adhere to a particular style and embraces many different materials, forms and details, it still appears consistently ordered and rational. This project was completed just two years before the opening of the Tate Modern in London; it is considerably more modest, both in scale and bravado, and yet it contains the same astuteness in the manipulation of detail and light.

The Hans Grothe collection of post-War German Art is housed in a converted brick warehouse in Duisburg's redeveloped inner harbour area. This imposing ten-storey building had a monumental quality that ensured it became a significant landmark. The new museum contains a series of modified gallery rooms and a new circulation area. When remodelling the Küppersmühle, Herzog and de Meuron indelicately reworked the building and in particular the façade, in order to expose the new use and to reinforce the building's monumental character. They used the productive strategy of subtracting and eliminating specific parts of the building in order to clarify and emphasise its character. This is an example of the constructive powers of removing sections of an existing building to accentuate its appearance.

The host is a tall imposing brick building. Its organisation was in four distinct parts and all of these, apart from the storage containers, were reused for galleries, offices, and a restaurant. Unlike the architect's project for the Tate Modern in London, where necessary additions were made to the building to accommodate the complex specifications, this building can easily accommodate the necessary but quite simple requirement of the provision of gallery space for a provincial museum.

Most of the load-bearing structure was retained and the main internal intervention was in the middle two sections of the building, where some of the existing floors were removed in order to open up a number of five-metre high gallery spaces. These were necessarily high and echoic in order to incorporate large works of art. They were finished with the standard white walls and stone floors to provide a benign neutral space for the contemplation of the works on show.

The removal of the floors activated a far more robust intervention, the extreme expression of which is exposed upon the façade of the building. The modifications in the remodelled building drew their cues from the existing building yet deliberately went against the grain of it. The harbour-side façade was composed of a series of small arched windows methodically arranged in vertical stripes, each stripe edged by a brick pier. Between the ledge and upper arch of each window was a colourful vertical motif, made by the placement of a coloured brick alternating with the regular brick of the warehouse. The bottom two storeys were a solid masonry plinth, punctured by windows arranged in the same vertical lines but without the articulation of the brick piers.

This rendered the lower part of the building as a solid base. This original composition expressed the verticality of the façade, accentuating its monumental height and presence. The architects wanted to strictly control the natural light and the view of the harbour from within the gallery spaces and therefore many of the window openings within this central area of the building were closed. These were deliberately sealed with the same type of bricks as used in the construction of the original building and the rest of the masonry was repaired and cleaned so that there was little apparent discrepancy between the closed openings and the façade. Once prepared, a number of incisions were made into this sheer wall. Tall thin slots were cut that had absolutely no respect for the former arrangement of the façade and sliced through the windows, the arches, the decorative brickwork and anything else that got in the way. This new fenestration for the new spaces inside the building and were designed to reflect the five-metre high gallery spaces within the warehouse. The monumentality of the façade was accentuated by the closed windows and then heightened by the new tall thin narrow slots that were cut through it. The windows from within describe views across the harbour as well as controlling the entry of natural light into the gallery. The glazing was placed on the outside edge of the building to accentuate the thickness of the walls and to allow the window reveal to become part of the gallery space.

The intervention is so successful because the host building dictated the quality of most of the spaces inside the gallery; Herzog and de Meuron increased the scale and verticality of the façade and so heightened the monumentality of the building.

Fig. 2. The slice of light accentuates the pure space of the gallery and heightens the relationship with the harbour

Fig.1. The cuts
reveal previously
unconnected
spaces

Office Baroque

Location: **Antwerp, Belgium**
Date: **1977**
Artist: **Gordon Matta-Clark**

Gordon Matta-Clark was a pivotal figure in the SoHo art community in New York during the mid-1970s. His media were the houses, warehouses, old office spaces and dock buildings that were abandoned or about to be demolished. He would intervene upon these buildings by using a chainsaw to literally slice them open, cut holes in them and score the very fabric of the building to reveal the previously unmade connections between floors, ceilings and walls, the exterior and the interior. Some of the cuts were large-scale and involved removing huge panels of exterior walls and others were much smaller, the size of window openings. All of the cuts were made to expose the hidden layers of life and relationships that had taken place within the confines of the spaces and release previously hidden connections.

In the project Office Baroque, Matta-Clark made a series of cuts in an old office building, an intervention that was designed not only to reveal the physical conditions such as light and dark, movement and connections between floors, but also to provoke reflections on aspects of the relationship between the spaces which were previously not made or impossible to make.

The act of intervention is a process that can be extremely powerful; it can reorder, reconnect, and reveal the narrative of an existing building. Matta-Clark regarded the process of cutting open a building as 'undoing' it.

This undoing of a building not only exposed the previously hidden connections but also created new meanings and a reactivation of the space. The modifications were extremely intrusive and brutal, and arguably did not complete the work but instead offered a critique or judgement of it. The complex layers of human inhabitation and relationships offered scope for action but the cuts were also guided by the structure of the building. Matta-Clark's training as an architect enabled him to remove just enough to retain the structural integrity of the building or, conversely, sufficient to undermine it.

Office Baroque had its generative origins in the bizarre accident of the teacup ring stains left upon a drawing of the building; these suggested organising the undoing around two semi-circular areas of slightly different diameters. The cuts began on the first floor of the five-storey building and were a constant motif as the floors, walls and ceilings were sliced into. This process created large open spaces at the bottom of the building and small interconnecting rooms towards the top. The intervention was completely internal: the structural integrity of the building was not violated. Beams were left exposed and, where the cuts crossed, pointed shapes were created. The very thinness of the walls and floors was revealed, showing how small these seemingly solid barriers really were. Each intervention was relatively small and it revealed and connected with other areas but the only way to comprehend the whole piece was to wander through and appreciate the whole building. Matta-Clarke describes it:

Besides the surprise and disorientation this work stimulates, it creates an especially satisfying mental map or model to help the eye remember.[4]

The building was in a prime location but the local authorities forbade any external representation of the piece and Matta-Clarke rather sadly summed it up as 'another esoteric hidden work in the history of inaccessible projects'.[5]

The intervention was expressed as a series of lacerations. The cuts opened up the building, connected parts and spaces previously unconnected and exposed the containerisation of the usable space. This process of creating three-dimensional relationships within a building is a device that has obviously influenced the work of such architects as Steven Holl and Bolles+Wilson.

Fig.1. Strategic cuts
in the building allow
movement and natural
light to penetrate
the museum

Fig. 2. View from
the stair towards the
first floor main rooms
of the museum

Cathedral Museum

Location: **Lucca, Italy**
Former Function: **House, Church and Store House**
Built: **13th-17th century** Architect: **Unknown**
New Function: **Museum** Remodelled: **1993**
Architect: **Pietro Carlo Pellegrini**

The remodelled Museo Della Cattedrale is a microcosmic representation of the development of the city – consisting of a 13th century town house, a 16th century church and a group of 17th century storehouses all arranged around a courtyard garden. The actual site of the museum is a block of the city alongside the Cathedral San Martino. The buildings exist as neighbours, yet the chronological development and therefore the style and character of each are very distinct from the others. The museum, designed to house the collection of religious artefacts from the nearby cathedral, is the result of the sensitive joining together of three buildings.

The development of the museum involved the sensitive restoration of the three buildings, which was then followed by their selective stitching together. This was achieved by the addition of a new circulation route cut centrally across the spaces of the buildings. The journey through the new museum traverses the three different buildings, each with their respective scale and composition of different rooms left intact. This journey is populated with carefully positioned religious artefacts.

In this building the strategy of intervention is used to sensitively re-appropriate the built fabric in order to make something new. The transformation of the old is heavily informed by the forms, volume, and the history of the original buildings. Intervention is used here to draw together pieces of disparate buildings. Parts have been creatively destroyed to reveal the building's true characters. The chronological differences between the disparate set of buildings have been brought together, while their different formal qualities have been left intact.

An element of vertical circulation was placed in the storehouse linking to a series of walkways and bridges that are attached to the other buildings and spaces. The steel stairs and lift and the steel and timber paths are fragmentary and complement the disjointed nature of the original buildings. A journey through the various rooms of the buildings, linked by the new circulation route, is like walking through the city, with its narrow passages and courtyards opening out to the viewer. The character and specific qualities of the original buildings, and the character of the city in which the museum is based, informs the Cathedral museum.

The urban fabric of Lucca itself is a dense weave of compacted buildings from differing periods and architectural styles. The larger scale is the landscape of the city; its terrain and identity grew through incremental development. The analysis and understanding of this context led to a museum which reflects the grain of its host buildings and city. At the smaller city block scale, the context is provided by the museum, its neighbours and the spaces between them. The analysis of these contextual factors led to a thorough understanding of the hosts and subsequently to an intuitive yet subtle intervention.

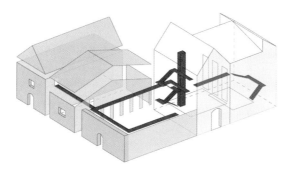

Fig. 3. A circulation route is imposed upon the buildings, which both links them together and highlights their differences

Fig.1. Upper mezzanine level. The brutal 1970s beams are reused to hang the new floor. The new truss mimics the old arch of the vault

Santa Maria La Real Regional Museum

Location: **Najera, Spain**
Former Function: **Monastery**
Built: **11th century**
New Function: **Museum**
Remodelled: **1987** Architects: **Javier Bellosillo, Barbara W. Baluffi**

The Monastery of Santa Maria La Real, based around a cave set into the sandstone hills surrounding Najera, was established in the 11th century. Its foundation was based upon a miracle that occurred in the cave. The young King Garcia of Spain was hunting in the hills when, pursuing his prey, he entered the cave and found a statue of the Virgin Mary and a vase of lilies. The King went on to gain many victories in battle and consequently dedicated much of the spoils to the building of a monastery to commemorate the miracle. Since its inception in 1045 the building has undergone a series of renovations and additions right up to the present day. The last major and yet disastrous set of works before remodelling took place in the 1970s but were never finished. This was the starting point for the new works by Bellosillo and Baluffi.
The architects were commissioned to design a museum, for religious works from the local Rioja region, and a library for the Monastery, to repair the tower and part of the cloister and to restore and maintain the complex of buildings that had suffered considerably over time.

As we have seen, intervention is a procedure that utilises the specific characteristics of the original building to provide the impetus for change. In the case of the Najera Monastery, the architects took the view that the story of the building had been formed by the extensions and accretions to the complex. Even the really insensitive additions had become part of the narrative and it was from this beginning that they formulated their strategy.

They isolated three areas where, in order to expose the plot, the necessary remodelling and interventions were to be made. These were the upper cloister, the main volume of the refectory and the bell tower.

During the unsympathetic 1970s renovation, the refectory and upper cloister were partially demolished and many of the existing vaults were removed and replaced with a series of concrete beams. This work was left unfinished and both spaces remained incomplete. Rather than ignore or replace these insensitive additions, the architects embraced them. The condition of the original building was such that it was in danger of collapsing and most of the existing floors could not be loaded with any further weight. In the cloister a new pre-cast concrete vaulted ceiling was hung from the concrete beams and in the refectory space the beams became the new structure for the mezzanine level of the museum. This floor was suspended with the lightest of touches and connected to the ground level by a combination of raked seating and stairs. The ground floor was deliberately kept relatively clear for performances and functions.

The form of the remodelled refectory space is dictated by the form of its host. The refectory space is L-shaped and the new mezzanine exactly echoes this. This mezzanine is constructed from steel and untreated concrete and is positioned respectfully slightly away from the original stonework. It consists of two landings connected by a steel walkway. The larger landing is hung from the beams while the smaller one relies heavily for support on a part of the existing floor that is still structurally sound. The larger floor is strapped to the 1970s beams with steel braces looped through the structure and arched over the top of the beam, successfully evoking a memory of the old vault shape. The old form influenced the new form. Once again, form follows form.

The third space is the bell tower. This tall square-sectioned chimney-like space, affording dramatic views from the top, required a new staircase. The journey from the refectory space up the bell tower, the enclosure of the tower and its particular qualities imposed a specific three-part solution.

The old stairs were removed and an unfinished concrete and lightweight steel construction was hung from four new steel beams spanning the top of the tower. At the base the stair is heavy and static and is rendered in concrete. The upper section is made of steel and appears lighter and contrasts strongly with the heaviness of the concrete base; and suspended between the two, in the middle of the tower, hanging like a cork-screw in space, is a helicoid staircase. At the top of the tower the final galvanised steel stair projects out of an opening and a small platform floats over the roof of the monastery.

The eclectic quality of the original buildings, where no one part was joined to another with a discernible rationale, led the architects to an interventionist approach. An understanding of the nature and growth of the building allowed them to formulate a strategy which uncovers and depicts the disparity between the moments of addition and subtraction. They created their own distinct architectural layer contrasting and complementing the existing one. They showed that, however out of favour a particular approach to architecture might be, it is still part of the pattern of the history of a place and in that respect, is part of the narrative. They composed a complete picture of the monastery in which over a thousand years of development and change have been exposed and revealed as a continuous story.

Fig. 2. The new tri-part staircase in the existing bell tower

Fig. 3. The final part of the ascent. The galvanised steel floating platform and stair provide a stunning view from the top of the bell tower

P. S. 1. Contemporary Art Gallery

Location: **Queens, New York, USA**
Former Function: **School**
Built: **1893–1906** Architect: **Unknown**
New Function: **Gallery**
Remodelled: **1997** Architect: **Frederick Fisher and Partners**

**Fig. 1. Existing 'scissor'
stairs are retained
to lend a distinct
atmosphere to
the new gallery**

The P.S.1. Contemporary Art Gallery was set up in a derelict school in Queens, New York in 1976. The school was built at the turn of the century and was the first public school in Queens. It was closed in 1963 and was left derelict until 1976 when Alanna Heiss, a curator and collector, started to use the school for the display of installations by local artists. In 1995 Heiss commissioned Fred Fisher to transform the school into the P.S.1. Gallery.

The gallery had to retain its autonomy from the Manhattan art scene, yet it had to contain sufficient gallery space and enough high quality work to justify its existence. Contrarily, in order to attract visitors from Manhattan, it was important that the gallery had an angle; it was not sufficient to be another anonymous building with white walls and a flagged floor. Fisher, the architect, took the view that the old school had a unique atmosphere and its preservation was the design generator.

Fisher's desire to retain the qualities of the building led him to an approach where he intended to 'reinforce the existing structure … maintaining and revealing historic elements and surfaces in combination with neutral forms and details in the new construction'.[6]

The remodelled P.S.1. manages to reactivate the building because the architect sympathetically appreciated the layers of the previous use of the building and exposed them to convey character and identity for the new gallery. The previous function imbues the new gallery with a municipal aura reminiscent of the old school. Corridors are left relatively untouched, with timber wainscoting and highly varnished parquet floors. Old doors to gallery rooms are the same schoolroom doors with a single panel of frosted glass. Everywhere in the building the aura of the school is retained. In some places Fisher peels back the surfaces of the walls to reveal graffiti or notices, left from many years ago. The old is used to directly infuse the atmosphere of the new. The

ambience of the school house still looms large in the corridors and rooms of the building. The patina of history, the scratches and marks of the old classrooms, the assembly hall, and canteen, are, where possible, retained. In among the rooms and spaces of the old school, artists install their works. In the basement occupying a coal bunker are pristine white works by Robert Ryman, and a ladder climb up to the top of the old school bell tower reveals an installation by Julian Schnabel, and so on. Even the name, P.S.1. from public school, is generated by the history of the building.

Fisher opened up the building, and moved the entrance, realising that the separate Girls/Boys doorways could cause organisational problems, and instead re-ordered the entrance sequence to the back of the building through the old schoolyard. This allows the gallery spaces to extend out of the building to create an enormous open air sculpture court with the additional bonus of re-presenting the building to the subway exit and thus making it the access route used by most visitors. The gable end of the school is reused for advertising. The sculpture court is terminated by a grand stair which adjoins the back of the school and monumentalises the new entrance. It also serves as informal seating for performances in the yard.

Intervention is a strategy that exposes the historical narrative of the building. The act of cutting and exposing the scars of its previous use, the joints of new additions, or the layers of accretions built up over the years, require a forceful attitude to the host and a sense of risk through investigation. The narrative of the P.S.1. is etched into its surfaces; the separate entrances, stairs, doors and rooms are manifestations of its former use as a school. The main infrastructure of the building is maintained while the rooms are reused for galleries, the stairs for the different level circulation and the playground for exhibitions.

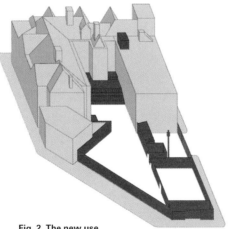

Fig. 2. The new use for the school is signified by the sculpture courtyard entrance at the back of the old building with the entrance to the gallery through the yard and up the monumental staircase

Fig. 3. The new
entrance courtyard,
enclosed by smooth
concrete walls, is the
host to temporary
exhibitions

Strategy
Insertion

The insertion of a new functioning element not only provides a use for an often redundant or neglected space but also serves to enhance and intensify the building itself.

Insertion is a practice that establishes an intense relationship between the original building and the remodelling and yet allows the character of each to exist in a strong and independent manner.

Insertion, as the word suggests, is the introduction of a new element into, between or beside an existing structure. The inserted object can often be seen as independent and confrontational, a single large powerful element that establishes surprising dialogues between itself and the existing structure or volume. It is at its best when the clearest possible distinction between the crisp new contemporary work and the crumbling antiquity of the existing is established and therefore the style, the language, the materials and the character of each are different.

Although the inserted element is independent, particular qualities are derived from the original building. This is inevitable because the insertion always has a direct architectural relationship with the absolute physical properties of the existing space. It is built to fit. Factors such as the scale and the dimensions, the proportions, the rhythm and the structural composition of the existing building influence the design of the insertion. At times perhaps, the insertion can be seen as some sort of interpretation of the past.

It is necessary for the form of the host building to be sufficiently powerful to accommodate the addition of a new and autonomous object so that it is not overawed. It is also important that the host building is relatively physically unaltered, that it retains its original integrity. Often it is necessary for the architect to do little more than address any structural or environmental problems, although the complete restoration of the building to its original majesty may be required but the recognition of the distinction between the original building and the insertion is important. Equally, the insertion must be sufficiently strong to sit easily within or around it; a counterpoint or balance must be realised. For a successful dialogue to be established, the two components must be speaking equally loudly, albeit in different languages.

The tension and the ambiguities in the relationship between the two can also strengthen and reinvigorate the existing building allowing it to be looked at afresh, as though new life had been drawn into it.

At the Royal Exchange Theatre in Manchester, the structure containing the theatre was inserted as an alien element into the original exchange building. Levitt Bernstein designed the steel and glass 'space ship' in direct contrast to the formidable classical marble and stone of the existing building. It provides a focus for the space. The open hall of the Exchange building is so huge that the theatre can comfortably sit within it as a sculptural object and can be accessed from all sides. There is no confusion about what and where the theatre is. Both the original building and the insertion have strong independent characters and yet the theatre depends upon the exchange for such measures as scale, proportion, size and support. The floor of the exchange was not structurally capable of supporting the new structure, so the weight of the theatre was loaded onto long legs, which actually raise the theatre from the ground and transfer the load onto the columns of the original building. The insertion of this new object reinvigorates the original building. A symbiotic relationship between the two elements is established based upon juxtaposition, counterpoint and contrast, and this relationship heightens the quality of both.

The insertion of a new functioning element not only provides a use for an often redundant or neglected space but also serves to enhance and intensify the building itself. The strong relationship of attracting opposites, each complementing and enhancing the other, generates a building of a new and greater worth.

Fig.1. The Royal Exchange theatre, Manchester, relies on the old building for its structural support

Fig. 2. The theatre was inserted into the old Exchange building

De Trust Theatre

Location: **Amsterdam, Netherlands**
Previous Function: **Lutheran Church**
Built: **1792** Previous Architect: **Abraham Van Der Hart**
New Function: **Theatre**
Remodelled: **1999** Architect: **Mecanoo**

The fringe theatre group, the De Trust company, needed a permanent home that would embody the ethos of such an avant garde group, that would not overpower their performances, that they were not completely rooted to and that was within their limited budget.

Mecanoo embedded this ethos in the conversion of a disused church, into the heart of which new theatrical elements were inserted. They carefully separated the new elements from the old, allowing both to be easily distinguished.

The old Lutheran church is on the edge of the red light district in the Kloveniersburgwal. It was built in 1792 at a time when Protestant churches did not look like conventional churches. The classical façade was austere and contrasted with the interior, which was rather grand and elaborate.

The two-storey building contained a huge void in the centre and this, combined with the open ceiling, created a massive three-storey space in the middle. This was the great hall where the congregation once gathered. It was ringed by a series of very attractive carved timber columns. At the far end of the hall an ornate three-storey organ once dominated the space. In the 1950s a banking organisation acquired the building; they removed the organ (donating it to a church in Arnhem), and inserted an enormous archive into the void space. The building was sold in the 1980s and remained empty until De Trust group acquired it. Their requirements were for an auditorium, a bar, a foyer, rehearsal and office spaces.

The strategy of the architects was to design two new elements that were inserted into the voids left by the organ and the congregation area. The new auditorium was placed within the former worship area and the ancillary activities in the space vacated by the three-storey organ. Francine Houben of Mecanoo explains:

I want to design a piece of furniture that will make the space a theatre just as the organ makes the church. It stands on its own in the empty space and does not touch the colonnade of the old building...old and new do not come into contact, that is the principle of the details.[7]

The volume of the existing building and the arrangement of the columns in the space

Fig.1. The auditorium sits exactly in the congregation space. The natural light in the side aisles can be blacked out by drawing curtains across them

Fig. 2. The ancillary activities were designed as a single piece of furniture inserted to fill the void left by the old organ

Fig. 3. The new
elements are brightly
painted to
distinguish them
from the existing
surfaces

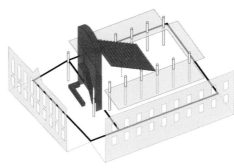

Fig. 4. The theatre
seating and the
ancillary services were
inserted into the
building without
touching the existing
structure

determined the strategy for reuse. The insertions have a very direct relationship with the physical properties of the space, in that they are built to fit into the church's void spaces.

The architects inserted the new function according to the existing volumes and dominance of the structure. The large opening on the upper floor immediately suggested where the largest requirement of the accommodation should go – the auditorium. Obviously, the view to the stage could not be obstructed. The architects calculated that a rake of 21 seats across and 15 high, with sufficient circulation, could slide between the columns at first floor level. The volume was high enough to accommodate suspended lighting and sound control, and was designed to be wrapped in a theatrical blue curtain during a performance. To allow the daytime users of the space some natural light, the curtain could be pulled back. This left a series of colonnaded residual spaces around the auditorium which are used for circulation and gathering before the show.

The bar, the kitchen, the technical control box and the vertical circulation were combined to produce a single element not unlike a piece of furniture, which was dropped into the void vacated by the organ. This clever insertion linked all floors and was painted red on the outside and gold inside, to reflect the light and to clearly distinguish between the old and new. Houben revealed that this new piece of furniture had similar qualities to that of the original organ. They both connected and facilitated the life of the space; both were inserted into the space and did not even touch the walls and, like the old organ, one day the new piece of theatrical furniture might be removed to another place.

This new insertion establishes an intense relationship with the original building. The character of the new is derived from an understanding of the old space. Its physical properties are directly informed by the available space of the host. The new theatre is a combination of the austere, almost foreboding qualities of the original building and the playful, temporary essence of the new.

Bull Staircase

Location: **Prague**
Built: **11th century**
Previous Function: **Palace**
New Function: **Presidential Palace**
Remodelled: **1921-1935** Architect: **Jože Plečnik**

A castle is a great symbol of the monarchy and yet ironically after the First World War when the new Republic of Czechoslovakia was created, Prague Castle was at the heart of this new independent state. Plečnik was requested to make a physical embodiment of democracy by reconstructing Prague Castle in a style in which the features of democracy would be clearly visible to everybody. The dilapidated castle, as well as other prominent feudal buildings, were to be remodelled as symbols of the newly gained independence.

The castle itself had developed over almost a thousand years into an enormous complex of churches, palaces and government buildings, connected by a series of courtyards and gardens. At the centre of the castle is the St Vitas Cathedral, which consists of a 13th century Gothic chancel with a 19th century Gothic revival nave.

Fig.1. The entrance to the bull stair sits provocatively in the corner of the courtyard

Plečnik was commissioned to make Prague Castle more uniform architecturally and to rebuild it in the image of the new state to meet the functional requirements of the time. The project involved the remodelling of the gardens, the ramparts, the official residence of the President, and the courtyards between them.

The strategy of insertion was used, a process in which a new element is introduced into, around, beside or over an existing building. At its best, the new is quite distinct from the old; but some of the fundamental qualities are shared because the insertion is built to fit.

Plečnik deliberately disrupted the monolithic impenetrability of the castle and, by doing so, successfully met his brief: the thrusting new Czech state had disrupted the monolithic old order. The insertions respected tradition, and yet at the same time were modern as he sought to find a new language to express the new Czech identity.

Throughout the castle complex Plečnik made a large number of alterations, new works and additions. These changes to the existing site and fabric of the castle were delicately laid out, based upon the sightlines and views across the site. On the west side of the site, the access to the castle was through a courtyard into a series of public spaces including a second and a third courtyard. Plečnik remodelled these spaces in the early 1920s by simply and effectively adding new paving. In the first court, two paths were delineated with huge slabs of differently treated granite, one path leading to the presidential apartments, the other to the columned hall in the second courtyard. Plečnik had to reconcile a succession of different levels and a series of archaeological excavations in the third courtyard. To achieve this, the whole courtyard was levelled and a series of objects such as the monolith originally intended for the gardens and the St George's fountain were carefully repositioned within it. To the south and southwest of the castle the Eden and Rampart Gardens were remodelled. A monumental staircase was inserted leading to the gardens, and the positioning of the fountains,

Fig. 2. The void
of the staircase
unites the city with
the castle

Fig. 3. The bull
staircase from the
lower garden

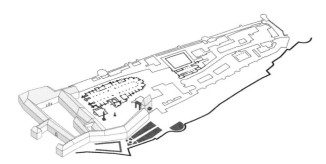

Fig. 4. The castle
complex, with the stair
penetrating through
the building

the vase on the stairs, the pyramid and obelisk, and the landscaping of the entire garden were all reorganised.

Probably the most important and relevant insertion into the castle is the Bull Staircase, which now links the corner of the upper third courtyard with the lower garden to the south side of the castle. Tomáš Valena describes this as 'a descent into the mythical history of the place'.[8]

The staircase is a symbol of democracy; it slices right through the castle walls and thus creates a connection between the castle itself and the city below. It contains a number of flights and the descent frames exceptional views through the space and over the garden to the city. The staircase is pulled back into the body of the castle, with just the projecting balconies breaking the line of the wall. Each floor contains a pillar instead of a central wall, a device used at the palace staircase at Knossos, allowing the view to be opened up. Plečnik acknowledged this reference with the use of Minoan columns. The covered entrance in the third courtyard is constructed from two wooden beams resting upon four columns which are literally draped with a canopy of copper. On top of the columns sit the bulls and it is from this that the staircase gets its name.

The staircase is an element inserted into a void cut from the castle walls. As important as the element itself is the gap or empty space that provides the views and the link between the castle of the late monarchy and the people of the city. This is a symbolic act of cutting through the old impenetrable royalist kingdom to create the new democratic state. The bull staircase insertion illustrates and narrates the history and identity of the new state.

Fig.1. Visually, the
space slips beyond
the boundary of
the building to the
sunken pool

Canova Sculpture Gallery

Location: **Possagno, Italy**
Former Function: **Sculpture Gallery (Gipsoteca)**
Built: **1836** Previous Architect: **Guiseppe Segusini**
New Function: **Sculpture Gallery Addition**
Remodelled: **1955-57** Architect: **Carlo Scarpa**

In celebration of the bicentennial of the birth of the Possagno-born sculptor Antonio Canova, Carlo Scarpa was commissioned to expand the Gipsoteca. The existing gallery could not adequately display the sheer numbers of original plaster models, casts, marble works and small sketch models that they possessed. The existing building was very formal in arrangement, with a tall magnificent vaulted roof and a large imposing space for the exhibits.

Scarpa was instructed that nothing need be preserved and yet, far from destroying any of the original, he revolutionized the space. He created an additional building that was positioned beside the formal basilica plan original building. The new gallery provided extra space for casts and models which had been in storage and it also alleviated the congestion of the original gallery, and became the home for a cast of Canova's most famous sculpture, The Three Graces.

Fig. 2. The dramatic light of the cube is accentuated by the darkness of the ante-space

In Possagno, the new element inserted was a whole new gallery alongside Segusini's Gipsoteca. The very act of this placement initiates a conversation between the existing and the insertion, yet each exists in a strong and independent manner.

The Gipsoteca interior is immense in scale and proportion. As the floor advances so the ceiling appears to rise and frame the final sculpture in an architectural denouement. The space is rendered in white and light pours in from the roof adding to the theatricality of the room. Scarpa's new gallery counterpoints the monumental unity of the hall. It respects and understands it, reworks some of the ideas and yet provides a gentle contrast. Scarpa creates a small space that unites the fragmentary nature of the site and uses some of Segusini's architectural devices to make an insertion that complements the fierce independence of the Gipsoteca. The site of the insertion contained some inconsequential buildings; Scarpa removed these but retained their outline or memories, which were incorporated into the new space. The junction between the old and the new was clearly defined. The sidewall of the original ante-space was opened up and the floor raised, thus creating distinctly different types of space.

The new gallery consists of two interconnected elements. The first is a cubic volume, lit from above by four prism-shaped windows. The second is a narrowing wedge, stepping down and following the shape and contours of the site.

Assimilating the formal devices of the Gipsoteca gallery, Scarpa reworked the stepped cascading roof theme into the new addition. Stepping the roof and the floor down to the thinnest end of the space allows him to contrast it with the tall cubic volume of the initial gallery. The journey toward the thin end of the gallery is framed by the roof and a small glazed opening at the far end. Repeating the conclusion of the Gipsoteca north wall, Scarpa uses this point to place the statue of The Three Graces. This journey, however, continues beyond the end wall, to the exterior where the boundaries of the site allow for a narrow pool of water. Reflections from the sun wash into the space and onto the statue, animating it within the gallery. It is at this point that the contrast between the static axial space of the original building and the dynamic qualities of the *promenade architecturale* of the new are at their greatest.

As well as this change of level, Scarpa clearly differentiates between the new insertion and the sidewall of the old hall by separating the two buildings with a screen wall. A strip of land is left free between the west wall of the Gipsoteca and the new addition. This strip, a light court, divides the old and new, both physically with structure and atmospherically with light. The new wall is a steel structure that begins as an open frame, is then glazed, then become solid with small windows to protect and frame the Three Graces, and in the final section, as it slides toward the nose of the building and through the end, it is masonry. This treatment offers a deliberate contrast with the heavy stone of the adjacent Gipsoteca's west wall. A glazed reveal ties the extension

to the existing building and allows the heavily articulated exterior masonry of the Gipsoteca to form part of the inside wall of the new addition. In the main cube Scarpa manipulates the light in order to animate the arrangement of the sculptures in the space. The corners of the cubes are removed to diffuse light into the tall space and create an incredible variety of shadows and light throughout the day. The frames are concealed and so a direct relationship with the sky is established.

Through the distinct architectural separation of old and new, the insertion by Scarpa is clearly distinguished from Segusini's Gipsoteca, yet a tension is created by the ambiguities of reworking many of the themes prevalent in the old building. A powerful dialogue between the original building and the new insertion is created, and it is this dialogue which strengthens and reinvigorates the existing and allows both new and old to be considered in a way that creates a unity of a much greater worth.

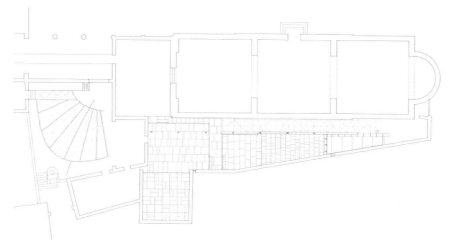

Fig. 3. Plan showing the relationship between the orthogonal original building and the wedge of modernist space

German Design Centre

Location: **Essen, Germany**
Former Function: **Colliery Power Plant**
Built: **1927-1932** Previous Architect: **Fritz Schupp, Martin Kremmer**
New Function: **Museum / gallery/ offices**
Remodelled: **1997** Architect: **Foster Associates**

The Ruhr area of Germany was probably once the most industrialised place on earth, but in this post-industrial age, in parallel with much of the western world, it had to search for a new focus. The Zeche Zollverein coal mine in the Ruhrgebeit area was just one of many in the region to close in the 1980s, leaving a vast tract of land riven with miles of underground tunnels and occupied by a series of enormous structures, including the washing plant, the boiler house and the enormous pithead shaft that contained the winding gear.

From the 1990s onwards many parts of the coal mine were regenerated and re-opened to house a business park that accommodated offices, design studios, and even a restaurant. Foster Associates remodelled the cavernous space of the boiler house to turn it into the German Design Centre. The museum was inserted into the engine room of the coal mine, an area that once supplied power to the entire complex. This vast echoing industrial building is very much of its time. Extremely rational, it was rigorously constructed from

a steel frame with brick and glass infill. The new Design Centre displays examples of good quality German product design, everything from cars to taps.

When the project began, four of the five boilers were removed and the unstable chimney was demolished. In order to retain the atmosphere of the original building, its dramatic interior was exposed and left unrestored. The existing fabric of the building was strewn with the raw detritus of the working life of the mine. Steel columns and beams were exposed, pipes, dials, gauges, and conveyors littered the space, but the most significant aspect of the building was the space left by the removal of the enormous boilers. On the first floor, the outlines of the boilers can be seen and on the ground floor, the undercroft is dominated by the furnaces and the structure for the support for the colossal engines.

In among the elements of the old space, Foster inserted new circulation routes and display areas. These loop around the perimeter of the building and to all sides of and in-between the furnaces. This strategy

Fig.1. Shiny new objects placed against the decaying hulk of the original building ensure maximum contrast

of insertion allows the original to exist relatively untouched. Unfinished and incomplete buildings can inform the placing of inserted objects. The boiler house was meant to house six furnaces but only five were ever installed. The missing sixth furnace left a space and an incomplete symmetry and it was in this area that Foster Associates restored the balance by inserting a new stack of circulation and display space. This fair-faced concrete insertion contrasts with the rugged exposed fabric of the host. It rises through the space to connect with the upper floor offices and contains a glass and steel lift and a concealed stair well. On the ground floor in the only part of the space that was column-free, due to the lighter load of the new circulation and gallery tower above it, the architects placed the auditorium.

In this project Foster used the incomplete geometry of the building to inform the placement of the new inserted object. The tower is built to fit yet it is clearly

distinguishable from the old building by the textures and finish of the surfaces. By imposing upon the existing building in the lightest of ways, Foster Associates expose the drama and scale of the space.

The contrast between the textures of the rough exposed boiler house and the smoothness of the new insertion enhances the drama and scale of both. In this theatrical space, the new German Design Centre products are displayed against the backdrop of the wreckage of the host, an explicit demonstration of technological and industrial progress. The power of the existing and its atmospheric condition contrast with the sleek modern insertions that Foster Associates deploy throughout the space. The new glass and steel circulation walkway and the concrete and glass tower and lift counterpoint the rusted decayed qualities of the boiler house and the furnaces. The tension between them reinforces the integrity of the original building.

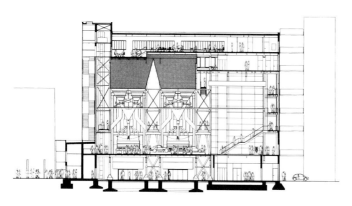

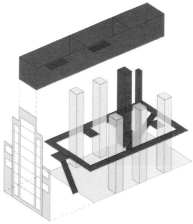

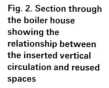

Fig. 2. Section through the boiler house showing the relationship between the inserted vertical circulation and reused spaces

Fig. 3. New vertical circulation inserted into the space for the missing sixth boiler. A walkway is slung around the edge of the building and a strip of offices inserted at roof level

Fig. 4. Main hall of the
building where objects
are exhibited amongst
the detritus of the
boiler house

Fig. 1. This atmospheric drawing 'captures the long abandoned sounds of architecture'

Museum for Pre- and Early History

Location: **Frankfurt, Germany**
Former Function: **Carmelite Monastery with Church**
Built: **Unknown** Previous architect: **Unknown**
New Function: **Museum with shop and café**
Remodelled: **1989** Architect: **Josef P. Kleihues**

Frankfurt anticipated the rise in the popularity of cultural tourism. It was one of the forerunners of the idea of the museum as a recreational activity and the regeneration of a place through art and tourism. Many cities are now defined by their cultural institutions, and museums, like cathedrals, attract visitors. Frankfurt recognised the ability of architecture to enrich the urban landscape and initiated the cultural regeneration of the city with a series of museums strung along the south bank of the river Main and through the urban landscape. These include: the Museum of German Architecture by O. M. Ungers, the Museum of the Federal German Post by Behnisch and Partners, the Museum of Modern Art by Hans Hollein, the Museum of Arts and Crafts by Richard Meier as well as the Museum for Pre- and Early History by Josef P. Kleihues.

Fig. 2. New roof over the church expresses the formal qualities of the original building

John Hejduk described Kleihues as a long-distance runner architect whose work was getting both sparser and richer:

He captures the long abandoned sounds of architecture. He celebrates the ancient laws and mysteries of the rites of construction. He brings forth through his knowledge of materials and detail of the density of brooding stone, the dark soul of steel, the thought/reflection of glass, the ecclesiasticalness of wood, the softness of earth and the crystallization of air. He is the architect of pewter. He polishes architecture with the palm of his hand and places it in the landscape with the care that the painter Giorgio Morandi gave to his still lifes.[9]

Kleihues is an architect who strives to combine the present day with the historical, to create a dialogue between the modern and the traditional. He has designed more than twenty museums or exhibition halls and Hejduk's comparing him to a long-distance runner is apt because each building is, in terms of thought, a continuation of the last. His theoretical ideas about the relationship of recollection and 'the concept and practice of remembrance have supported planning, detailing and the choice of materials for the Pre-history Museum'.[10]

The museum was placed in an old monastery building, making use of the deconsecrated church for the main exhibition space. The nave of the derelict church was repaired and re-roofed. Kleihues reinstated the street line and made provision for the necessary museum services by creating a long thin additional building between the main building and the street. This thin sliver of space contains the entrance, foyer, bookshop, offices and exhibition space.

Insertion is a method of attaching and connecting an autonomous element to an existing building and although each may have an extremely personal identity, a close association is created.

Kleihues creates two such relationships in the Museum for Pre-History. The first is the long slender ancillary building attached to the nave of the church, yet separate from the great hall, which gives the museum a new presence and street façade.

This addition makes no concession to the language or properties of the original building; it is clad in alternate bands of red and grey sandstone and, contrarily, is actually a reference to the Frankfurt Stock Exchange, which was destroyed during World War Two.

The second relationship is the new cut steel roof structure that spans the great hall of the church. This slender structure is reminiscent of the original stone vaulting and creates a feeling of being both old and new at the same time. The new construction seems completely natural, as though it has always been there and unnatural because it obviously cannot have been. Hejduk was 'aware that something profound has occurred. A healing has taken place.'[11]

The insertions ensured that the separate identities of the new and old elements making up the building remained intact and yet their relationship is such that together they create a strong, articulated character totally appropriate to the ideas of a Museum for Pre- and Early History.

Fig. 3. Old and new
are simply butted
together

Sackler Galleries, Royal Academy

Location: **London, England** Former Function: **Diploma Galleries and Light Well**
Built: **Burlington House 1665. Diploma Galleries 1867**
Previous architect: **Burlington House, Sir John Denham, Diploma Galleries, Sydney Smirke**
New Function: **Galleries, circulation and foyer**
Remodelled: **1991** Architect: **Foster Associates**

In the late 1980s, the president of the RA, Roger de Grey, asked Foster Associates to consider the out-of-date Diploma Galleries and install some air conditioning. Foster's approach is to always question the brief and if necessary step beyond the boundary of the programme. He quickly realised that if the request of the patron was to be acknowledged ('Dr Sackler is not interested in loft conversions'), then the project had to be considerably more involved.[12]

The Royal Academy is a complicated set of buildings and extensions. The front section, Burlington House, was designed as a family home by Sir John Denham in 1665. A Palladian façade by Colen Campbell was added in 1715 and the garden house was completed by Sydney Smirke in 1867. Smirke also remodelled the original Diploma galleries and rooms at the same time. He added these third floor toplit galleries to Burlington House, cleverly disguising their impact upon the front courtyard by hiding them behind a blind niche wall. Since its original construction as a country house, the

building had been extended or remodelled fourteen times, by such illustrious architects as Colen Campbell, William Kent, James Gibbs, Samuel Ware, Sir Charles Barry and Norman Shaw.

The contemporary requirements for galleries meant that the problems of inadequate environmental control and the difficulty of access made the Diploma Galleries unsuitable for holding exhibitions and Foster Associates were commissioned to address these concerns.

As we have seen, insertion can be used to reinvigorate a place through the placement of a powerful element within an existing building. The position of such an element can create an exciting dialogue between itself and the context into which it is placed. It can be used to generate a new function in a previously unoccupied space or draw new life into neglected parts of a building. It is important that the host space is strong and is of great integrity so that one does not overwhelm the other but rather that the two can co-exist in tension.

Fig.1. Self-supporting inserted structure only lightly touches the original walls

A gap of about 14 ft had been left between the back of Burlington House and the Garden house extension during construction; this was allegedly discovered by Foster during a meeting in an adjoining office. This grimy space, open to the elements, contained plumbing, lavatories and other ancillary equipment collected over the hundreds of years of the building's existence. The light well proved to be the key to the solution of the design problem. In an analysis of the existing building, Foster Associates concluded that the new gallery renovations were useless unless access was improved to the upper floors of the building and this 4.2 m wide vertical slice of free space could provide exactly that.

Julian Harrap Architects were commissioned to restore – completely and beautifully – the decaying façades that directly faced onto the light well. Inserted into this slot was a highly contemporary steel and glass element of circulation and entrance. It had a progressive, industrially-refined finish that contrasted strongly with the classical style of the existing building.

Resting upon the existing walls, a finely-crafted square-section steel and glass balcony was placed right at the top of the light well; indeed the cornice on the outside of the main RA galleries was appropriated and turned into a long low sculpture plinth. Connecting this enclosed balcony to the ground floor is the vertical access to the Sackler Galleries. The stairs and lift rise enigmatically towards the light from either ends of the well. They are supported by just four round-section white painted steel columns and barely touch the original building. The lift is predominantly glass and the stairs have glass treads and both appear almost to float. The edges of the balcony floor are also made of glass, which allows light to fall through the space, illuminating the journey and accentuating the brightness of the elevated entrance platform.

The picture galleries are entered from the high-level balcony and are finished in the 20th century style of white walls and maple floors. They are of course meticulously detailed and the air-conditioning is notably efficient.

This project was quite unusual for Foster Associates. It lacked the usual bravado and obsession with an overtly engineered solution; instead, it modestly and sympathetically handled the relationship between the existing building and the intervention.

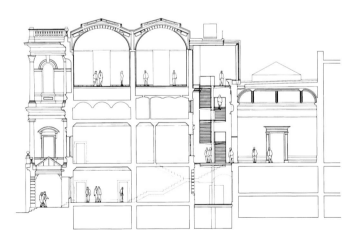

Fig. 2. Section showing the vertical relationship established by the Sackler Galleries

The Sackler Gallery insertion changed a previously unused space into a functioning gallery. The new access route and the sculpture promenade narrate the development of the building's growth. The Smirke and Ware façades were cleaned and repaired and provide the backdrop for the ascent to the galleries. Their strength as architectural compositions can now be read at close quarters; they were never intended to be read as whole elements but as fragments, which visitors can now view as they ascend the stair. The strength of this backdrop is counterpointed by the new insertion. This element is independent but gains in strength and magnitude when compared to the host. The language is of a very different time yet it is of a similar magnitude. Foster described the project as entirely his own and as 'a deliberate interpretation of how you relate the old to the new and get something richer and more dynamic out of both.'[13]

Fig. 3. Foyer area at the top of the building is a pure light-filled space

Fig.1. View from the
courtyard to the
chapel. The new roof
emerges from the
depths of the
orthogonal building

Gerona University

Location: **Gerona, Spain**
Former Function: **University buildings including a chapel**
Built: **14th to 16th century** Previous Architect: **Unknown**
New Function: **Administrative headquarters, library and information area**
Remodelled: **1995** Architect: **Josep Fuses, Joan Maria Viader**

The University was once at the very heart of the provincial capital city of Gerona, situated just to the south of the cathedral. But as the city became industrialised, the historic centre became more and more marginalised. The university buildings were abandoned and were allowed to fall into ruin. The architects' restoration of the Les Aligues area demonstrates the contribution that the university can play as a key element in the cultural and historical regeneration of the city. The architects were commissioned to provide accommodation for an information area, an administration area and a library.

Josep Fuses and Joan Maria Viader spent approximately ten years refining and assembling this building. This long incubation allowed for endless reflection and refinement, ensuring a design of high quality. The site of Les Aligues is congealed into its context and comprises a series of chronologically and stylistically disparate buildings set around a courtyard (Plaça Sant Domenec). The site was bounded by the Roman wall of the city. There was a 14th century retaining wall on the south side, an adjoining Dominican Monastery with two chapels, only one of which was on this site, and a 16th century University building. The site was in a ruinous state

when design work began: the Chapel had no back wall or roof, and the university building was in total disrepair.

The architects' approach was to complete the courtyard. To accomplish this they designed a totally new wing to accommodate the university library, positioned the administrative area within the existing north and west buildings and inserted the information centre into the ruined chapel.

The L-shaped university building was carefully restored and the administration area placed within it as a sensitive series of new elements juxtaposed against the rustic fabric of the original building. The new two-storey rectangular library wing completes the courtyard and has a sense of continuity with its context. But it is the conversion of the chapel that is most relevant. The remodelling takes the form of an insertion that appears to be floating up from inside the chapel; it is very effective because the original building and the new element display their own character and still develop an intense relationship. The insertion is completely dependent upon the original building for its scale, mass, size and position and yet the style and the materials are obviously 20th century. As in all good insertions, the tension between the two heightens both.

The chapel occupies the heart of the composition. It is situated upon roughly the central axis of the site and in its ruinous state had no back wall or roof. The architects reduced the height of the three remaining walls, removing the late addition high gable from the front façade and two windows that were structurally weakening the building. They then took the approach of accepting the history and difference of the building:

We decided to maintain the three façades, with all of their history plainly visible, without doing the slightest restoration work on them. We were attracted by the variety of textures resulting from aged stuccos, occasional holes, different types of stones, all distributed at random across the surface.[14]

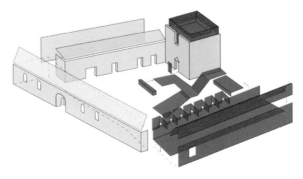

Fig. 2. The courtyard is completed by the insertion of a wing attached to the university building and a roof rising from the shell of the old chapel

The designers also preserved the doorway, an opening framed with Renaissance-style ashlars. The details were retained in order to maintain the character of the original building. Despite this preservation of historical details, the power of the removal of the top of the building and the austerity of the walls gives the building a distinctly modern feel.

The architects enclosed the chapel by adding a new wall and then using the three existing and one new wall for structural support, completing it with what appears to be a hovering roof. This startling new addition seems to float free from the chapel, giving the appearance of the interior sliding out from the inside of the building.

The new roof is constructed from huge concrete beams spanning the top of the walls and supporting concrete half vaults, which fold out of the chapel roof and in turn support an upside-down pyramid roof and glazed walls. The half vaults allow the structure to sit away from the edge of the building and therefore the glazed walls of the roof section appear to be sliding up, out of the main body of the chapel and the roof seems to float. The architects explain this approach:

We felt that the roof should be seen as one element of the whole … added with the intention of not being especially differentiated, an element which could be at the same time very heavy and very light, whose gravity would be counteracted by the suspension of its support, effected tangentially and with no apparent exterior contact with the old walls on which it would rest.[15]

The pure square of the black marble floor is separated from the walls by a strip of white travertine. This reflects the construction of the roof and reinforces the concept of the modern element having been inserted into the building. Although at ground level the insertion is not physically apparent, the natural light around the edges of the room, the dark floor and the hovering roof element all combine to create a seemingly visible element from the slot of space. The furniture in the new information centre is minimal and free-standing,

maintaining the echoic atmosphere of a religious building and so the enormous top-lit roof insertion dominates the internal space, its brutal modernism balanced by the simplicity of the exterior walls.

The Gerona University remodelling is a careful and sensitive appropriation of an existing building's fabric and character. Fuses and Viader use the identity and language of the existing to construct a solid yet appropriate response. The new chapel and wing insertions are of sufficient strength and simplicity of language to be clearly distinct while not seeking to overpower the host. The form of the chapel is robust, its orthogonal geometry influencing the new moves to its fabric. The heaviness of its stone shell is counterpointed by the light glass screen and half-vault ceiling rising from within. The new insertion clearly takes its cues from the existing.

Fig. 3. The roof of the chapel appears to soar from the top of the building, allowing light to penetrate to ground level

The Ondaatje Wing

Location: **London, England**
Former Function: **National Portrait Gallery**
Built: **1896** Previous Architect: **Ewan Christian**
New Function: **Galleries and circulation**
Remodelled: **2000** Architect: **Jeremy Dixon Edward Jones**

The best design solutions always appear to be so obvious and so simple that it is surprising that no one has thought of them before. This is the impression given by the design for the Ondaatje Wing at the National Portrait Gallery. In a daring and imaginative deal the National Gallery gave the National Portrait Gallery a service yard in exchange for the gallery space along St Martin's Place. The gallery space nicely tidied up a ragged corner for the National Gallery, but the service yard had a massive implication for the National Portrait Gallery. It enabled them to enlarge the entrance area, construct a foyer space fit for a nationally important gallery and to construct a series of galleries so that a considerably larger proportion of their collection could be on show. A new element was inserted into the old service yard, holding the foyer space, two new galleries, a lecture theatre, IT facilities and a new rooftop restaurant all linked together with a dramatic circulation route.

An inserted element will establish an intense relationship between itself and the host building and often the character of each will be heightened by the connection. At the National Portrait Gallery, the huge white box insertion certainly contrasts greatly with the original classical galleries; it is squeezed into a grubby internal service yard but has a liberating effect. It frees the gallery from the tortuously clumsy old circulation route, throws light into the heart of the building and provides the building with a 21st century image.

In 1994 a competition was organised to obtain ideas for the remodelling of the gallery spaces. Visitor numbers had risen yet few people were making the journey to the top floor of the building where the bulk of the collection was displayed. Jeremy Dixon Edward Jones won the competition.

Previously when entering the building on the ground floor from Charing Cross Road the visitor to the gallery had immediately to

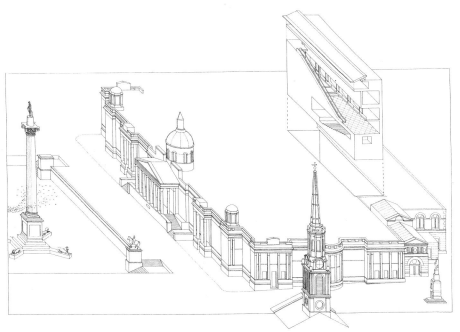

Fig.1. The wing is inserted into a former loading bay between the buildings

Fig. 2. On entering, the view of the long escalator is established. The dramatic light emphasises the hanging mezzanine galleries

take a sharp right turn to reach the main ground floor collection. To get upstairs they had to locate the great staircase, which was hidden behind the upper landing of the main lobby, and was off-putting because it was long and imposingly monumental. The more straightforward route, which was straight ahead, was occupied by a service yard, the rights to its natural light being held by the neighbouring National Gallery. The Portrait Gallery owned the ground floor and basement while the upper floors provided light to offices in the National Gallery and could not be blocked off.

The architect suggested negotiating with the National Gallery and exchanging space in order to build an insertion that would fit into the yard and allow generous access and gallery floor space. This was a most ambitious proposal but one strongly favoured by the National Portrait Gallery, who embarked upon detailed and extensive negotiations. A swap was agreed and the yard was handed to the Portrait Gallery in return for some of its East Wing provision.

The inserted box contains all the required functional accommodation and fits into the service yard exactly. It derives its proportions and scale from the host space between the two galleries, but it not only has to fit the yard but it also has to correspond to the various levels of the existing staircase and gallery floors. The multi-layered insertion adds a monumental presence to the previously secretive, hidden nature of the Portrait Gallery.

In the new form, the triple-storey height entrance space immediately makes the visitor aware of the organisation of the building. The clerestory windows allow light into the third floor lobby area and this is linked to the entrance area by an very long escalator. The visitor is invited to take this and as they rise, they can catch glimpses into all the galleries. The new insertion monumentalises this ascent in the top-lit white box, on the longest escalator outside the London Underground. The clarity and light is shocking and contrasts deeply with the top gallery where the Tudor and 17th and 18th century portraits are hung on dark grey fabric in darkened rooms. Starting from this second floor where the exhibition begins, visitors take a chronological journey down through the building to the 20th century on the ground floor. At the very top of the new insertion above the galleries is a rooftop restaurant and bar that has a fantastic aspect and provides views over the domes and cupolas of the National Gallery roof towards Nelson's Column.

The new insertion into the old service yard reorganises and revitalises the gallery in a radical manner. It simplifies movement through the building and is sufficiently powerful to complement the host by acting as a foil for the reorganisation of its entire contents. 'The new east wing is an extremely complex project that responds intelligently to its historic site'.[16] The contrast between its pristine white walls and the old galleries leaves the visitor in no doubt that it is of a different time, yet the success of the insertion is as a result of that dialogue between the two.

Fig. 4. Light cascades into the foyer space

Fig. 3. A perspective drawing depicts the complex and sophisticated purity of the insertion

Fig.1. The monumental
scale wall, by Christo
and Jeanne-Claude,
overawes the visitor

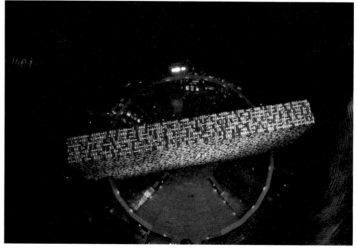

Fig. 2. The gasometer
is 25 storeys high
and the new drum
wall 12 storeys

Strategy
Installation

Installation is a process where the elements of remodelling exist independently from the building; the two simply touch each other.

Installation is the placement of a series or group of related elements within the context of an existing building. This is a process that, while recognising the oeuvre of an architect, will heighten the awareness of an existing building and successfully combine the two without compromising or interfering with either.

The character of the objects or elements that constitute the installation is usually dictated by the style or the passion of the commissioned architect or artist. There are generally a number of related imported objects, concepts and ideas that embody the character of the creator and are positioned in groups or in series. The objects are usually of a limited size and often have a limited lifespan, such as an exhibition.

The objects are not necessarily without a relationship with the host building; they can be grouped together or placed in position to give maximum impact, both to the building and to themselves. They can be used to organise and delineate space or to create order in a confusion of buildings and volumes. Considerations such as adjustments of scale and appropriateness can be dictated by the building itself. The site can set up the parameters and be part of the reason for the installation. It can inspire the installation; the existing materials, structure, quality of space, history, context all may directly provide the impetus or generate the design of the new installed elements.

The host building generally needs few physical modifications. The architect will repair or even restore it but these changes generally have nothing to do with the installation.

Sometimes the host building is little more than a stage for the performance of the objects but the best installations actually expose and reveal the beauty and qualities of it, allowing it to be read and understood in its own condition. The installation will enliven and reveal the true, possibly hidden or lost character of the building.

Christo and Jeanne-Claude created an installation in a disused gasometer in Oberhausen, Germany. This huge structure was a very unusual host building; circular with a diameter of over 50 m, the empty space was 25 storeys high, that is, about 100m. The artists constructed a high wall made from oil barrels in the middle of the space. The coloured barrels, which were stacked ten deep and reached to about half the height of the building, were intended to provoke reflections upon the scale of the space and its former function. The barrels were imported objects intended to enliven the space; they were neither built to fit, having been collected and placed within the space, nor did they alter the building in any way. At the end of the exhibition, the installation was dismantled and removed, the two elements returning to their original state.

Installation can be seen as the generation of a symbiotic relationship between a building and the series of elements placed within it. The two often have quite different characters and it is their juxtaposition that provides life and vitality for both.

Magna Centre

Location: **Rotherham, UK**
Former Function: **Steelworks**
Built: **1917** Architect: **Unknown**
New Function: **Science Adventure Centre**
Remodelled: **2001** Architect: **Wilkinson Eyre Architects**

The Templeborough steelworks in Yorkshire was once the largest smelting plant in Europe. Built in 1917 to meet demand for steel during the First World War, the enormous steel workshops were housed in a shed that measured 350 m long by 50 m wide. This colossal space was organised along the lines of the linear production process, from the creation to the storage and then distribution of vast amounts of steel. During the 1950s more than 10,000 men worked there. In 1993 the steelworks were closed and left unused until the late 1990s when the local authority embarked upon the reuse of Templeborough as a museum of steel-making. Their ambition was to create a heritage centre that would commemorate the huge commitment made by Yorkshire to the steel industry. This idea developed into a successful National Lottery bid which

widened the programme into a broader-based 'Science Adventure Centre'. Wilkinson Eyre Architects were commissioned to turn this into reality. They were already known for their knowledge on the subject of large buildings, Chris Wilkinson being the author of 'Supersheds'.

The Magna Science Adventure Centre is an experience-based attraction, designed to convey the story of the steel-making process through an exploration of the four elements; fire, earth, water and air. Each element is represented by an enormous pavilion containing interactive exhibitions and displays dedicated to each particular element. The pavilions connect to the building and to each other with new circulation; a metal catwalk elevates visitors away from the dark and dangerous ground floor of the steelworks. The size of the host

Fig. 1. Remnants of the steel producing plant, hoppers, cauldrons and cranes are reminders of the building's original function

allows for future development in the form of temporary galleries, and other exhibition spaces. For reasons of economy and practicality, the heating and air conditioning is restricted to the pavilions, the huge shed becoming a sort of inside/outside area.

A particular characteristic of an installation-based approach to remodelling is that the host building is treated as a stage for a performance. The beauty and qualities of the existing building are allowed to be read and understood in their own condition but act as a backdrop. This approach at the Magna Science Adventure invigorates the decrepit shell of the steelworks and revitalises it, showing the building in a new light. It does not compromise the host's character but on the contrary allows its natural beauty and awe-inspiring scale to shine through.

Inside the shed space the architects installed four pavilions. They are designed to be read as independent of the existing fabric, their appearance at odds with the host building. Each pavilion is intended to evoke

the image of their title and reflect the contents of the exhibition inside. The dirt, dust and darkness of the interior of the steelworks is in stark contrast to the brilliant appearance of each object.

The exhibition has two aspects: an educational interactive science display and a dynamic, noisy, spirit of steel-making spectacular extravaganza. The roaring noise of the the old steelworks is reproduced, the retained arc furnace spits, sparks and crashes, and these, with the atmospheric lighting, come together in front of the huge stage set of the steelworks.

The Air pavilion is a tensile structure that hangs from the original crane rail in the shed. It is cigar-shaped and appears almost to float like an airship through the space. It is enormous, about 40 m long, and yet is dwarfed by the sheer scale of the shed. Directly below it is the Earth pavilion, fittingly buried in the floor and seemingly carved from stone and concrete with a rough unfinished quality.

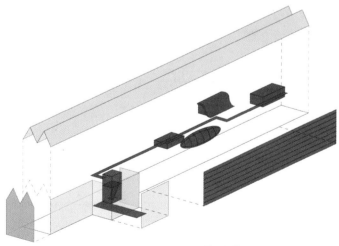

Fig. 2. The raised walkway connecting the individual pavilions within the long twin bay shed

The Water pavilion has an elliptical wave-like form and is lit with rings of blue neon. Resting on the floor, it seems fragile and light in comparison to the massive shed and discarded structures and debris around it. Fire, a black steel box, is the final pavilion in the journey and provides the denouement of the series of experiences. The re-enactment of the process of steel-making within the arc furnace demonstrates its hazards and noise which, combined with the reflected red light from the shed cladding, all add to the atmosphere of danger.

The pavilions are positioned to afford the visitor maximum drama as they negotiate the shed. The pavilions are accessed from the former transformer building, the original control tower of the whole plant. This now houses lifts and stairs. Much of the steelwork machinery was too difficult and costly to remove; objects such as cranes, hoppers and cauldrons were left where they were when the works closed down. Some objects that could be removed are now exhibited on plinths outside the building as industrial sculptures. The appropriation of these objects into the installation leads to further instances of the juxtaposition of old and new. These objects become industrial artefacts. Their appropriation sets the scene for the new installations inside.

The generation of a dynamic dialogue between the existing structure and a series of new elements placed within it revitalises original space through dynamic contrasts. The two may be different but it is their juxtaposition that provides vitality for both.

Fig. 3. The Air pavilion appears to float in the shed space

Mandarina Duck

Location: **Rue St Honore, Paris**
Former Function: **Retail space**
Built: **Unknown**   Architect: **Unknown**
New Function: **Shop**
Remodelled: **2001**   Architects: **Droog Design (Gijs Bakker & Renny Ramakers)**

In this age of innovation, shoppers are looking for a heightened experience and expect to be enticed into a shop. They need to be wooed, to be surprised, delighted and amazed. Retailers sell not only products but also an image. The personality of the shop and the products will be transferred to the consumer. Whether cool, minimal and sophisticated or down-to earth and trustworthy, by wearing the clothes, carrying the accessories or using the goods, the image projected by the retailer will rub off on to the consumer.

Mandarina Duck, an Italian luggage company also selling clothes, have a funky, high design yet slightly off-the-wall image and it was this look that they wanted to project with a series of shops in major cities across

Europe. Droog Design, whose previous work was sympathetic to the design ethos of Mandarina Duck, were commissioned to create the transferable overall concept and also the flagship shop in Paris.

The location is one of the most fashionable streets in Paris, situated in the heart of the designer showroom area. The two-storey corner site was so modest in size that the upper floor was enlarged to take over the first floor of the adjoining building. This led to an unusual plan form, with the upper floor overlapping the ground floor of its neighbour, creating a considerably larger area at the upper level.

The strategy of installation is the arrangement and display of a series or a group of elements within an existing building. The objects have a relationship with each other but not necessarily with the building or space that they are placed in, although they are often displayed in a manner that provides the building with maximum impact.

Mandarina Duck adopted an unusual strategy to develop their identity. In order to differentiate their shops across the world,

Fig.1. As the visitor enters the shop, the cocoons become visible

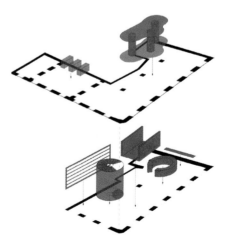

Fig. 2. The store is designed as a series of installations inside the envelope of the building, each display object having a distinct character of its own

they commissioned Droog to create a concept that could be translated in a variety of ways. Local designers would then be approached to interpret the idea in each retail location. The concept was to install in each shop an identical series of free-standing objects called 'cocoons'. These elements were intended to display the products for sale, but the exact method depended upon the individual designer. The cocoons were described as: circle, tunnel, wall, curtain, and enclosure.

Droog organised the cocoons in the Paris shop with no real relationship to the host building apart from the fact that they were bounded by its enclosure. It was treated as no more than a minimal white-painted backdrop, a neutral space that did not detract from the impact of the installations, and the objects were placed independently of it and of each other, in a way that reinforced their autonomous nature.

The cocoons were designed to display the Mandarina Duck products, and the articles for sale were actually concealed within them. It was intended that the process of discovery ensured that the products became precious, that the beauty of each item was examined.

Each of the cocoons is radically different. They bear no physical relation to each other but this very fact, combined with their playful nature and their 21st century-language, actually connects them together. In the Paris shop, Droog selected the display method for each cocoon: a curving curtain of thin translucent plastic lines directs customers through the shop; a three and a half metre diameter metal doughnut hides clothing within it; a stack of internally-lit plastic pallets holds handbags; a wall of metal pins grasps luggage while another wall of elastic bands suspends purses; and a crop circle of long white fibreglass canes defines the changing rooms. The playful nature of this farrago of components makes them stand out from each other and from the building. It reinforces the fact that they are independent objects in space.

The installation of these objects ensures that the building becomes little more than a stage for their performance. The signature of Droog architects is quite explicit and reinforces their identity as unusual installation-based designers.

The witty playful nature of each of the cocoons enlivens the interior space, impressing the identity of Mandarina Duck on to the visitor.

Galerie de l'Evolution

Location: **Paris**
Former Function: **Natural History Museum**
Built: **1889** Architect: **Jules André**
New Function: **Gallery exhibiting vast collection of animals**
Remodelled: **1994** Architects: **Paul Chemetov, Borja Huidobro, Rene Allio**

The Natural History Museum was renovated and reopened as one of President Mitterrand's hugely ambitious and successful *Grands Projects*. It had been closed to the public for thirty years. Constructed towards the end of the 19th century, it is just one of a number of buildings arranged around the Jardin des Plantes, on Paris's left bank. The new Galerie de l'Evolution, previously the Galerie de Zoologie, occupies the main atrium hall of André's building. This is an imposing space lined with cast-iron columns that support three floors of side gallery spaces that rise to the glass roof. The architects reordered the museum's collection of zoological specimens to create a new gallery that is as much about sheer spectacle as it is about education.

The Galerie de l'Evolution is an installation that reveals the striking qualities of the original building, allowing it to be understood as André intended and at the same time it serves as a dramatic backdrop for an awe-inspiring exhibition.

The architects made some adjustments and alterations to the original building. The ground floor was excavated to give more space to the temporary exhibitions while the library and storage facilities were removed to elsewhere in the building. The entrance was changed from the garden side to the street side of the building, which allows evening access when the gardens are closed. Visitors now enter at the front of the nave, thus heightening the impact of the imposing central hall space. Other

Fig.1. The building is a spectacular setting for this extraordinary exhibition

modifications included the cleaning and restoration of the main space, and the repair and conservation of the large glazed roof. All of these changes primed the space to create a magnificent backdrop for the installation of the objects.

The galleries were remodelled to display the museum's collection of taxidermy and the installation is governed by this. The theory of evolution is embodied in the character, selection, grouping and positioning of the objects. The bones and stuffed animals appear to be marching through the gallery assuming their correct position in the evolutionary tree.

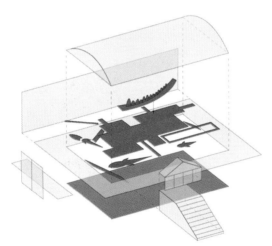

Fig. 2. The main hall is entered on its axis, with the museum based around a central island installation

The main exhibition space is the ground floor of the large hall. On its upper side, on the diorama, is a cavalcade of animals. They appear to roam across the floor as if making for Noah's Ark, elephant next to giraffe alongside hippopotamus. Underneath this floor are the sea animals. The designers gathered shoals of fish that are displayed against sheets of planar glass tipped with blue light. This subterranean level appears to float free from the edges of the existing building and in the gap is where whalebones hang in space, as though floating somewhere between land and sea. Ascending from the lower levels up to dry land the visitor passes underneath and then past large sheets of sandblasted glass. Sea lions, walruses and polar bears occupy these. The journey is from sea to dry land. The upper galleries encircling the main hall are the home to exhibits of climbing animals such as monkeys and higher up are the birds. Perhaps the most poignant exhibition is that of the extinct or near extinct animals, displayed in an almost completely dark side gallery. Each animal is faintly picked out by a single spotlight illustrating its fading chance of survival.

The use of the existing building in this way organises such pragmatic concerns as circulation in an allegorical fashion. Visitors enter the gallery at the subterranean level and from here are guided vertically through the space. This journey from water to dry land mimics the earliest beginnings of life and brilliantly narrates the story of evolution.

The relationship between the old building and its new use is closely entwined. The previous function was not entirely different to the new one, but the site-specific installation generates a powerful dialogue between the qualities of the original and the character of the new function.

**Fig. 3. The line
of animals walk
across the 'plain' of
the ground floor**

Fig.1. The light
distribution plan
becomes a
decorative surface

Fig. 2. The installations
hover expectantly
in the space

Zumtobel Staff Lighting Showroom

Location: **Lemgo, Germany**
Former Function: **Storage facility**
Built: **Unknown** Architect: **Unknown**
New Function: **Lighting showroom**
Remodelled: **1996** Architect: **Bolles+Wilson**

The idea and nature of shadow had always had a fascination for Bolles+Wilson, revealed in the deep blackness so often employed in their enigmatic drawings of the ninja. Peter Wilson describes the ninja as an electronic shadow ('Remember ninja were often refered to as shadow killers, night stalkers, anti-figures to samurai'.)[17] When Zumtobel Staff Lighting approached the architects, it was natural that the shadow or more accurately the exact opposite, the brightness cast by a fitting, should generate the design.

The Zumtobel Staff lighting showroom is situated in a 1,000 sq m industrial shed on the outskirts of Lemgo. The showroom and customer centre is used for demonstrations of the company's various lighting products and to house conferences on new developments in lighting. Zumtobel Staff commissioned designers and artists including James Turrell and Sauerbruch and Hutton to create the concept and realisation of their other showrooms. In Lemgo, they asked Bolles+Wilson.

The strategy of installation can react to and make a studied response to a building, but the character of this particular building

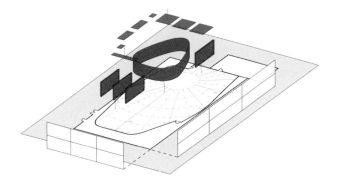

Fig. 3. The anonymous host shed building hides the distinct interior showroom

and its location is anonymous. In many examples of installation, the context is used to derive character or a starting point from which the design may enter into a dialogue with the original building. The anonymity of this host for the showroom offers none of these possibilities. Instead the designers used the building as merely the container for the new use; it simply limits the scale and size of the installation.

When confronted by a building with no discernible characteristics, the designers imported their own. Bolles+Wilson imposed a lighting distribution diagram directly onto the floor slab of the shed and used this to organise the space. The edge of the space was lined to provide the showroom with a positive definition, to accommodate and conceal offices and storage, and to control the entry of natural light. A series of objects was then arranged within the space, their position dictated by the lighting plan. The diagram was used not only to arrange the elements but also to define their form. An oval of light in the centre dominated the space and this created an oval conference room. The room is clad in rich cherry wood, with the walls raised from the ground and lit from below, which confers an ephemeral feel of transience and movement. Radiating from the conference room is a series of movable elements that can be positioned in various ways to illustrate the different light qualities of the products.

The anonymous character of the original building hides the jewel-like quality of the installation within. The strategy of installation is utilised to inhabit the interior of the shed and to provide it with character. The colour and light of the new showroom is radically different to the shed, its black walls and soffit in stark contrast to the rich cherry cladding of the conference room and the white screens of lighting products. All this rests upon the floor of light grey resin with the white marked lines of the lighting diagram. The installation intensifies the insignificance of the existing building and this anonymity heightens the displayed objects; the two hardly relate to each other yet work together well.

**Fig.1. The space
provides a stimulating
environment for visitors
before and after going
to the galleries**

The Basement Children's Galleries

Location: **Science Museum, London**
Former Function: **Basement**
Built: **1928** Architect: **Sir Richard Allison**
New Function: **Children's Galleries and school group entrance**
Remodelled: **1995** Architects: **Ben Kelly Design**

Ben Kelly is known for the industrial chic look that he developed in the 1980s in the infamous Hacienda Club and Dry Bar in Manchester. His work is characterised by the use of industrial materials and motifs, bright colours and the reuse of 'found' objects. Traffic bollards were used to distinguish the edge of the dance floor in the Hacienda and road marking chevrons, plastic garage doors, rubber and steel tread plate combined with the huge screens and raw cavernous space created a place appropriate for the post-punk generation.

The basement of the Science Museum was remodelled to create the Children's Galleries. Ben Kelly was responsible for the master plan, whereas Casson Mann Designers created the Garden Gallery for 3–6 year olds and for older children, and Gilles Cenazandotti designed The Things Gallery.

The new basement consists of a new entrance and a large stepped terrace, which act as an antechamber to the galleries and allow the large groups of schoolchildren to gather. It also doubles up as an informal lecture and performance space and somewhere for the children to eat lunch.

**Fig. 2. The language
of the installation
is derived from the street**

The strategy of installation is the placement of a number of connected elements into an existing context. The objects can embody the ideology of a designer and it is the nature and positioning of these that can project the concepts and ideas developed by the architect. The import of ideas and motifs from other contexts creates installations that have a particular vibrancy and character and their juxtaposition in the existing building dramatically enhances and accentuates both.

The terrace area of the basement galleries reflects the design ideology developed by Ben Kelly Design. The space is stripped down to leave only the essential elements, and it is then animated with 'industrial' objects and motifs to create a open place where children can feel sufficiently relaxed to enjoy themselves, yet suitably stimulated to become curious.

Once the terracing was positioned, there were very few structural changes to be made to the original building; most of the remodelling was purely modification to the surfaces. The concrete ceiling, the pipework and the trunking were all exposed. Columns were decorated with brilliant yellow, red, orange and blue chevrons and the walls were equally vivid. Imported objects were then installed within the space; a long sloping ramp directs the children into the area, traffic lights control the flow of movement, huge plastic signs hang from the ceiling and the lighting is brutally exposed. Even the lift and air conditioning machinery are revealed to become found objects and therefore to be examined and explored. In front of the terrace a large electronic advertising hoarding was positioned which slowly turns, first to reveal publicity for the gallery and then in another turn to offer information. The billboard has been appropriated from the street, and reused in the basement. The children further animate the terrace as they wait to enter the galleries or just sit and eat while watching a performance.

The installation of a series of elements has generated a new and lively place from a dark and lifeless basement.

Fig.1. The size of
the bulkhead
compartments makes
them ideal for human
inhabitation

Figs. 2-7. The containers
had to be lifted
by crane into the
apartment

Morton Duplex

Location: **Manhattan, New York** Former Function: **Parking Garage**
Built: **Unknown** Architect: **Unknown**
New Function: **Apartment** Remodelled: **1999**
Architects: **LOT/EK**

Using ready-made and found objects can be a fruitful approach to remodelling. LOT/EK, a New York-based practice, reuse industrial containers, bits of lorries and all sorts of other found materials to create spaces. Taking their name from William Gibson's book, *Johnny Mnemonic*, LOT/EK's work is characterised by off-site installations. The previous works of the two architects, Ada Toller and Giuseppe Lignano, include the use of stacked shipping containers as blocks of flats, the sides of lorries as screen walls in exhibitions, and container lorry units as rooftop penthouses. When Josh Morton acquired the fourth floor of a carpark, LOT/EK were the obvious architects to fashion a two-bedroom apartment from it.

Ada Toller of LOT/EK explains:

I get inspiration from the view of the West Side highway from the studio windows, the machines for moving meat, the water tanks on the roofs, the fire escapes and air conditioners that seem to grow out of the sides of buildings. It's an artificial environment but at the same time very powerful.[18]

The character of the objects or elements making up the installation is usually dictated by the style or passion of the commissioned designers. The Morton Duplex project is distinguished by the installation of two petroleum lorry containers imported into the otherwise empty space. The open plan car park has a relatively high ceiling, therefore the designers were able to install one of the containers at high level across the space, and the other vertically towards the back of the space. The insides of the aluminium containers were separated by bulkheads that were necessary to stabilise the petrol while in transport; these corresponded to human proportions and formed natural partitions in the vessels. The horizontal bridge container is used to house two double bed spaces, while the vertical vessel houses two bathrooms, one on top of the other. The service vessel is stacked at the back where there is less natural light, while the bedrooms are at the front, nearest to the glazed façade. They have new doors and windows worked by a hydraulic action. A stair and raised walkway were constructed from steel and clear resin to provide access to the high levels.

The installation is positioned to afford maximum impact. It provides what was previously a parking space with a new distinct identity, ironically providing a final parking place for two tankers. The objects are not necessarily without any relationship to the original building; it dictates the size of available space and the containers are trimmed to fit. Whether the previous use of the host influenced the choice of objects is open to speculation but the installation certainly embodies the ideology of the commissioned architects.

Chapter Three
Tactics

**Previous pages:
Walkway, British
Museum, London.
Foster and Partners**

Tactics
Introduction

Tactics express the
very qualities of the
building, what it looks
like, how it sounds
or what it feels like.

Although details are perhaps considered late during the conception of a building, they play just as important a role as strategy in the realisation of a project. They are but a small part in relation to a larger whole, and yet the selection of details and style gives the building its character.

Frascari in his essay, 'The Tell The Tale Detail', used the conceptual analogy of total architecture; that is, the plot plus the details equals the tale. Frascari explains:

> In the details are the possibilities of innovation and invention, and it is through these that architects can give harmony to the most uncommon and difficult or disorderly environment generated by a culture.[1]

The tactics employed in the remodelling of a building can be seen as the manipulation of the elements or details in support of the overall strategy. These elements are an expression of the use and of the character of a building. It is these elements that distinguish or make one place different from another. The elements give character; they define the quality and provide the features of a building, and it is the tactical deployment of them that gives the remodelled building its individual nature. The whole building can be understood through the reading of its details. As Umberto Riva puts it:

> I like to confer nobility on an interior, make sure that no window, door or sequence is taken for granted. Knowing how to construct space is fundamental. Sometimes positioning a wall at an angle is enough to capture and reflect more light. You can bring tension into an environment simply by adding something 'out of scale' like a door that's bigger than all the others in the same room. You might draw attention to a door or window frame, or enhance the relationship with the exterior by inserting a carefully designed window. This is what nobility means to me: non-obviousness, care over detail, intelligent economy.[2]

This chapter is divided into six sections, each focusing quite specifically upon the use of a particular element or tactic and its relationship with the whole building. Whether vertical or horizontal, a *plane* will define space. The walls, the floors and the ceilings can control the visual and physical limits of a space, but they can be so much more than a pure surface. They cannot only be dealt with in terms of their usefulness or ease of maintenance.

A precisely placed *object* can manipulate space, movement and visual direction. A number of objects placed in series or clustered together can be loaded with significance and meaning. An object, whether it is a piece of furniture, a sculpture or a large structural pod, can actually enhance the space it occupies.

Light can control space and form, it can direct, movement can be suggested, objects and places can be illuminated and accentuated and it can be used to change the perception of things. Whether natural or artificial, light is an essential element and the skilful articulation of it can influence the experience of a building.

Surface is the tactile element that establishes a direct relationship between human contact and the building. The surface of any element, that is, the specific materials that it is made from, not only provides for environmental and ergonomic control but also renders the very character of the building.

Openings are crucial punctuation points in buildings. They have obvious uses such as facilitating movement and admitting light, but they also have the less obvious function of creating views, providing orientation and direction and most importantly, they establish relationships between places.

Movement through or around a building is generally either vertical or horizontal, by means of stairs or a lift, or a path or corridor. Movement through a building not only provides access to different areas but also serves to bind together separate or disparate spaces. Staircases in particular, but also bridges and balconies, can prove to be more than purely functional, forming sculptural elements and focal points.

**Fig.1. The pivoting openings
within the façade can be
reconfigured to allow a variety of
views into and out of the Gallery.
Storefront Gallery, New York**

Planes organise and
seperate space.

A plane, whether horizontal or vertical, is a major element of design control, used both inside and outside a building and is probably the most obvious and easily recognisable detailed element in any building.

Whether permanent or temporary, walls provide visual, acoustic and environmental protection, they enclose areas, they surround or confine activities, they divide spaces, and they provide intimacy or even complete privacy. A wall can be much more than a pure vertical surface; for example, it can contain storage, cupboards, bookcases and even whole rooms (such as a kitchen). The library wall in the Villa Mairea by Alvar Aalto is curved and movable; one side contains the books, the other is sheer. The ephemeral quality of the whole thing is accentuated by a glazed section at the top. The undulating wall does not appear to reach the ceiling and therefore encourages movement. Of course a wall need not be vertical. The expressive qualities demonstrated in the changing room wall at the Vitra Fire Station, designed by Zaha Hadid, emphasise the dynamic character of the project. The wall need not be flat; the huge balcony walls of the Tate Gallery in Liverpool, England, are an echo of the massive structural arches of the original warehouse.

Screens placed in a large room can control, divide and shape a space. They can provide shelter, conceal, suggest direction and partition. Eva Jiricna created an undulating flexible screen that fitted very much around the perimeter of the Way In clothing shop occupying a whole floor of Harrods in London. This now dismantled adaptable wall could be folded or pinched to provide changing rooms or specific sales areas or shifted away from the building to allow clutter to be stored behind it. The simple grilled orthogonal screen placed off-centre at the end of the long first floor gallery of the Castelvecchio serves to deflect the eye and suggest that the journey is not complete but continues beyond the end of that gallery.

The problem of how to treat the original walls in an existing building can be approached in a number of ways. The walls can be left very much in the condition they were found, with no more than the necessary structural repairs taking place, as, for example, in the P. S.1 Institute for Contemporary Art in New York by Fred Fisher and Partners. Here the architects were anxious to reveal the history of the building, once a school, and so the internal conditions were retained, graffiti and all. Alternatively, a building can be restored to its original glory in anticipation of accepting a contemporary insertion. When designing the Sackler Galleries at the Royal Academy in London, Foster Associates benefited from working with Julian Harrap Architects, the conservation consultants who completely restored an early 18th century elevation designed by Samuel Ware.

Fig.1. The walls separating the changing areas from the main social space of the Vitra Fire Station are sculpted to modulate light and view

A casting or shadow of the wall can be created. At the Keltenmuseum in Hallein, Austria, Heinz Tesar built a 16 m high concrete reflection of the original mid-17th century almshouse wall, with just an enigmatic 80 cm gap between them. The new wall not only provides stability, attached as it is to the original with perforated steel plates, but it also presents the idea that something new has occurred. However, by far the most common approach to walls is to simply re-plaster those of the original building and paint them white, as can be seen in hundreds of galleries all around the world.

According to Rob Krier, 'The façade is the most essential architectural element'.[3] It is capable of communicating the function and significance of a building. It speaks of the era in which it was built and adaptations to it can compound the sense of history of a place. When attempting to adapt a number of adjacent buildings for the same purpose, a new plane can stitch together the different buildings to present a continuous façade, as shown by Karl-Josef Schattner in the remodelling of the School of Psychology in Eichstatt.

In modern buildings, both new-build and remodelled, the ceiling is often expected to take on a huge amount of work; not only must it contain the lighting but it must also carry and conceal air-conditioning systems, smoke and other detectors and alarms, sprinkler devices, pipework, as well as power and telecommunications arrangements. No wonder it is usually white, flat and suspended! However, ceilings can be adapted to emphasise certain areas. When remodelling the Manchester City Art Gallery café, Stephenson Architects created a lowered white plastered ceiling over only half of the café, which contained all the mechanical and electrical necessities, thus leaving exposed the other half, the original, early 19th century intricate and gilded Charles Barry ceiling. Lowering the ceiling created a considerably more intimate area, and the general arrangement of the furniture echoed this. Where the ceiling was higher, the more open aspect provided for a bright, casual, more sociable space. Interestingly, the tiled floor pattern installed by the architects in the lowered area reflected the form and rhythm of the ornate ceiling.

Ceilings need not be a single consistent element; for practical, environmental and aesthetic reasons, Fielden Clegg Bradley fixed horizontal white fabric screens to the windows and fitted them far into the offices of the Green Peace Headquarters in London. These are attached just above head height but below the height of the top of the window. This serves a number of purposes: to conceal any mechanical and electrical pipework, to shield those working by the windows from the worst of the sun's glare, and to allow sunlight to bounce off the top surface of the screen and then to be reflected from the ceiling into the far reaches of the room.

The ceiling can be emphasised. Bolles Wilson felt the views from the Blackburn House in London were so undesirable that they positioned the windows high up on the walls, adjacent to the ceiling, throwing light horizontally, thus deflecting the eye to focus on the pure qualities of the ceiling. Inevitably, the ceiling or soffit has a close connection to both the floor above it and the one below it. It does not have to be flat: it can undulate, step, be raised or lowered – the horizontal plane above our heads is more than a purely functional issue.

Fig. 2. The Manchester City Art Gallery Café by Stephenson Architects

We have a greater relationship with the floor than with any other element. We walk on it, touch it, stare at it, we have a close physical connection with it. The floor can be used to manipulate movement, control circulation and flow. It can articulate and define the design strategy, and can be used either to link and connect or distinguish and separate space. The floor of the Post Office in Vienna designed by Otto Wagner echoes the pattern of the structure thus giving a clarity and direction to the building. The materials that the floor is made from are a crucial consideration; O'Donnell and Tuomey created a circular pattern from limestone on the floor of the covered courtyard of the Irish Film Centre in Dublin. This reinforced the exterior qualities of the space, tied the many disparate spaces and elements together and supported the interventionist strategy employed by the architects.

Fig. 3. On the exterior of the Kelten Museum in Hallein, Austria, Tesar creates a concrete shadow that echoes the original medieval wall

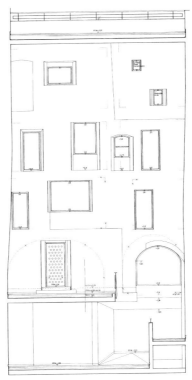

Fig. 4. Tesar's drawing shows how from the interior of the museum the dimensions of the new wall are dictated by those of the existing

**Fig.1. The Palladian
arch–lintel combination
of the bays allows
for variations in the
rhythm and proportions**

Basilica

Location: **Vicenza, Italy**
Remodelled: **1546-49**
Architect: **Andrea Palladio**

One of the best known examples of building reuse is Palladio's masterful extension of Palazzo Della Ragione. The existing palace, which had partially collapsed, had arcades on three sides and was wrapped in a new façade – Palladio's solution gives an impression of uniformity to an irregular building and site while allowing maximum flexibility to deal with each bay.

Palladio's structure could not be called a building; it is a screen around the existing building that functions as both a buttressing device and an elegantly decorated wall. It cleverly disguises the irregular trapezoidal plan of the original building and hides its Gothic façade. Much of Palladio's construction was predetermined by the form of the original building, the position and the height of the two storeys and the width and number of bays. The problem that Palladio had to solve was one of proportion and rhythm. Classical architecture demands that columns are equally spaced. To have an arch of exactly the same height, the width of each bay had to be identical.

Palladio used an arch–lintel combination of bays to surround the building, combining arches, oculi and balustrades on two levels. He utilised an order that Serlio had perfected in the design for an arcaded Venetian Palace. The Serliana was a flexible system that allowed Palladio to absorb the differences in the rhythm of the palace building and the three zones of circulation. Columns flanked each bay; while the central pier and wall retained the same proportions, the lateral ones could be expanded or contracted and parts of the frieze were almost imperceptibly included or excluded. The narrow openings of the corners were absorbed, while allowing the centre of the façade to open up.

The building, referred to as the Basilica, has a significant position on Vicenza's main square which helped Palladio to gain his reputation. Despite the fact that the arch–lintel combination of the bays was invented by Bramante and popularised by Serlio, the style became known as Palladian.

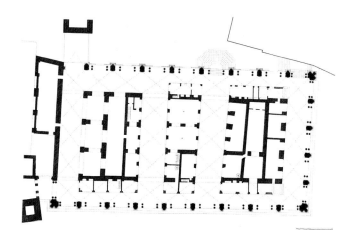

**Fig. 2. Plan showing
how the irregularities
of the existing building
are absorbed
by the plane of the
Palladian façade**

Fig.1. Christo and
Jeanne-Claude
Wrapped Reichstag,
Berlin 1971-1995.
The wrapping simplifies
the form of the building
and increases
its impact when seen
from a distance

Wrapped Reichstag

Location: **Berlin, Germany**
Date: **1995**
Artist: **Christo and Jeanne-Claude**

To enclose a building with a new cover or façade ensures that the manner in which the building is presented to its surrounding environment is altered.

Christo and Jeanne-Claude developed an extraordinary method of changing the meaning of a place by actually physically wrapping the building or structure. This is a process they developed and perfected over a series of projects, including the Wrapped Kunsthalle, Bern, Switzerland 1968 and the Pont Neuf Wrapped, Paris 1985. The Reichstag was a much more controversial project as it is a major political symbol, not just of the reunited Germany but also of the whole of European 20th century history. There was much discussion about the proposal in the German Parliament and although the project polarised opinion, the majority felt that wrapping the building like a present would be an appropriate symbol of a new beginning in German history.

To construct the wrapping, a specially manufactured steel structure was positioned upon the upper part of the building. It was designed in such a way as to accentuate the contours and features of the building and to avoid any accidental damage. The Reichstag was then completely covered in an aluminium coated polypropylene fabric which was held in place with polypropylene cables. These were tensioned to large steel weights at the base of the building.

The wrapped Reichstag still resembled the inherent form of the building. The new cover, although a different material – a heavyweight metallic fibre in contrast to the sandstone of the host – was not responsive to the detail of the building but accentuated the mass or bulk of the Reichstag. The result was a dramatic experience of great beauty. The presence of the building was emphasised and the symbolic beauty of the politically loaded gesture was realised.

Fig. 2. The Reichstag as depicted in one of the many preparatory drawings by Christo

Fig.1. New cladding
wraps the old building
with scant regard for
existing rhythm or
openings. The insulation
and structure are
apparent and exposed
like a rip in the lining of
a padded anorak

School for Fashion and Graphic Industry

Location: **Utrecht, Netherlands**
Remodelled: **1997**
Architect: **Eric Van Egeraat**

Eric Van Egeraat was asked to complete the building of the School for Fashion and Graphic Industry in Utrecht. Most of the building was already in place so that all Egeraat had to address was the problem of what the building looked like. He chose to reconsider the elevations, in effect to design a dynamic final cladding for the façade and ensure that it did not compromise the works already completed. (He was also to redesign the auditorium.) He had to make certain there were no visible scars or disjunctions between the old core and the new enclosure.

Egeraat questioned the nature of the glass façade. He realised that by divorcing the façade from the structure and the internal arrangement of the building, the creative possibilities were endless.

The architect described this as:

It can be anything from a free suspended membrane to a load bearing wall. It allows for an architecture in which the outline of the structure is unresolved. Is it a display case? Is it a quotation? Is it the unsentimental acceptance of the nature of the materials? The answer to all these questions is that it is both, or even better, all of them.[4]

Egeraat's approach was to wrap the building in a new glass façade. This new addition was developed as an even and consistent surface layer that revealed the presence of the original building behind it. Egeraat imposed a new geometry upon the building to veil and absorb the irregularities of the existing. The new façade relentlessly disrupted the order of the previous work. This new façade consisted of glazed panels supported by aluminium mullions spaced at uneven intervals and positioned 150 mm from the face of the original building and at a uniform 12 m height. The rhythm did not correspond to the existing windows of the school; sometimes the mullions missed the openings and sometimes they crossed them. The concrete structure and insulation panels are also revealed behind the new wall. This irregular geometry of openings and mullions creates a tension and a disharmony between the inside wall and the new façade.

This new façade is imposed upon all sides of the school. Where wing heights differ, the new façade remains constant. The uneven and potentially banal qualities of the original building are relieved and absorbed by the placement of a new element immediately in front of it.

Fig. 2. The new façade sits in front of the existing with its ad-hoc pattern of mullions and transoms

Fig.1. The floating
ceiling allows natural
light to illuminate the
periphery circulation
areas and accentuate
the central table

Sir John Soane's Museum

Location: **Lincoln Inn Fields, London**
Date: **1794-1824**
Architect: **Sir John Soane**

Sir John Soane created great beauty in interior spaces by the manipulation of natural light in combination with sculpted form. This skill is probably at its most evocative in the breakfast parlour in Sir John Soane's own house. The room is not large. It looks out on to the monumental courtyard and is approached through three different entrances. Soane focused the room centrally by hanging a shallow dome that is detached from the walls from the ceiling. A lantern placed in the middle and skylights around the edge of the canopy give the illusion that the soffit is floating.

During the day natural light falls into the room, highlighting the centre of the table and the circulation routes around the edge of the space. Soane wrote of this room:

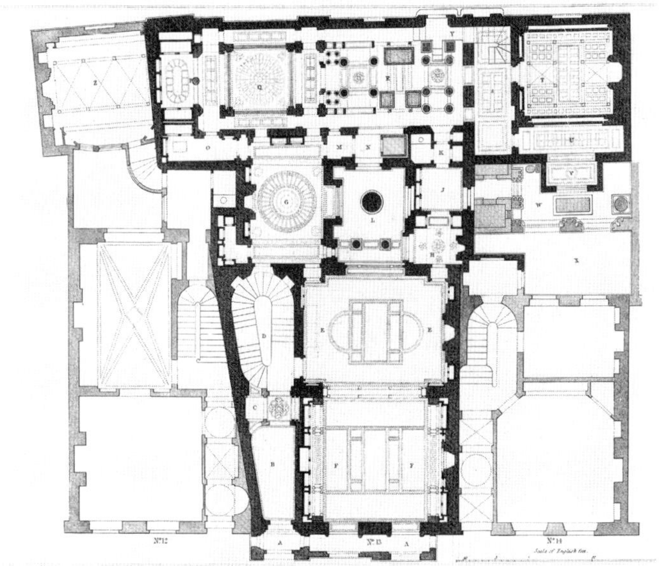

The views from this room into the monumental court and into the museum, the mirrors in the ceiling, and the looking glasses, combined with the variety of outline and general arrangement in the design and realization of this limited space, present a succession of those fanciful effects which constitute the poetry of architecture.[5]

Sir John Soane (1753-1837) was born the son of a bricklayer and rose to become one of England's greatest architects. For forty-five years he was architect to the Bank of England and during this period he oversaw the rebuilding and enlarging of the Bank's buildings. Perhaps his greatest work, though, was this house, now a museum and library, at numbers 12, 13 and 14 Lincoln's Inn Fields. He spent over half of his life rebuilding, remodelling and extending the property to accommodate his collection of paintings and artefacts. The façade of the building is austere and classical, but it is in the interior that Soane's ability to manipulate form and light created spaces of extreme beauty. The building is an extraordinary collection of spaces, changes of level, top lighting, allusions and scenic complexity that make it the leader of the picturesque movement in neo-classical Britain.

Fig. 2. Plan showing how the breakfast room is a completely internal space within the house

Fig.1. The space left by
the missing gable end
enables the existing
buildings to project out
from under the new
covering and engage
with the street

National Studio for Contemporary Arts

Location: **La Fresnoy, France**
Remodelled: **1998**
Architect: **Bernard Tschumi**

The soffit can be used to unify and gather a series of disparate elements quite literally under one roof.

The French architect Bernard Tschumi remodelled La Fresnoy Art School in Lille, northern France. The intervention was a response to the programme of the school and embodied the collectivity between the creative practices that went on underneath it. The existing site consisted of an auditorium called 'The Fun Palace' and a host of other buildings that so closely resembled the proposed requirements of the new school that it was at first anticipated that little more than basic maintenance would be required before the school could open. However the condition of some of the existing building was poor and the requirements of a number of the new programmes, such as sound recording, needed far better facilities.

Tschumi's approach was to restore and repair the existing buildings while covering them with a giant roof, which would provide extra protection against the elements. The new soffit over the roofs of the old buildings provide space for service equipment that can be plugged into the old buildings, maintenance stairs, and a series of new catwalks and public walkways. These give views across the roofs of the existing buildings and into the various rooms and spaces.

This solution not only provided sufficient room for the school but also created extraordinary interstitial spaces that were neither inside nor outside. These extra or accidental rooms, which are sheltered by the giant roof but not within any of the existing buildings, are very special and are intended for student interaction and relaxation.

Fig. 2. The plane wraps the existing buildings

Fig. 3. The new soffit, placed over the existing collection of buildings and their interstitial spaces, turns the whole site into a huge multi-spaced room

**Fig.1. The interior
is dramatised
by the roof of
glass and steel**

Lawyers' Office

Location: **Vienna**
Remodelled: **1989**
Architect: **Coop Himmelb(l)au**

As well as heightening sensation by modulating light, or gathering disparate buildings under one space, a soffit can be used just to create a startling statement in order to shock and surprise the viewer. Still as striking as it was when the design was first published in 1985, this office for a chamber of lawyers inhabits the roof-scape of a traditional building in Vienna's first district. Completed in 1989, the building is virtually hidden from view at street level and yet it has drastically altered the Viennese skyline.

This insertion is an add-on that radically re-interprets the roof and soffit of the existing building to make new office space in the attic below it. The extent of the collision of the roof and the new office space within the existing building becomes clear only from inside the building.

The new meeting room is situated in the corner of the building and the new twisted and contorted roof has been driven through this corner to enclose the room. The ridge of the new roof, resembling the spine of an animal, springs from the rear of the building to overhang at the front and is then pinned back to the existing stair tower. Along this axis are some new internal stairs that slice through the existing roof to access the roof terrace.

The complex geometry of the roof addition has no direct formal relationship with the proportions of the existing building, but the whole object is placed at the point where the roof would have turned the corner of the building. The spine or central beam of the new glazed canopy sits just slightly off the line of the old ridge, and protrudes just to the right of where the original truss would have rested. Where the new addition touches the old roof, the original is peeled back. It is as though the new has burst through the old, a manoeuvre that gives the insertion the dynamic of flight.

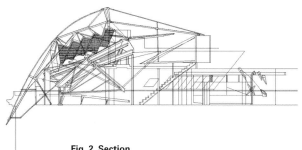

Fig. 2. Section revealing the complex geometrical form of the new addition in relation to the regular layout of the attic space

Fig. 3. Almost invisible from street level, the roof top element is a dynamic addition to the roofscape of Vienna

Location: **Eichstatt, Germany**
Remodelled: **1990**
Architect: **Karl-Josef Schattner**

The work of Karl-Josef Schattner has been compared to that of Giancarlo de Carlo, Aldo van Eyck and Eric Gunnar Asplund. He believes in a continuity in architecture, that buildings can be interpreted and reused without destroying their memory, and that the solution lies in the context and the constraints.

Between Nuremberg and Munich is the ecclesiastical town of Eichstatt; strangely, it has a medieval layout with a Baroque appearance. The religious status of the town had ensured a turbulent history; indeed, the town has been razed to the ground on a number of occasions. During the 17th and 18th centuries the town was rebuilt. The architects to the prince-bishop were three Italians who reconstructed it in the Baroque style, which is still remarkably well preserved.

Schattner, the principal architect in the town, had already restored and converted many buildings for the University. This project was the reuse of a pair of large neighbouring Renaissance houses dating from 1581 and 1695. They were originally combined by one of the Italians, Maurizio Pedetti, in the 18th century to create an orphanage. Pedetti joined the two houses using a central core that contained a chapel. The children could be kept separate from each other, the boys in one house, the girls in the other. The slight angle on the front façade and the fact that one building was slightly deeper than the other gave Pedetti a problem with the geometry of the roof. This he solved by constructing a new back wall to square the two buildings up, thus creating a clarity that could easily be used as a base for the new single roof.

Schattner was commissioned to restore and re-order the houses, which had fallen into disrepair and had been unused for many years. The problem was one of authenticity. Should he remove the additions of Pedetti and restore the buildings to their individual Baroque natures or should he ignore the earlier phase and use the 18th century conversion as the basis for the remodelling? Schattner's approach was to reinterpret the buildings. He restored what it was possible to restore. The chapel was removed, but the link between the two buildings was retained. The roof of this area was glazed and the space used for circulation. However the most relevant intervention was Schattner's reinterpretation of Pedetti's connecting back wall.

In the remodelling Schattner unites the buildings by placing a new abstract screen façade at the rear of the houses. The screen is spaced and separated from the back of the buildings to create a loggia. When in the space, the original rear façades of the houses are revealed, a reading that the street façade denies. The new façade consolidates the buildings yet at the same time allows them to still be read as separate entities.

The screen wall is constructed from rendered block work. The space created contains emergency exits and allows natural light to reach the rear of the original buildings. The façade does not attempt to copy or match the openings of the existing buildings but instead it has a particular rhythm and geometry of its own.

**Fig.1. The new
rear façade unifies
the two buildings**

Basis Wien, Information Centre for Contemporary Art

Location: **Museumsquartier, Vienna**
Remodelled: **1997**
Architect: **propeller z**

Vertical planes can link and unite disparate spaces. When they are divorced from the task of containing space, walls can become symbolic dynamic elements. The architect, propeller z used a long horizontal plane to link the inside and the outside of the Basis Wien, a single-roomed artist information centre, situated on the ground floor of an 18th century block on the edge of the huge and newly created Museumsquartier. The function of this element changes as it travels into and through the space. The elongated plane is lit from behind and below and appears to float; it is used for storage of archives and display and to accommodate computer and other communication equipment in the public area. It then glides out through a transparent glass door set into the Baroque façade to signal the entrance and to advertise the centre with a simple yellow logo. The screen unites the outside with the inside. It was obviously quick and easy to build, constructed in a most simple manner: cut sheets of aluminium are attached to a straightforward steel frame using kitchen cabinet fittings. The lack of polish in the construction is balanced by the decaying qualities of the original room. The impact of this long aluminium element is huge, but the damage to the original vaulted space is minimal.

Fig.1. The wall slides through the room, organising the books and files, then through the entrance to signal the information centre

Fig. 2. The wall is lit from behind and below accentuating the illusion of floating

Edizioni Press, Storage Display Divider

Location: **Edizioni Press, New York**
Remodelled: **2000**
Architect: **LOT/EK**

Planes can separate and link spaces. Once this basic tactic has been established, then the finish or materiality of the plane can be determined.

Paint, timber, metal and glass are the more traditional materials used for wall finishes but more unusual or incongruous ones can create a distinct identity or character.

In a publishing house bookshop, a series of stainless steel sinks were assembled in a most unusual wall. They were used to create a bookshelf and screen wall dividing the shop from the office and conference room.

LOT/EK collected 20 stainless steel sinks, each 12 inches square and 12 inches deep.

These were riveted to a steel frame and coated with orange paint and rubber. The screen was then attached to a central pivot which was fixed to the floor and ceiling, and which allowed the wall to be spun into place or opened as a door. The sinks quite adequately hold the books in place, provided they are no more than 12 inches in height, and act as a display shelf. The plugholes become peepholes to the other space when the screen is closed.

The object is quite simple and, while it certainly gives the space a distinct identity, appears to be quite natural and appropriate to the nature of the shop.

Fig.1. The screen is an entrance to the conference room. The unusual qualities of the element lend a distinct identity to the shop

Fig. 2. The plug holes allow glimpses of activity beyond the screen

Prada Store

Location: **SoHo, New York**
Remodelled: **2001**
Architect: **Rem Koolhaas/OMA**

OMA are regarded as being at the forefront of both technological and theoretical issues in architecture. Prada are equally ambitious fashion designers and retailers, and therefore any collaboration was bound to be controversial. The technology installed within the Prada store in the former Guggenheim museum space is equal to the architecture and, of course, the clothes.
The changing rooms have a wall of glass that turns milky white when the space is occupied. The sales assistants hold mini-computers that keep them up to date on stock levels and other database information. Clothes are suspended in cages from the ceiling. One long interior wall is made of translucent back-illuminated plastic sheets while the other is covered in wallpaper with a grossly oversized motif.

But the most striking and significant element within the shop is the undulating floor plane. The store itself occupies the very deep ground and basement floors of a typical 19th century warehouse with an internal cast-iron column and beam structure connected to a masonry envelope. A new surface, a landscape floor or plinth, stretches through the whole length of the building. This floor undulates and swoops to rise then drop dramatically into the basement, thus creating a sunken amphitheatre and a three-dimensional link throughout the height of the building. Clothing dummies are clustered together in small groups on this planked floor of blonde zebrawood and shoes are arranged on the steep incline from the basement to the ground floor.

This store, situated within the museum area of New York, is the first of a series of 'epicenter stores' that deliberately market the clothing as high art. It exploits the notion of the customer as a discerning individual who would rather purchase from a gallery than a boutique. Is this an exhibition or a commercial operation?

Fig.1. The floor dips to reveal the basement level and the shop opens up. The rolling floor acts as a plinth for the flexible display system

Visitors' centre

Location: **Arles Abbey, France**
Remodelled: **2001**
Architect: **Rudi Ricciotti**

The Romanesque ruins of Abbaye de Montmajour lie up on a hill overlooking the picturesque Provençal landscape. Rudi Ricciotti won the architectural competition to create a new visitors' centre within the vaults of the building. His sensitive design inserted elements in among the massive stone walls and vaults of the cellars without touching or compromising the new or the old.

The visitors' centre marked the beginning of a circuit around the abbey grounds and it therefore required a ticket booth, toilets and reception.

The first part of the scheme was to clean and repair the building. The old apertures of the cellars were reopened and simple sheets of clear glass were placed over them. Ricciotti then inserted two beautiful but completely opposite floors into the building. The first, of black polished concrete, was literally poured into the basement reception area, its sumptuous deep darkness held slightly away from the edges of the space by troughs. Concealed lights fitted into the troughs further accentuate the impression of a still black lake. The other floor is threaded through the tall vaulted corridors that link the entrance with the reception. This glass and steel inclining structure is supported on slender columns and is lit from below, thus appearing to float delicately, suspended in mid-air.

Ricciotti's attitude of only touching the building very lightly created two exquisite elements of great contrast both in relation to each other and to the original building.

Fig.1. The solid dark polished concrete floor looks as if it has just been poured into the reception area

Fig. 2. Lightweight steel and glass floor floats between the heavy masonry walls

Fast Forward

Location: **Vienna**
Remodelled: **1999**
Architect: **propeller z**

Jan Tabor in *Frame* magazine[6] claims that propeller z are 'classical exponents of Vienna's neo-avant garde. Classics. Trendsetters and trend-accelerators.' Their work is inventive and precise; it is bizarre and functional and, most importantly, contains the vitality of youth.

Fast Forward is an exhibition of fashion and propeller z created a floor-scape that resembles a giant green computer chip to accommodate it. The landscape almost fills the whole floor of the gallery and is made up of a series of puzzle pieces that simply sit upon the existing wooden floor. To emphasise its transient character, it is lit from below and can be reconfigured in a variety of ways. These strange elements are constructed from painted plywood and also contain provision for seating and display for multimedia access to the exhibition. Gaps in the puzzle reappear as pieces of furniture. Giant projections complete the exhibition.

In this way the materials and surface treatment of a floor can convey the identity and character of a space or activity.

Fig.1. The new floor accommodates temporary exhibitions

Fig. 2. Layout of the raised platform was based upon a computer chip

'Every architect who loves his work must have had his enthusiasm dampened by a prophetic vision of the hideous furniture with which his clients may fill his rooms, and looks all the more incongruous as the rooms themselves are architecturally beautiful.'
–Mackay Hugh Baillie Scott[7]

A purposefully placed object is loaded with meaning; whether it is a small piece of furniture, a large sculpture or a number of pieces clustered together, it establishes a physical and cultural relationship with its environment. It can influence the way in which the space is viewed, it can deflect the eye towards something else, it can form a focal point or even a landmark. This reaction is compounded by the perceived quality of the piece; a genuine LCl2 armchair is sat upon with reverence while something from the local furniture shop may be dismissed as inconsequential.

Furniture is an element that expresses human scale and use. It can be worn and used and barely noticeable or have beautiful sculptured qualities. The furniture can be fitted and totally appropriate to its surroundings or deliberately juxtapose and clash with its environment. The choice of furniture echoes and supports the function of the building. The leather corporate seating of a bank is quite different to the funky stuff acceptable in an advertising studio whereas the Barcelona chair by Mies Van Der Rohe has managed to transcend all classification and is acceptable everywhere.

Furniture is of a definite scale; that is, it is designed to fit the human body. Too small or too large and the pieces become sculptural or bizarre, and they lose functional qualities. Zaha Hadid exploited this in the Fire Station at the Vitra Headquarters in Weil am Rhein in Germany: the furniture and the fittings were ridiculously oversized thus reinforcing the notion that fire fighters are big, strong and brave.

The grouping of a number of pieces of furniture can induce a specific response. The manner in which they are arranged can suggest definite activities such as eating or playing cards or more ambiguous responses such as socialising or intimacy. The meaning comes from the precise position of particular pieces of furniture within a definite place. As noted by Mackay Hugh Baillie Scott:

It is difficult for the architect to draw a fixed line between the architecture of the house and the furniture. The conception of an interior must necessarily include the furniture which is to be used in it, and this naturally leads to the conclusion that the architect should design the chairs and tables as well as the house itself. Every architect who loves his work must have had his enthusiasm dampened by a prophetic vision of the hideous furniture with which his clients may fill his rooms, and looks all the more incongruous as the rooms themselves are architecturally beautiful.[7]

Fig.1. The decorative
screen, which cuts
across the route,
encourages the
visitor to turn around
and view, once again,
the spectacle of the
Farnese Theatre

Kevin Lynch, in *The Image of the City*, describes how a person looks for legibility within the city by building up patterns of relationships between one area and another.[8] He lists the four elements that build this image as paths, edges, districts and nodes. This idea can equally be applied to individual buildings, and it is the node or landmark that is most relevant here. The node is a reference point from which observers can orientate themselves. For a form to become significant enough to be viewed upon as a reference point, it has to stand out from its surroundings. This need not necessarily mean a difference in scale; an object with a different character to adjacent forms will be sufficiently conspicuous. A void will be obvious next to solids and an organic form will stand apart from a grid. Significance is attached to a specific object which when artfully placed can become a pivotal element within a building. In much of his residential work, Frank Lloyd Wright placed an open fireplace in a central position at the heart of the building. Stanley Abercrombie, describing the significance of this element, offered the opinion that, 'If one could kill one of these houses, one would know exactly where to shoot'.[9]

A precisely placed object can also induce movement. Carlo Scarpa did just this when he designed the extension to the Canova Plaster Cast Gallery in Possagno, Italy. A sculpture placed just off-centre in the limbo of the entrance area served to deflect first the eye and then the body away from the strong axis of the original building towards the brightly-lit animated space of the new galleries.

This is a device used to equal effect in the redesign of the Farnese Theatre Galleria Nazionale in Parma by Guido Canali. A simple circulation route was installed throughout the building. A ramp leads the visitor through the centre of the theatre and on to the stage and a small screen placed exactly across the path forces the visitor to turn and suddenly the sheer spectacle of the theatre is apparent – a beautiful view that could be overlooked without this manipulation.

The history of a building can be discussed through the re-examination of found objects. Ben Kelly at the Dry Bar in Manchester, England, appropriated a huge casting of a curtain, which was painted and then hung on the wall near the entrance. This not only gave a clue to the past use of the building, a soft furnishing shop, but also added to the collection of elements that threaded through the length of the bar.

To take the idea of the object to its logical conclusion, existing buildings can themselves be taken to be objects and subsequent remodellings should reflect the qualities of the huge sculptural element within a space.

Fig.1. St Jerome in His Study, Antonello da Messina 1450-55. This extraordinary piece of furniture derives its nature and proportions from both the place that it inhabits and the functional requirements of the occupant

St Jerome in His Study

Location: **National Gallery, London**
Date: **1450-55**
Artist: **Antonello da Messina**

Antonello da Messina is said to have
changed the course of Venetian painting.
He is credited with having introduced the
Venetians to the technique of painting in oil,
or at least how it could be used to give
previously unknown atmospheric, luminary
and colouristic effects to landscapes,
interiors and figures. He was the son
of a stonecutter and inherited the sculptor's
sensibility for three-dimensional form. He was
obviously influenced by Flemish painters; it
was recorded that he studied the work of
Jan van Eyck while in Naples and thus:
He was able to blend a Netherlandish
passion for the details of visual reality and
the saturation of vision in light and shadow
with quintessentially Mediterranean purity
and clarity of form.[10]

St Jerome in His Study is one of his
earliest paintings; it depicts St Jerome
reading quietly at an extraordinary desk in
a monastic library. He is viewed through
an illusionistic stone arch, on the cill of
which are sitting a peacock, a brass bowl
and a partridge. They are lit from the left and
the same light throws a shadow from the
arched frame far into the depth of the
picture. This shadow allows his celebrated
lion to hide and the views from the windows
behind St Jerome to be highlighted. The
desk is positioned in the brightest part of the
picture, with light from the clerestory
windows shining directly onto the book.
Every little detail is complete and clear,
particularly characteristic of Dutch painting.

The study appears to be constructed from
timber and is positioned to sit within the
rhythm of the monastery's structure.
It seems to be part of a larger element;
maybe his is just one of a pair of desks linked
by an arch, and contains all that an academic
monk would require for learning and
contemplation: a desk, a chair, storage
shelves, a trunk and other personal effects.
It is completely closed on one side and
raised off the ground. St Jerome is depicted
as small relative to the size of the painting
but he is framed a number of times to
become the central focus, firstly by the true
decorative frame, then by the painted stone
arch, next by the terracotta tiled floor and
the monastery in shadow, and lastly by the
fantastic study.

The furniture element on which
St Jerome sits derives some of its formal
qualities from the space it inhabits. The base
of the plinth is arched and the desk shape is
a half arch that has a back shelf that rises
to form an arched doorway. The object feels
comfortable and is well proportioned
and scaled in response to the great hall that
it occupies. The painting demonstrates
the harmony that can arise from an object
built to fit a specific space and function.

Apartment

Location: **New York**
Remodelled: **1975**
Architect: **George Ranalli**

A modern interpretation of Antonella da Messina's portrait of St Jerome in His Study is the design of an apartment to fit into a tiny space in a converted furniture warehouse.

A compact free-standing element was inserted into the space. The principle was to provide the basic service requirements in the smallest amount of space, thus allowing the maximum amount of free or lounging area. The element split the tiny apartment laterally; the service areas were positioned next to the entrance and the relaxing space at the naturally-lit side, facing the large arched window. The transitional activities were then collected in the free-standing element, the dining space, the sleeping platform, the bookcase and the winding staircase that links them all together.

The Ranalli element is informed by the scale of the existing, a neutral, white-walled space. The new element also adopts this neutral tone, the space animated by the timber stairs and the upholstered seating and, of course, the occupants.

Fig.1. A modern interpretation of the painting of St Jerome. The Ranalli object incorporates seating, dining space, sleeping platform and bookcase all into one element

The Flying Steamroller Project

Location: **MAK- Austrian Museum of Applied Arts, Vienna, Austria**
Date: **1996**
Artist: **Chris Burden**

A steamroller is extraordinarily and explicitly heavy and has a very small turning circle.

Chris Burden attached a 12-ton yellow steamroller to a counterbalanced pivoting arm. He then drove the massively heavy object in circles around the pivot in a small gallery room until it reached its optimum speed of 30 mph. At this point the counterbalance shifted and the steamroller slowly and magically rose from the ground and continued its extraordinary circular journey in the air. The steamroller was flying.

This thunderous and breathtaking experience lasted for just a few minutes until the momentum was lost and the spinning action exhausted, the counterbalance was returned and the steamroller landed and slowly came to halt.

Chris Burden is probably one of the most controversial and influential American artists of the present day. Since the mid-1980s he has worked with things that society has discarded. This particular steamroller was selected for the project because it had already flown. It was a relic from the Vietnam War and had been transported there by helicopter.

A steamroller is a symbol of extreme heaviness and yellow is the symbolic colour of constructional machinery. It fulfils all our preconceptions of what an inert, immense, industrial object is. We do not associate it with elegance and grace, and we would not expect it to leave the ground at all. The Flying Steamroller confounds our expectations; despite its massiveness, it rises into the air and the beauty inherent in the movement evokes an extremely emotional experience.

A familiar object placed in an unfamiliar situation can create feelings of surprise and admiration. The unexpected causes us to re-evaluate our attitude to the object, its condition and the situation that it is in. Our position and preconceptions are challenged provoking unexpected emotions.

Fig.1. The steamroller laden with energy patiently awaits within the gallery

Fig. 2. The steamroller is flying

Musée des Arts et Métiers

Location: **Paris**
Remodelled: **2000**
Architect: **Andrea Bruno with Francois Deslaugiers**

Objects that contrast with and accentuate form and space can be of a variety of scales. A specifically placed chair can stimulate a moment of reflection and is of a human scale. The opposite end of the spectrum is the use of a huge element to contrast with large-scale spaces.

The Parisian Musée des Arts et Métiers is devoted to the collection of artefacts from the industrial revolution. It was created during the age of Enlightenment and was the first museum in the world dedicated to the study of science. It occupies a corner site among an impressive collection of buildings, some of which date back to the Gothic period. The buildings had already been the subject of conversion and remodelling; the chapel of Saint Martin des Champs was constructed in the 11th century, was converted to the Conservatoire des Arts et Métiers in 1794, was used for a period as a school, then an arms factory before, at the end of the 19th century, it was reconverted to a museum. As part of Mitterrand's *Grands Projects*, a competition was held to renew and restore the museum, which Andrea Bruno won in 1991. Bruno was known for his sensitive work with historic buildings, most notably the Rivoli castle near Turin.

Bruno's strategy was to work with the existing building. He deliberately touches the building lightly and modern changes and additions contrast with the old. The museum has a rectangular court enclosed by four thin wings with the chapel attached to the south side. Care and importance were placed upon the repair and restoration of the mixture of buildings and additions, and where necessary new insertions were made to facilitate the new museum design.

The work within the main museum was a mixture of restoration, sensitive reuse of existing display systems and cases, and modern additions designed to evoke the industrial nature of the objects on display. The fabric of the building, such as plasterwork, windows, staircases and glazing, was repaired and restored by Bernard Fonquernie, architect for the Monuments Historique de France. He also restored the interior of the Chapel, a complex project that involved peeling back the layers of accretions and additions and reinstating the colour scheme to its original glory.

An impressive display device was placed in the chapel designed to accommodate all those artefacts that could not fit into the main museum. Bruno collaborated with Francois Deslaugiers to create a striking steel and glass insertion, which was not only sufficiently large to accommodate and display the artefacts, but also allowed visitors to access all areas of the chapel.

The unreserved structure is in stark contrast to the newly restored interior of the chapel. Although the display system is well ordered – the display and the vertical circulation on one side with the space for viewing and the horizontal circulation on the other – the objects are placed quite chaotically. This gives the whole room a dynamic quality. Aeroplanes hang from the rafters, cars look as if they have been badly parked and a replica of the Statue of Liberty rises through the whole structure. This room is brash and dynamic and quite different from the subtle, well-controlled nature of the rest of the museum.

Fig.1. The new steel and glass display 'cabinet' houses the variety of the left over objects in the museum's collection

The Tectonic Garden

Location: **Museum of Modern Art, New York**
Modelled: **1998**
Architect: **Ten Arquitectos with Guy Nordenson**

An object can be specifically constructed to define a certain point in a space. Its purpose may be to articulate a particular view, frame a scene or even to encourage someone to reassess their attitude to something.

The Museum of Modern Art in New York asked four architectural practices to create an intervention in the sculpture garden of the gallery in order to accentuate a particular aspect of the space. The Mexican architects Ten Arquitectos, with New York-based artist, Guy Nordenson, responded to the sculpture of Balzac by Rodin. This piece sits quietly in a corner of the garden, almost lost next to the blaze created by the Matisse, the Picasso, the Moore, the Judd and the other modern masters. The Rodin is set upon a marble plinth and positioned quite close to the façade of the gallery.

The Installation was conceived as a place to contemplate the sculpture and to understand the story of the piece. A three-metre square of ground was excavated and into this was pushed a solid timber seat. The chair part of the seat was fairly normal, but it had a narrow base as wide as the seat that stretched from the viewer's feet across the rough ground of the excavation and pointed directly at the sculpture. Above the chair, suspended horizontally from a stainless steel frame, was a cantilevered glass screen.

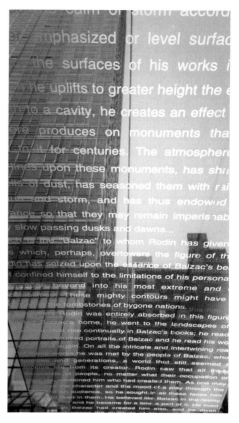

Fig.1. The seat is positioned immediately in front of the statue of Balzac

Fig. 2. Balzac's writings are etched onto a plane of glass, positioned in front of the screen wall of an adjacent skyscraper

Fig. 3. While sitting
on the fabricated
seat in the busy
courtyard the viewer
feels disconnected
from the surrounds
and focused on
the sculpture ahead

When sitting in the chair, the viewer became directly focused upon the statue and disconnected from the activity in the garden. A story by Balzac was etched on the glass canopy and, as the viewer looked up, the words were overlaid onto the façade of the opposite skyscraper. The slightly sunken seat positioned the viewer as though in deference to the sculpture and the edge of the glazing framed the view of it. Upon leaving this sanctuary the viewer was immediately thrown back into the noise and commotion of the sculpture garden.

This temporary installation took an existing part of the courtyard and used a specifically created object to narrate and accentuate what was once overlooked.

Reactor Film Studio

Location: **Santa Monica, Los Angeles**
Remodelled: **1996**
Architect: **Pugh and Scarpa**

In 1917 Marcel Duchamp exhibited a work of art entitled Fountain. This extraordinary, revolutionary and controversial art represented a great leap in the theoretical and conceptual direction of art. The work of art was an industrially produced urinal that Duchamp signed on the base: R. Mutt. He contended that Fountain was a work of art because he selected it, removed it from its natural context, gave it a new name and therefore provided the object with a new meaning. The value and the identity of the object were altered. The concept of the ready-made had become the subject of the gaze. By removing the object and placing it in an unfamiliar setting its value had been reassessed, the familiar had become the unfamiliar and the usual, the unusual.

The use of ready-made objects can still create excitement; the placement of something completely out of its normal context can provoke surprise and interest. This approach can communicate a distinct identity and is still regarded as a provocative and creative act.

Pugh and Scarpa were given the difficult task of designing and building the office and production space for the Reactor Film Company in just 14 weeks. The building was a 1930s Art Deco masonry building just 6 m high. The building also had an unusual bye-law attached to it that insisted that the shop window of the building had to engage with the street.

The architects designed well thought out cellular office space to contain the majority of the functional requirements, but in the shop window they placed a huge ready-made object. An enormous, used, rusty brown shipping container was fork-lifted onto an in situ concrete base in the centre of the window display area. It was positioned with its end facing the street and adapted slightly to hold a 12-seat conference table. The side wall was opened to make an entrance landing and to insert a small staircase. Most importantly, though, it served to signal the creative process that was taking place within the building.

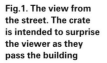

Fig.1. The view from the street. The crate is intended to surprise the viewer as they pass the building

Fig. 2. The reworked shipping crate contains the conference room

Fig. 2. The three
openings in the
façade, each
expressing a different
aspect of the insertion
– the left filled with
the cascade of
aluminium, the right
with the stair, while
the centre is clearly
the entrance

Fig.1. The organic
platform clambers
across the space

Atelier Baumann

Location: **Borsplatz, Vienna**
Remodelled: **1986**
Architects: **Coop Himmelb(l)au**

An object can be more than a piece of furniture that is artfully placed in a space. It can, for example, be an integral and controlling element that creates a new floor and organises circulation and space around it.

Atelier Baumann is a studio/workshop for a graphic designer situated in a single space on the ground floor of a neo-classical building. The room has three tall arched openings to the street, the centre one being used as the entrance.

The space is designed as somewhere for the client to work and to display his collection of art. Coop Himmelb(l)au deliberately kept the existing room fairly neutral and created a dynamic mezzanine across it, which is juxtaposed against the orthogonal plan of the space. This increases the available floor area, provides a tiny drawing studio, allows pictures to be hung from it and supports a collapsible staircase that hangs through one of the side windows and into the street. The final window contains an extraordinary rush of aluminium sheets sliding from the gallery level. This provides insulation, breathable barriers, several windows and a small radiator! The mezzanine is a prefabricated steel and plywood deck supported in the centre by slender steel columns and at the edges by the walls of the host building, but it is also a tense collection of flying beams, floating platforms and swaying screens. The mezzanine is light, balanced and appears almost to be stalking across the room like some strange deformed, half mammal–half machine.

In their work, Coop Himmelb(l)au question the strategies constructed by modern society to govern human action and interaction. They strive to create a freedom within their architecture. This freedom is derived from interpretations of the writings of Jacques Derrida, who posits that society is built upon a series of given strategies or assumptions that govern our actions. Robert Mugerauer in his essay, 'Derrida and Beyond', describes the approach of Coop Himmelb(l)au as 'insistently stripping away the pretence of safe… and the refusal to assert determinate spaces for proper programmed use.'[11]

It is their refusal to accept predetermined conclusions for the distribution of spaces and activities that makes their work so radical. Coop Himmelb(l)au were asked to design the atelier because of their philosophical approach to architecture and the completed scheme really bears little relationship or relevance to the existing building.

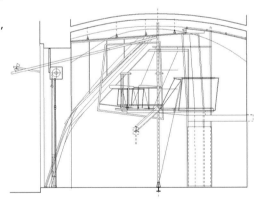

Fig. 3. The section shows the simplicity of the existing building in contrast with the complexity of the layers of materials used to realise the object

Fig.1. The front façade of the library, the original buildings apparently peering over the cage walls of the new plane

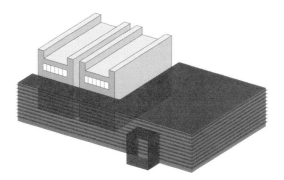

Fig. 2. The old buildings are treated as 'objects.' The slaughterhouse halls are wrapped by the new façade, enveloping and absorbing them into the organisation of the building

Public Library

Location: **Landau, Germany**
Remodelled: **1998**
Architect: **Lamott Architekten BDA**

The contrast between a given object and its surroundings can be greatly intensified by an increase in scale. An existing building can be treated as a single huge element when provided with new surroundings. This was the approach adopted by Lamott Architekten BDA for the design of the new public library in Landau. They wrapped two neighbouring existing buildings in a shed of such a different size, shape, construction and materials that the new and the old appear almost to exist independently, yet each complements the other.

The old slaughterhouse in Landau was once a notable landmark, celebrated for its vast size and operational prowess. The main buildings date from the late 19th century and were constructed mostly from sandstone and brick and were just part of a much larger complex. The costly renovation and improvements demanded by the European Union regulations of 1989, combined with having been poorly maintained, meant that it was cheaper and easier to build a new abattoir elsewhere and shut the buildings down.

In 1989, the town held a competition to reuse the abandoned buildings and Lamott's winning submission proposed a mixed-use urban arrangement that included a new town square, the first phase of which was the construction of the public library. The strategy was to remove any late additions and unworthy buildings from the site and then work with what remained. The listed buildings were too small to accommodate the requirements of a modern library and too structurally unstable to support the addition of mezzanine floors. The solution was for the old halls to be enclosed within a contrasting new structure, which would organise the building and provide the necessary extra space, environmental control and other vital services.

The slaughterhouse buildings are treated as objects in space. Indeed, the new surrounding walls are somewhat shorter than the original and the masonry upper levels of the halls peer out over the top of their new surroundings. The very straightforward modern containing building unifies the site. It is constructed from a steel frame that supports a glass curtain wall and positioned in front of these on all sides are fixed laminated plywood louvres. These brise-soleils cover only the top three-quarters of the building and thus the horizontal emphasis of the whole composition is accentuated.

At ground level the front and the adjacent walls of the original buildings were removed, which promotes transparency, eases movement and provides a much greater area for the storage of the 75,000 books. The retained sidewalls act as a baffle separating the noisy and hectic entrance and café areas in the new space from the quiet reading rooms in the old. The juxtaposition of the new and the old lends a great energy to the original buildings. Their majesty is restored, their presence is intensified, as they appear to be silently waiting behind the walls of their cage.

A brightly lit space beyond the place occupied can indicate the continuation of rooms, it can signal the relationship of one space and another and can reveal and suggest a route.

Light is probably the most important element necessary for the understanding of space and form. For fear of stating the obvious, without light, space cannot be visualised. Whether natural or artificial, light can indicate space and define form. Light can influence the attitude towards a place. Low subtle lighting can, in the right circumstances, make a room appear inviting or in the wrong, very threatening. A bright sunny room can induce feelings of happiness while a dull one can be dispiriting.

Natural light can be manipulated to illuminate specific places and channelled through quite large distances to great effect, as is shown in the house that Sir John Soane designed for himself in Lincoln Inn Fields, London, now the Sir John Soane Museum. Natural light is directed into building through roof lanterns. These allow light to reflect through the whole height of the house, illuminating certain sculptures and spaces as it falls, eventually reaching the cellar and creating a series of semi-lit extremely atmospheric rooms.

A brightly-lit space beyond that which is occupied can indicate the continuation of rooms, to signal the relationship of one space to another and can reveal and suggest a route to follow. The Irish Film Centre in Dublin is entered through long low dark corridors. The top lit courtyard at the heart of the complex beckons visitors along these alleyways, very much the light at the end of the tunnel.

If the quality of light changes through the length of a space, it can indicate movement; the altering conditions show that there is something beyond the space occupied. Each area is given presence and differentiated from those before and after. The light will accentuate the changing narrative.

Foster and Partners created a rich sequence of contrasts in the entrance of the Sackler Galleries at the Royal Academy in London; from the dimness of the entrance hall, up the stairs and lifts with their strangely external quality to the cold white daylight of the reception area. Opaque white glass focuses attention on the interior, horizontally along a series of sculptures on top of the cornice of the exterior of the main galleries. The viewer is engaged immediately and a strong relationship is generated between the idea of the sky, the recognition of having reached the top of the building and the presence of the silhouetted sculptures.

The entrance area of the D. E. Shaw & Co. offices in New York is a perfect white triple storey cube designed by Steven Holl. Alcoves and niches are carved into its walls. These and the routes to other areas are coloured and lit from within by both natural and artificial light. The illuminated colour is reflected in and around the notched spaces thus projecting the colour towards the room and making it very apparent that there are spaces beyond the entrance area, although the deliberate ambiguity about which of the alcoves is functional adds to the mystery of this extraordinary place on the 39th and 40th floors of a mid-town skyscraper.

Fig.1. The artificial
lights concealed
between the inner
wall and outer façade,
colour the wall, pick
out the edges and
promise further
spaces within the
offices of D.E. Shaw,
New York

Natural light reveals the seasons of the year and the daily weather. Sunlight can present challenges but in the northern European climate it is nearly always welcomed into buildings, especially in the winter. There is great pleasure to be derived from the gentle warmth of the long winter sun as it reaches the depth of the interior space. In hotter climates the problem is too much sunlight, not too little. Le Corbusier developed the brise-soleil, which allows the winter light to be thrown deeply into the interior, and yet stops the hotter, higher summer light from entering. Morning light is strong and pure, while the sun shining through the dust-laden atmosphere of the day gives the evening light a rich golden quality.

Artificial light is used to supplement natural light; as the darkness arrives, electric lighting compensates for the lack of sunlight. Artificial light is capable of considerably more than this; the glass pyramid that marks the entrance to the Louvre in Paris is by day an impressive lightweight structure but at night it glows, taking on a monumental quality and scale. Artificial lighting allows a single object to be dramatically highlighted. In darkness, a single action, event or element can be spot-lit.

The use of pure light as an artistic medium was developed by James Turrell in the late 1960s as part of the California-based 'light and space' movement. He used the actual brightness of light itself as the material to be manipulated. In a series of installations, Turrell experimented with the observation and the experience of the object when the object was nothing but pure light.

I use the material of light to work in the medium of perception.[12]

This principle has been adopted by a number of architects. When Philippe Starck remodelled the St Martins Lane Hotel in London he ensured that when the building is viewed from the exterior, each room glows with a different colour. The colours in the bedrooms can be changed to suit the occupant and the spectacle has become an inseparable part of the image of the hotel. The experience of this relatively anonymous modernist building has been intensified and an intriguing yet dynamic façade has been created. Herzog and de Meuron have also exploited the impact of pure light. The long horizontal bay windows that look down into the turbine hall at the Tate Modern in London are places for rest, conversation and contemplation, but seen from the great hall itself, they appear as huge floating bodies of light. The enormous glazed roof contains the restaurant and during the day draws natural light into the great hall but at night it projects itself as a block of light, glowing and signalling the presence of the building.

**Fig.1. Night Passage
(1986),
James Turrell**

Date: **1969 onwards**
Artist: **James Turrell**

Turrell is preoccupied with the effect of light on space. He regards light as the three-dimensional material of the artist and his installations play on the perception of what is really there and what is illusion.

The early works of Turrell were installations made indoors, in which light was perceived as a physical presence and the nature of the space was seen in an unexpected way. Since 1969 he has produced a number of works called the Wedge Works and the Veil Series. These consisted of spatial and light manipulations in rooms and galleries, using a partition wall and hidden lighting. The effect was to produce a sort of optical illusion, where the presence of the light was observed, but it appeared not to be contained by the physical constraints of the space.

Turrell realised the Veil Series in different coloured lights, which were constructed in a very simple manner. All the natural light was excluded from a space and a screen was constructed parallel with and a short distance in front of a wall. The screen had a huge rectangle cut from the centre of it and the gap between the two was lit with concealed lighting. Turrell was always particularly careful to ensure that the light levels were consistent and that the intensity of it did not diminish towards the edge of the space or the fitting. The quality of the light within the room was also controlled; it was always kept dim, and was sometimes the same colour as the screen and sometimes its opposite. The effect was to disorientate the viewer; it took time for the visitors' eyes to adjust to the darkness. They became aware firstly of the room and then of the screen wall. It was impossible to understand the dimensions of this wall, because the space seemed to recede into infinity. It became a space of pure light.

My works are about light in the sense that light is present and there; the work is made of light. It's not about light or a record of it, but it is light. Light is not so much something that reveals, as it is itself the revelation.[13]

The Wedge Work installations were equally clever. Light was projected into the corner of a room in such a manner that it appeared to float in front of the solid walls. The shape of the projected light was such that, instead of conforming to the shape of the right-angled walls, it created the optical illusion of a rectangle. Rationally, the projection could not possibly be contained within the corner and so the eye was tricked into thinking that the rectangle of pure light was hovering just in front of the walls.

Turrell also created a sequence of works called sky spaces which encouraged the viewer to become intensely aware of the qualities of the changing sky. Turrell constructed a small room with continuous bench seating around the edge. The space had no ceiling, but the gap where it should have been was framed like a picture. On the bench, the viewer was positioned so that they could contemplate the changing qualities of the sky without any visual interruptions. The experience was especially poignant at dawn or dusk, when the relationship between the qualities of light inside and outside became interchangeable. The work of art was the sky itself.

In more recent works he has altered architectural objects, such as the Kunsthal in Bregenz, and the Museum of Applied Arts (MAK) in Vienna, to create different readings of the objects in the city. These temporal changes alter and transform the buildings and the manner in which they are comprehended.

Turrell's work manipulates our perception of space and how light inhabits that space. His installations are very influential and a number of architects cite him as a major influence upon their own work – MacCormac Jamieson Pritchard, for example, in the design of the Wellcome Wing at the Science Museum, London, England.

Sky

Location: **Neue Nationalgalerie, Berlin**
Date: **2001**
Artist: **Jenny Holzer**

Fig.1. The soffit of the Neu Nationalgalerie holding Holzer's light installation. Electronic signs are used to send poems across the vast expanse of the gallery ground floor and beyond reflected in the glass walls of the pavilion

Artificial light shines in the dark, its comparative brightness in the surrounding dimness bestowing it an urgency. Artists who work with light make particular use of its striking qualities to make a definite statement.

Ever since the late 1970s the artist Jenny Holzer has been exhibiting works worldwide under the title 'Truisms'. These consist of a series of sayings, poems, slogans, and manifestos. Her work emerged from the radical art scene of 1970s New York, when art started to spill out of the galleries into public spaces where it could get more attention and provoke more reaction.

Holzer's work uses posters, adverts, billboards and t-shirts, appropriating the methods of communication used by advertisers. Her work is displayed in streets, offices, public squares or transmitted into unusual places such as airports, shopping centres, and cathedrals, in order to provoke or at least warrant a second look from passers-by. The messages or signs are usually deployed to shock. Her favourite medium is the flashing electronic billboard; moving messages can be very arresting.

One of the key ideas behind Holzer's approach is to position the installation where the slogan or message deployed is an observation or reflection upon the space where it is shown. The statement sums up the context or the inhabitants. An electronic sign placed in the New York Stock Exchange on Wall Street repeated the slogan 'MONEY CREATES TASTE', an advertising billboard outside Caesar's Palace in Las Vegas read 'LACK OF CHARISMA CAN BE FATAL', and at a concert for Nelson Mandela in London, a billboard flashed up the slogan 'PROTECT ME FROM WHAT I WANT'. Holzer's work is site specific, ephemeral, poignant and highly charged.

In Berlin, Holzer uses the massive soffit of the Neue Nationalgalerie designed by Mies Van De Rohe to house a series of electronic strips that display impertinent messages. The visitor is invited to lie on the elegant Barcelona chairs and read the stories as they race overhead in a non-stop electronic stream of words. Strangely the installation is so site specific that it renders the floor plane of the building free from the 'clutter' of art and objects to become a modernist's dream!

Landschaftspark

Location: **Duisburg, Germany**
Remodelled: **1994**
Designers: **Lighting by Fisher Park,**
Landscaping by Peter Latz

**Fig.1. The Fisher Park
light extravaganza
transforms the
steelworks
at night into a giant
stage set**

Artificial light is a most ephemeral medium. During the day it is often completely unnoticeable but at night it can be awe-inspiring and dramatic.

The Kommunalverband Ruhrgebiet of mid-west Germany is a huge area that contains over five and a half million people living in the industrial towns of Essen, Duisburg, Oberhausen and Dortmund. This area was once the heavy industrial centre of Germany, producing steel and mining coal for the rest of the country. The shift of industrial production to other cheaper parts of the world effectively rendered the industries obsolete and resulted in the closure of the steel works, smelting plants, coal mines, gas refineries, and many of the other industries that relied on the by-products of these enormous plants.

This left an architectural legacy of colossal buildings, packed with machinery of varying size and scale and occupying enormous tracts of land often poisoned and scarred by the raw materials and processes of the various production systems. The region is littered with vast relics of steel, coal, and gas production. Rather than demolish or attempt to remove them, the cities and districts of the Ruhrgebiet came together to form the Kommunalverband, a council made up of the districts of the region, and formulated a strategy to reclaim and reuse these places.

Among the industrial detritus and wreckage are a series of new spaces, made from the old. One of these is in the city of Duisburg, which is situated at the confluence of the Rhine and Ruhr rivers. The Thyssen steel works, in Duisburg-Nord, was a massive complex set in 200 hectares of land and was one of the principal steel works in Germany until its shutdown in the early 1980s. Rather than destroy or demolish the site, the landscape architect Peter Latz turned the site into a public park, replanting the slag heaps with birch trees and rare plants and trying to 'clean' some of the contaminated land for planting and landscaping. The blast furnaces, water tanks, storage bunkers for the raw materials, coking plants, and assortment of bunkers, outbuildings, factories, finishing and storage warehouses were retained and became host to a variety of new uses from outdoor cinemas to artist workshops. Underwater playgrounds were created in the cooling towers for the scuba divers to explore the cavernous underground cooling tunnels in the plant. The park became a host for plants and landscaping, some formalised and imposed, some wild with some quite rare plants having arrived in the various imported ores and minerals from the Americas and South Africa.

The landscaping of the park and the variety of new uses has transformed the works from a previously inhospitable place into a park for the city's inhabitants.

The steelworks were reused in a way that transformed their presence and scale (albeit temporarily) through a lighting strategy devised by Fisher Park. The Thyssen steelworks become a different place at night as this vast site was transformed through special lighting effects, to make it appear like an enormous set design in the landscape. Fisher Park were responsible for designing the stage sets of the massive world tours for bands like the Rolling Stones and the Who. Here they treated the steelworks in the same way. The 80 m-high chimneys and the main structure of the blast furnaces were lit in solid blocks of colour. Secondary architectural features such as gantries and pipework were lit in blue and green, while pipes into the blast furnaces were in red to symbolise the heat of the pig-iron process. The chimney tops were ringed in white bands of neon, symbolising their new 'environmentally clean' use as signposts for the nearby autobahn. Computers controlled changes throughout the night, with colours becoming more intense and shifting according to the time and day of the week.

Bunker

Location: **The Atlantic Wall, Western Europe**
Date: **1995**
Artist: **Erasmus Schröter**

The photographer Erasmus Schröter uses light to change buildings. His raw materials are relics from the Second World War, the bunkers, batteries, and command bases of the old Atlantic Wall that stretches along the western coast of Europe. These gigantic monoliths, constructed from extremely thick reinforced concrete, were built to protect the German defenders from the air bombardment of the Allied forces. Although in various states of ruin and disrepair, many of the bunkers still exist, due for the most part to their phenomenally strong construction. Some are relatively intact, others have subsided or are lost to the shifting sand upon which they stand.

Schröter creates a performance with the bunkers. He swathes them in artificial light and then records the image. The photographs are taken using a long exposure time, and thus the resultant image contains slight movements or shifts giving a great intensity to the picture. The results are startling and dramatic. The bunkers are lit with strong colours; purples, reds and yellow are often captured during vivid skies or sunsets or at night against rough seas.

Schröter's images demonstrate the power of transformation through the application of artificial light. The function of the buildings – defensive bunkers shielding soldiers against air attack – hasn't been altered, but with specific lighting and photography Schröter complicates that straightforward message to produce a very different and romantic reading of the object.

**Fig.1. Bunker WB XVII, 1998.
The re-reading of the once
imposing defence bunkers created
by bathing them in artificial light
transformed them into beautiful
yet melancholic objects**

Wellcome Wing

Location: **The Science Museum, London**
Remodelled: **1998**
Architects: **MacCormac, Jamieson, Prichard (MJP), with lighting designer Rogier Van Der Heide**

Fig.1. The deep blue wall acts as a backdrop to the exhibition space, the combination of light and screen lending an uncertainty to the actual dimensions of the room

Richard MacCormac of MJP is very influenced by the work of James Turrell and Robert Irwin, both of whom heighten the awareness of a place by blurring its boundaries. Irwin uses a scrim or very light gauze stretched in front of a space and the virtual transparency of the material arrests the focal length of the eye and appears to distort the actual volume of the room. Turrell manipulates light to a similar effect and illuminates a room in such a way that it becomes impossible to ascertain the actual physical dimensions of it.

In the new Wellcome wing, MJP architects use light as a theatrical backdrop to the new exhibition space, which consists of a series of new floors suspended in space. MJP stretched a scrim wall about half a metre in front of the solid fire- resistant concrete wall. The space between was then lit with fluorescent lights containing reflectors and blue filters in the battens. Rogier Van Der Heide described the design:

I selected a very narrow bandwidth of deep blue, which makes it difficult for the eye to judge the depth of and focus on the blue plane.[14]

This creates a whole wall that appears to glow with an even blue light and, combined with the scrim, make it difficult to determine its exact position. It is as if the space is not bounded by anything solid but contained by planes of pure blue light.

Zumtobel Staff Lighting showroom

Location: **Berlin, Germany**
Remodelled: **2000**
Architects: **Sauerbruch and Hutton**

Artificial light can be combined with natural light and used in many ways to create a completely different and always changing atmosphere in a space.

The showroom for the lighting company Zumtobel Staff is quite appropriately housed in an old Berlin light bulb factory. The factory, in the Oberbaum City harbour-side location in old East Berlin, had been divided into units and this showroom occupies a 2-storey corner unit. It fronts the street and is framed on two sides by pedestrian arcades. The accommodation required consisted of showrooms, offices, meeting areas, exhibition spaces and client entertainment areas. The Anglo-German designers Sauerbruch and Hutton were asked to consider the project and their attitude was to regard it 'as an experiment in the transformative properties of light'.[15]

The architects' approach was to design the Zumtobel Staff showroom as a temporary space made up of elements that did not touch the existing building. These transient installations were intended to display and demonstrate the artificial light and manipulate the natural light of the building. They were not intended to last – they were transformable both physically and atmospherically. The partitions and the screens in the space are also movable and thus a space containing radically differing and always changing lighting effects has been created.

The building is ordered in a relatively simple fashion. The ground floor is the main public showroom, while the upper floors contain the private offices, meeting rooms and entertainment and display areas. The existing space was deliberately unaltered except for a spiral staircase to link the floors and on the ground floor the walls were neutral so as not to distract from the lighting show.

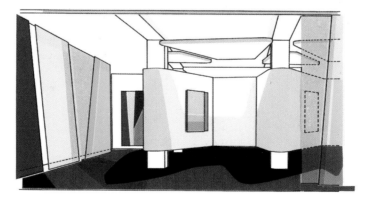

Fig.1. The designers intended this colourful space as a stage set for the lighting products

Fig. 2. Colourful translucent screens are used in the ground floor windows to reflect light onto the shiny floor

Once inside the space the changes can be dramatic. As the daylight changes so does the interior space, creating a constant shift in the light and atmosphere in the showroom. On the ground floor the natural light is modulated by a series of coloured translucent panels that are placed just inside the existing glazed façade. They are constructed from two sheets of glass with a coloured film sandwiched in between and then have been suspended by rods from the ceiling and supported by cast aluminium feet. They can be moved. The floor surface is made from highly polished black concrete and during the daytime the coloured natural light from the glazing panels creates a variety of effects upon and reflected from this.

From the ceiling hanging in formation across the space are a series of organically shaped lighting 'clouds'. They are suspended just below the original soffit of the existing building and carry a collection of the lighting products. A sculpted wall twists through the middle of the showroom. It contains niches and holes and these too hold examples of the company's lighting products. Printed onto the undulating wall is a series of quotes and poems about light. The intention is for the plaster-clad partition to become the blank canvas for the lighting effects.

It is on the stairs and first floor that Sauerbruch and Hutton's passion for colour is demonstrated. Fibre-optically controlled illuminated fittings in the walls continuously change colour to create dramatic effects. The void of the staircase contains a series of colour swatches that are lit by lamps from the Zumtobel Staff range. Not only does this give a magical coloured effect, but it also acts as a practical device for showing clients the effects of the lights on different colours.

Colour is an element of great importance to Sauerbruch and Hutton. They regard it as something to be considered right from the outset and to be treated with as much importance as the quality of the space or the materials used. Not only are they obsessed with the use of pure colour but it is the combination of it with the other elements that makes it fascinating; surfaces, light and structure all come together to create the complexity of the building.

Louisa Hutton described the intimate relationship that developed in their work between the existing building and colour:

We've used colour to create a certain atmospheric expression, similar to music. You can alter a space entirely with a coat of paint. You can make it warm, cold, distant, enclosing or opening. Kandinsky used colour in this way. Colour can also extend a space visually. The use of different tonalities and hues – cool against warm, for instance – can create depth and a play of space even when you're unable to alter the physical constraints of the site.[16]

Fig. 4. The showroom is organised around a series of installations; a folding screen used as a backdrop for light tests, a visitors' reception area and a stair to take guests to the offices and conference rooms upstairs

Fig. 3. The folded screen wall is washed with different colours of light

**Fig.1. Johan Menswear Shop,
Graz, Claudio Silvestrin.
The minimal effect is achieved
with just three materials,
pigmented plaster, polished
concrete and limed oak**

Surface is the use
of specific materials
to confer identity
and meaning.

It is the surface of an element that receives the most human contact. Doors can look strong but it is the handle that we actually touch; the light reflected off the water onto a ceiling can look beautiful but it is the velvet on the chair that we feel.

The specific choice of materials and textures can create identity and meaning. The character of a wall depends as much upon its textural quality as its structure or position. A coarse rough concrete finish has a quite different quality to that of polished marble and is different again to studded rubber or fun fur, even though they can all quite viably be placed in an identical position.

The manner in which materials are used creates atmosphere and mood. Many architects will use a similar selection of materials but it is the application or detailing of these that gives each building its individual quality. Claudio Silvestrin's very limited palette of exquisite materials epitomises his minimalist approach. The Johan Menswear shop in Graz, Austria uses just three quite common materials all of a similar subdued quality: grey-green pigmented polished plaster for the walls of the space, the changing rooms and also the fitted shelves; polished concrete for the floor and the top surface of the shelves and limed oak for the long thin display plinth placed centrally in the space. Silvestrin uses a fourth material, light, to accentuate the surfaces of the vaulted space. The identity is created by the manner in which the materials are put together. For a minimalist approach to work, the detailing has to be exact and well crafted; the precise 2 cm gap between the floor and the walls, the 3 mm joints in the flags, the module of the storage wall, all have to be synchronised with the other patterns of the shop.

Philippe Starck uses all these materials plus a lot more to create a much richer and more varied collection and deploys them in a shockingly sensuous way. When describing the Royalton hotel in New York, Kurtich and Eakin were quite excited by its dangerous quality:

Starck uses every aspect of the interior to create unfamiliar surroundings replete with symbols of horns, snakes, spermatozoa, caves, wombs, waterfalls. Sex is heavy in the air.[17]

The properties of the specific material will often determine its use. This is usually the case for the conventional architectural materials: timber creates warmth, steel is and appears strong, brick is traditional, concrete has modernist connotations and glass is transparent.

The application of a wide variety of surface materials, some drawn from unorthodox sources, can create an unusual identity. Materials such as steel mesh, plastics and acrylic, which were developed for industrial use, are now widely accepted as interior finishes. This crossover of use can create an odd yet often appropriate atmosphere and mood in a remodelled space.

**Fig. 2. The simplicity
of the changing
room drums
accentuates their
sculptural quality**

Fig.1. The felt is used
as a platform to support
laptops, catalogues
and accessories.
The lighting
emphasises the
simplicity of the space

OKI-NI

Location: **Savile Row, London**
Remodelled: **2001**
Architect: **6a**

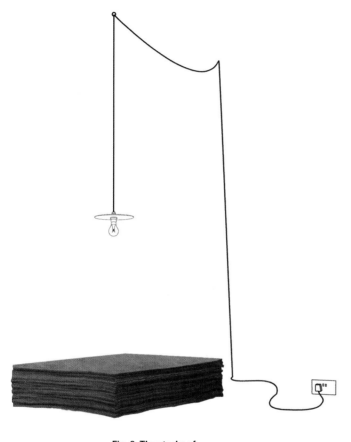

**Fig. 2. The stacks of
soft felt are used for
simple display**

There has always been a ritual to buying clothes from Savile Row in London, where the most exclusive tailors practise and the purchase of a handmade suit requires a number of fittings and a lot of patience. Only an extremely cheeky set-up would have the nerve to join this exclusive group and then mischievously play them at a very modern version of their own game.

6a architects were asked to create an unusual and dramatic space that displayed the clothes and provided changing rooms and somewhere to request the garment. The unusual approach that OKI-NI took was that, in common with the neighbouring tailors, the clothes had to be ordered.

The existing space was a small and roughly triangular single floor shopping unit with one existing central column and a glazed front façade. The architects wanted the interior to read as an extension of the exterior. The shop window display was therefore eliminated and a huge tall-sided wooden tray was inserted into the space. The floor and walls are made of a continuous half-sleeve of Russian oak boarding. It forms an uninterrupted landscape starting at the street edge and slides into the interior. This tray is a metre or so short of the ceiling, which gives the space a definite shape and creates somewhere for clothes to be casually displayed. In the centre of the shop an enormous pile of half-inch thick felt sheets was placed. This provides a soft plinth for clothes to be thrown onto and for the staff and customers to sit on. It is also where the clothes can be ordered by staff from laptop computers.

Traditional materials can be used in an unusual way and combined with other surfaces to make distinct spaces. The contrast between the timber and the felt is a subtle tactile shift between the hard surface of the walls and floor to the soft warm point of human contact.

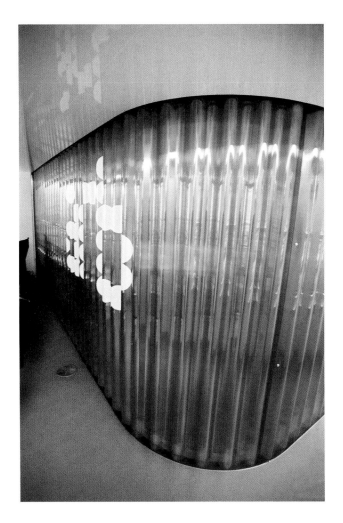

Fig.1. The polycarbonate wall refracts and diffuses light. The stretched vinyl soffit is cut back around the wall so that it seems to sink into the ceiling

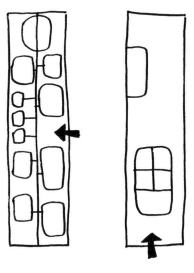

Fig. 2. The separated and contained organisation of the previous office (left) has been transformed into a transparent open space

The Architects Registration Board (ARB) Offices

Location: **London**
Remodelled: **1999**
Architect: **DDRM**

The ARB office is one project within a series that DDRM have designed entitled 'Off The Shelf'. Each project uses commonly available materials in an unconventional manner. This oblique approach creates spaces with unusual characters; the surface materials embody certain qualities, which then bestow a particular identity to the space.

ARB occupies the ground floor of a 1960s block in London. The brief was for a new modern office that reflects the ARB's new outlook. The policy of openness and friendliness was to be transmitted through the design of the offices.

Two simple curving polycarbonate walls slide into and through the space, one to surround the meeting room and form a backdrop to the reception, the other to enclose the toilets. The brief called for transparency, both psychologically and physically. The new screen is indeed see-through and although it allows plenty of light and reflection into the interior of the offices, it does tinge the interior of the space with a blue light.

The use of polycarbonate, conventionally a roofing material, endows the offices of the ARB with a bright, powerful new identity.

Fig. 3. The reception area has the look of a deli counter. The large glass top desk, continuous clean floor, stretched vinyl soffit and backdrop of blue polycarbonate wall are all bright, clean and open

**Fig.1. The rough
surface textures of
the factory are left
exposed to show the
many changes
undergone by the
building**

Media Centre

Location: **Hamburg, Germany**
Remodelled: **1993**
Architect: **me di um**

**Fig. 2. In contrast
with the old surfaces,
the new cinema
is rendered smooth
and blue**

The architects me di um describe their process of working with redundant building structures as 'soft architecture': they 'graft new forms and functions onto historical skeletons and roots'.[18] This produces new buildings of rich contrasts.

In Hamburg an old propeller factory was remodelled to house a cinema, design studios, shops, and restaurant/ bar. The surfaces of the old walls and the floor were left in their found state to counterpoint the crisp new interventions. The stains on the brick walls were celebrated together with the rust on the steel columns. Treasured and squashed next to these elements were the new insertions of crisp plaster, clean concrete, steel and glass. On the floor the old tracks of the trolleys that transported the enormous propellers across the factory floor were retained and instead are now used to direct the visitor through the building.

The surfaces and objects left over from previous use imbue the new with a strong historical atmosphere. The exposure of the old fabric makes a startling counterpoint to any new elements or surfaces imposed onto the building.

**Fig. 2. Like an archaeological
excavation, the layers
and surfaces of the theatre
are left exposed as
reminders of the building's
many transformations**

**Fig.1. The upper floor
bar area is rendered
and polished to
create a shiny
counterpoint to the
decay**

Location: **Sloane Square, London**
Remodelled: **2000**
Architect: **Haworth Tompkins**

New materials and surfaces are imported into an existing building when it is remodelled and these may or may not have a relationship with the existing material quality of the host. Often they will have no connection with it at all. A building interior may consist of years and years of accretions, layers of paper and paint, bits of materials, repairs, scratches and dents from the previous occupations. The discovery of this 'unintentional' surface may surprise and the exposure of the layers of use and addition can be a startling and delightful discovery. These surfaces can be used to generate an individual atmosphere of memory and respect. The exposure of the life and history of the building can lead to a distinct quality against which new surfaces and objects are then juxtaposed.

The Royal Court Theatre in Sloane Square, London, dates back to 1888. The building had undergone many changes since it was built. It was a theatre until 1932 when it was converted into a cinema, but this was blitzed in 1940. It was reassembled by the London Theatre Guild in 1952, who occupied it until 1996. Since its inception it had been renowned for its radical agenda and the fostering of new writing and directing talent. Appropriately, the directors chose the young practice of Haworth Tompkins to remodel the building.

By starting with a building with an interesting history, an exceptionally restricted site and a client who required a space that reflected their agenda, the architects decided that to erase the building and start again would be wrong. Instead they chose a strategy of intervention, one of cutting back and revealing the layers of history and accretion and illustrating these surgical incisions with new elements. The architects suggested that by using this strategy there was a 'sense of radical continuity, a feeling that the building is current, but has a strong relationship with its own past'.[19]

In the remodelling the complex history of the building is revealed. Inside, the method of excavation and exposure really comes to life. The fabric is stripped back to reveal the old steel beams embedded in walls, the ducts and even the builders' scribbles on walls. Steve Tompkins explains:

If we'd replastered the walls slippery and smooth it would have been wrong. It had to feel used and marked. It can't be pristine.[20]

Inside the auditorium, the underside of the balcony was stripped back to reveal the original riveted iron structure. The brickwork around the stairs and the old terrazzo floor were exposed and new insertions were made which are in character with the atmosphere that the architects created: new tan leather seats in the auditorium, untreated steel shutters in the dressing rooms and new furniture in the basement café.

Fig. 3. The box office sits upon the patchwork of repairs and changes of the ground floor surface

Maison de Verre

Location: **Paris**
Remodelled: **1931**
Architect: **Pierre Chareau**

Fig.1. From the courtyard the two-storey glass façade appears as a floating translucent screen

Richard Rogers, when discussing the link between high-tech architecture and the Maison de Verre, claimed in a *Domus* magazine article of 1966, 'This house of light is possibly the least known and the greatest of 20th century houses'. The house is actually the conversion of the bottom two storeys of a four-storey town house. The top two storeys were supported on steel columns and then a glass brick screen wall was cantilevered clear of them to create a free façade. This allowed the double height spaces created within the building real freedom that was further strengthened by the use of movable screens and free-standing storage units.

The exploration of a particular material or quality of a surface can form the principal characteristic of a building, thus shaping its identity. The house became known as 'The Transparent House' because of the dominating envelope of the glass brick exterior wall. The translucent glass bricks provided privacy while admitting ample natural light. This successful technique was imitated by numerous architects and is still being borrowed in the 21st century.

The surface treatment of a building formed its identity. The Maison de Verre established a significant position in architectural history based upon the ground-breaking use of a particular surface material.

A-POC for Issey Miyake

Location: **Paris**
Remodelled: **2000**
Architect: **Bouroullec Brothers**

**Fig.1. The 'cut to fit'
ethic of the garments
is expressed in the
furniture, which evokes
folded cutting tables**

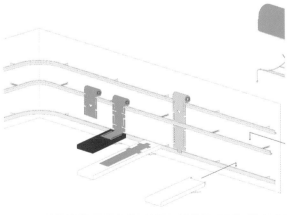

**Fig. 2. The clothing
and display elements
hang from the
horizontal bands
of the corian**

Corian is a remarkable material; it is a plastic with the ability to be both fluid and rigid. Although it is usually supplied in sheet form, it can be moulded to almost any shape and can have a satin smooth or sandpaper rough finish. It is sufficiently strong to support itself and the colour is solid throughout the moulding. It is the kind of magical material that all students of architecture and design dream of. Of course, corian does have some drawbacks: it always needs cleaning and is extremely expensive, but then Issey Miyake stipulated no budget for the A-POC shop and just requested that the Bouroullec brothers be remarkable!

The concept for the shop is also surprising. The customer is encouraged to participate in the creative process of the design of the garment; the space is both a boutique and a factory. The buyer can customise their garment by making different cuts or joins from the basic pattern.

The design of the space and in particular the surfaces of the shop characterise this concept. Three rows of thin strips of white corian loop around the edges of the space. This creates seamless bands that run through the pure white interior of the shop. The brightly coloured corian tables, screens and minimal signs that are attached to the bands then animate the space. The Miyake clothes, bolts of cloth and a rough vivid green wool curtain also hang from these flowing rails.

The fluid uninterrupted pure white background complements the radical qualities of the brightly coloured elements and the products for sale.

Tactics
Opening

Openings are crucial punctuation points within buildings, they can establish both physical and visual relationships between people and places.

Openings are important in buildings. They can signal physical or visual movement, and provide an idea of where to go or remind of a previous encounter. They also give an idea of context and suggest the extent of the journey. They can be ornamented so that the opening itself is accentuated or they can simply be frames for the passage of a picture-like view. Openings create sequences, giving rhythm and movement to a space. They guide circulation and allow views further into the journey.

Exhibitions can sometimes be so internally focused that the visitor loses contact with both the building and the outside world. The Picasso Museum in Paris by Roland Simounet allows the visitor glimpses of what is ahead, what has already been seen and of the outside. The rooms in the museum are linked together by means of a series of internal and external visual references. Openings are used to show previously visited or oncoming spaces to the visitor. For instance, upon entering the building there is a view of the final gallery in the strictly chronologically ordered exhibition, and halfway through the exhibition, the entrance courtyard is suddenly revealed from the first floor.

An axis through a building is a valuable controlling device. Venturi, Scott Brown and Associates use this in the design for the extension to the National Gallery in London. The strong cross-axis of the original building is continued through the extension, thus linking the two buildings. The new series of enfilade rooms culminates in Chima's great altarpiece, 'The Incredulity of Saint Thomas', a wonderful painting with a gilded arched frame. The diminishing perspective of the series of openings on axis causes the spaces to appear to continue into the picture.

**Fig.1. Picasso museum
in Paris, remodelled from
a French town house**

**Fig. 2. The Moller
House, Vienna, 1928.
Adolf Loos**

A door is much more than a mere opening in a wall: it is an important sign. It indicates the transition from one area to another and it prepares the visitor for the particular event ahead. The main entrance door of a building marks the position of the change from the public exterior to the private interior. It is not always the human body that will dictate the size of the door; a big door can be an indication of the importance of the entrance, an ornate door can signal prosperity and a heavy door, that there is something inside worth protecting. The new large sliding glass panel entrance door of the La Llauna secondary school in Barcelona by Miralles and Pinos, contrasts with the heavy masonry walls of the original factory and announces the change of use and modernisation of the building.

The most basic function of windows is to admit light. They also allow a view from the inside to the outside during the day and project an image of the interior to the outside at night. Steven Holl designed the front wall of the Storefront gallery in New York as a series of pivoted openings; during the day they provide the gallery with natural light and air and at night the odd-shaped openings glow with internal light and movement thus advertising the building's artistic function. The early villas of Le Corbusier were deliberately designed as vehicles of movement to provide a series of set views only visible as the occupant promenaded through the spaces. As Beatriz Colomina says:

The look is directed to the exterior in such a deliberate manner as to suggest the reading of these houses as frames for a view.[21]

This dual purpose can be disconnected and the separation of the admitance of light from the presentation of the viwer allows the internal spaces to be visually linked. In the words of Adolf Loos:

A cultivated man does not look out of the window; his window is a ground glass; it is there only to let the light in, not to let the gaze pass through.[22]

Adolf Loos removed the focus or gaze from the window by deliberately obscuring it and thus controlling the position of a person so their gaze instead of being towards the light and therefore the exterior, was directed to the interior. A person moving around the house would be presented with a series of set views through the three-dimensional space of the interior. The Moller house, for example, was provided with a view through the length and heart of the building. The view was from a sofa positioned with its back to the largest first floor window. The sitter gazed slightly downwards through the main living areas and entrance staircase towards the brightness of the garden. This scene, observed through a series of openings and spaces, allowed the viewer to comprehend the three-dimensional relationships of the space and observe the movements of anyone else in the building. Conversely someone entering the building was aware of the presence of the silhouette on the sofa in front of the veiled window, seen through the interior spaces of the rooms.

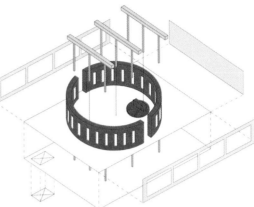

Fig. 2. The screen wall allows movement to occur around the outside, leaving the centre as a contemplative space of light and stillness

Fig.1. Framed views through the screen wall allow glimpses into the worship area

Grace Place Episcopal Church

Location: **Chicago, USA**
Date: **1986**
Architect: **Booth Hansen**

At the southern end of 'The Loop' area of Chicago is Printers Row, which consists of a series of late 19th century warehouses designed to house workshops and printing presses. From the 1960s the area was gentrified and is now the location for chic warehouse apartments, hotels and office spaces. The Grace Episcopal Church relocated to one of these warehouses in the mid 1980s. The intention was to attract a new congregation of office workers and apartment dwellers by offering religious services, concerts and a space in which to escape the daily noise and congestion of the city. The local architects, Booth Hansen, whose own office was based in a nearby building on the same street, were invited to remodel the warehouse by providing a flexible community space with a segregated area for more secular activities.

The robust and workmanlike character of the original building posed a particular problem for establishing the identity and atmosphere of the new function. The architects were determined to work with the existing yet avoid the clichés of stripped pine and empty space which was de rigueur in the surrounding new office and apartment developments. Another influential factor was the prerequisite that the space was to be used by a number of different denominations and therefore it could not overtly express any symbolism which might be important to one practice but offensive to another.

At a strategic level, Booth Hansen reorganised the building by placing the worship space on the upper floors while keeping the ground floor open and flexible for a variety of events. This gave the more religious area an elevated importance. It also allowed the architects to open the ceiling of the upper floor to allow light into the space. The existing building consisted of a masonry skin with a robust timber frame structure. Booth Hansen exposed the masonry and timber and cleaned them. They then intervened upon the space by adding a new raised floor for the altar, pews and a marble font salvaged from a previous incarnation of the church.

The worship space is designed to enhance the notion of a retreat from the outside city. The worship area itself is enclosed by a simple oval screen, constructed from timber and clad in plasterboard and rendered white. It curves around the room, flowing freely past the rigid posts of the structure and stopping just short of the beams of the roof. It is positioned inside the walls of the existing building to allow circulation around its outside and it maximises the contrast between its smooth white simplicity and the worn textures of the brick and the rough-hewn timber frame. This screen wall is punctuated by a series of openings, which articulate the wall and allow light and views into the main space from the entrance to the room. These openings are detailed with a pointed arch motif that evokes the Gothic style of church architecture. These abstracted motifs appear decorative in contrast to the robust, tough qualities of the host space, yet from entering the room, as the congregation circulate around the screen until they are allowed in through openings in either side of the hall, these give tantalising glimpses into the inner sanctum of the worship space.

Fig.1. Inside the gallery,
the panels can
be folded back to
reveal the city

Fig. 2. The Storefront
is a radical
intervention in the
ground floor of the
corner block of
Kenmare Street

Storefront for Art and Architecture

Location: **New York**
Remodelled: **1992/3**
Architects: **Steven Holl with Vito Acconci**

Fig. 3. The panels of the Storefront Gallery open to allow interaction between inside and outside

The Storefront Gallery is situated on the corner of a block at the intersection of three districts, China Town, Little Italy and SoHo and inhabits the ground floor of a three- storey domestic building. The gallery itself is the shape of a long narrow triangle and this, the architects considered, meant that the long façade was the only productive area for remodelling.

Acconci and Holl were interested in the idea of art being accessible to all and the permanence or impermanence of the façade. The layers of paint and the cuts of previous exhibitors had left their mark upon the interior of the wall. The architects used these as a base and inserted a series of hinged orthogonal panels into the façade, which linked the inside to the outside of the gallery. The panels are constructed of concrete mixed with recycled fibres. When the gallery is closed they appear as a strange pattern on the wall, but when it is open, the façade vanishes and the interior of the gallery expands onto the pavement. The director of the gallery summed up his attitude to the wall and the openings as 'no wall, no barrier, no inside, no space, no building, no institution, no art, no architecture, no Acconci, no Holl, no Storefront.'[23]

**Fig.1. Accentuated
view from the study
room toward the
neighbouring tree**

**Fig. 2. View through
the gallery space,
the glass window
on the left
emphasising the
complexity of light
and movement**

Blackburn House

Location: **London**
Remodelled: **1988**
Architects: **Bolles+Wilson**

Adolf Loos refers to the separation of light from the view. The purpose of a window is for the admission of light, not for generally looking out of. Views are to be set up, to be constructed, not by accident as you might get from idly gazing out of a window, but by the careful positioning of furniture and openings. The view from the Blackburn House was of the backs of unattractive houses that were far too close for a comfortable relationship.

When the architects were asked to remodel the top two floors of the mews building, their approach was to gut the building, and then to paint the resultant pure form white. The building was then animated with sculptural objects. These installed pieces of furniture or artefacts were placed carefully, at key points of articulation within the stark white interior.

The huge inclined bay window is the only element to penetrate the wall of the building. The void, the stairs and the window form a three-dimensional element that is placed diagonally against the rectilinear grain of the rest of the building and juts out from the façade.

This window admits a considerable amount of natural light into the building, but the glass has been sandblasted and the translucent quality obscures the view of the too-close neighbouring buildings. Small areas of untreated glass give the impression of bright lines trickling down the window. The focus has been forced back into the space of the room. The elements draw the eye along the room, and the translucent glass ensures that it is deflected back into the interior. The gaze of Adolf Loos's cultivated man is fixed on the three-dimensional space of the interior.

The only window that does have a clear view of the outside is in the study. This triangular room comes to a point directly opposite the desk, so that the perspective is accentuated and the viewer's vision is channelled towards the emphasised long thin window. However the scene that is visible is of a neighbouring tree trunk.

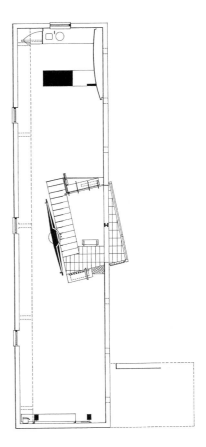

Fig. 3. Upper floor plan. The main window is twisted from the façade against the grain of the rectangular block

Henry Moore Institute

Location: **Leeds, England**
Remodelled: **1993**
Architects: **Jeremy Dixon Edward Jones, BDP**

Fig.1. The new opening is a slot cut into the enigmatic black granite façade. The intervention changes the orientation of the building by threading a circulation route through the gable end of the building linking the terraced houses

The gallery spaces and study areas of the Henry Moore Institute, situated in the heart of the city of Leeds, have been inserted into a row of elegant Georgian terraced houses. The Institute has been designed for the general study of sculpture rather than specifically focusing upon the works of Henry Moore.

The architects were faced with an awkward site and a set of intricate problems. The nature of the site at the front and the side differed greatly in scale and prominence. The front of the 18th century listed terrace faced on to Cookridge Street, a narrow street appropriate to the scale of the houses, but the clear gable end looked on to the Headrow, the civic centre of Leeds and site of Smirke's town hall and adjacent City Art Gallery. Cookridge Street had been the conventional entrance to the terraces, but the architects decided that it was more important to address the scale and proportion of the civic promenade and provide a new entrance that respected the importance of the Headrow and the cultural influence that Henry Moore has in Leeds.

The ambiguity of the site was addressed by taking advantage of this change of direction. A terrace or platform was built in front of the gable end wall to tie in with the line of the neighbouring cultural building and to hold and balance the enormous black granite false façade glued to the clear gable end wall of the Georgian terrace. A modernist element, it is slightly smaller than the original wall, has a partially crenellated top and just one huge central opening. This latter is a monumental entrance into the galleries, a huge element that signals the change of orientation. Once through it, the visitor ascends a long shallow stair to the reception; this circulation spine inserted through the opening links to the listed domestic scale gallery rooms. The massive orthogonal blackness of the façade is connected to the intimate whiteness of the interior by the monumental opening.

Public Library

Location: **Landau, Germany**
Remodelled: **1998**
Architects: **Lamott Architekten BDA**

Fig.1. The view through from the entrance to the 'quiet' library area inside the old slaughter halls, with the new black steel frame echoing the openings above and the columns repeating the natural structure of the building

Two old slaughterhouse buildings were remodelled and extended to create a public library. They were reused as huge objects sitting freely within an enormous new space. The masonry halls were literally wrapped in a contrasting structure of steel and glass with horizontal timber louvres.

The main studying spaces were situated in the existing areas and the supporting activities were placed in the new parts. Two major alterations were made to the fabric of the existing buildings, both of which cut sections from the walls to allow freedom of movement, physically, visually and psychologically. The two halls were very close together and the neighbouring walls created too much containment. At ground level, these were removed, and so at this level the buildings now appear as a single unit. Steel columns were inserted to support the high level walls and these were arranged with great sympathy for the form and rhythm of the existing building. In the new form the sheer thickness of the floating high-level walls oppresses the openings and the voids appear as enormous horizontal slots cut from the mass of the original buildings.

The second act of removal was in the contained front façade. Again, a section of ground floor wall was removed from each hall, thus making it possible to see right into the heart of the space. The view from outside now penetrates through the new façade and then through the removed façade of the original buildings.

The constructive demolition of parts of the existing buildings brought a clarity and order to the new library. The large heavy buildings were connected, given a lightness and charged with new life. The new openings link the areas of the building and prevent the existing structures from overbearing the design.

**Fig.1. Television
monitors placed in
the gallery show
visitors entering
the museum through
the revolving door**

Para-site

Location: **Museum of Modern Art, New York**
Date: **1989**
Architects: **Diller and Scofidio**

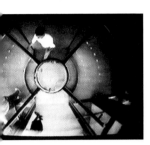

Fig. 2. Ironically,
the viewers become
the viewed

Openings create relationships between things, whether between people, spaces or objects and the established relationship can be physical, visual or by some other means. Diller and Scofidio developed a televisual link between the space of an exhibition in the Museum of Modern Art in New York and the people entering the museum. This very unusual exhibition was an attempt to comment upon the type of person visiting the gallery, the nature of the museum in society and, in particular, the edifying institution that is the Museum of Modern Art.

The installation was called Para-site, and as the architects Diller and Scofidio point out,

Para-site is a site specific installation [that] takes up the theme of a filtered vision in the museum. As parasiting is by nature site specific, a closer reading of the organism is unavoidable.[24]

The temporary exhibition used the visitor as the subject matter; they were observed and recorded from three locations within the museum's circulation system. The architects positioned cameras in the revolving entrance door on Fifty-third Street, above the escalators and at the entrance from the sculpture garden.

The recorded images were relayed to a series of monitors installed within the museum galleries. The pictures from the four revolving doors were displayed on four monitors, wedged into the corner of the gallery space. The monitors were held by a timber and steel structure, which reinforced the apparent invasive quality. The installation looked like an animal of some description that had invaded the gallery and clamped itself into position. On the ceiling was a chair which represented the 'fictive viewer'. The film footage was broadcast upside down (the right way for someone sitting in the chair). Inscribed upon the chair was raised inverted text from The Para-site, which would imprint itself on the body of the sitter and could be read the right way around, another invasive tactic.

The two escalator cameras (one escalator ascending, one descending), were positioned in the lobby, and were physically connected to the two television screens by a cantilevered arm that ran through the lobby and into the gallery space. The sculpture court monitor was positioned in the corner of the gallery and received a live feed from a camera pointing through the glass wall at a surveillance mirror. This convex mirror reflected the image of the very façade being looked through and therefore the received and broadcast image was also a reflection.

Diller and Scofidio suggest that the museum, and in particular the Museum of Modern Art, is of an era which is defined by the supremacy of sight or viewing. Looking, in all of its complexities, is governed by all sorts of composite encoded constructs. Para-site is a reading of this situation. Para-site recorded and monitored the movements and comments of the gallery users. Most of these visitors to the gallery had come to view some paintings or an exhibition, or even do some shopping; ironically, they also became the exhibits, a situation which obfuscated the normal rationale for going to a gallery. The self-conscious act of filming and then broadcasting people as they enter a building is a device that Diller and Scofidio reused in their design of the Brasserie restaurant in the basement of the Seagram Building. The images taken from the revolving doors are in this case shown in the bar area, ostensibly to inform anyone of a friend or colleague's arrival, but in reality, the visitor is so conscious of being filmed that the manoeuvre becomes a sort of catwalk performance.

Movement not only provides access to different areas within a building but also serves to bind together separate or disparate spaces.

Movement or circulation in a building occurs in a number of ways. It may be by means of something as inconsequential as the corridor that links a number of rooms. On the other hand, it may be by means of a dramatic gesture through a number of spaces, a dynamic series of stairs, ramps and bridges, or the building itself may be a massive circulation route.

The route through a building can be signalled by the use of directed light and specifically placed objects. The breakfast room of Sir John Soane's house in London is located in a pivotal position, occupying the central point in what was once a courtyard. The dome over the centre of the room contains a lantern and this focuses the attention centrally onto the breakfast table, thus leaving the sides of the space for circulation. The edges of the room are also top lit, illuminating the circulation zone and facilitating movement through this significant space and into the other areas of the house. In such a small area, just less than three and a half square metres, a remarkable sense of freedom is created.

Up until about the beginning of the 17th century, houses did not contain corridors. Doors were positioned in the centre of the internal wall and rooms were positioned as an enfilade. Rooms often did not have the single focused occupation, but rather were often used for a multitude of tasks and privacy was not the preoccupation that it is today. Robin Evans considers the corridor to have evolved during this period as a matter of expediently separating the gentry from the servants.

Fig.1. The Kunsthal is built around the circulation route through the building

Hence, in the 19th century, thoroughfares could be regarded as the backbone of a plan not only because corridors looked like spines, but because they differentiated functions by joining them via a separate distributor, in much the same way as the vertebral column structures the body.[25]

Le Corbusier used circulation to provide a dynamic counterpoint to the static geometry of the building, as an element that contrasted with the other spaces. His early buildings were designed as a sequence of experiences, the perception of which occurred while the viewer was in motion. The Villa Savoye is animated by circulation. The route begins as the site is entered, continues into the building through a series of doglegs, curves and ramps to conclude on the roof terrace. Geoffrey Baker, when discussing this *promenade architecturale* and the dynamic continuity of the route, describes the paths of circulation as 'arteries linking major organs'.[26]

Rem Koolhaas takes this approach to an extreme in the design for the Kunstal in Rotterdam. Although the building, a museum for exhibitions and performances, is new, the inclusive circulation system is both interesting and inspirational. The building is situated over the top of a small road and next to a boulevard that is on top of a 15 ft high dike. This difference in levels and the building's situation in the city provided the impetus for the unsettling system of circulation based upon what Koolhaas refers to as the city's 'culture of congestion'. The building is practically all slopes: the major areas are spaces of both exhibition and circulation, with views from one space to another and between the inside and the outside.

Fig. 2. Difference in levels through the Kunsthal building offers views and promotes movement

Movement through the whole length of a building need not be a boring activity; indeed the experience can be accentuated and the visual distance enlarged to dramatic effect. The length of the long linear lobby of the outrageous Royalton Hotel in New York is accentuated by being divided lengthways. On the east side is a long seating area which is situated upon two levels and separated from the circulation area by a row of obscenely fat columns. The west wall is a rich, gradually curving colonnade of doors and lifts, each headed by a large glowing protruding glass rhinoceros horn. Movement through this long immodest space is along a beautiful deep blue carpet runner laid against the whole length of the lift wall and accentuated by a row of down lighters. Philippe Starck, its designer, ensures that the extreme confidence necessary for the catwalk experience of walking along the carpet increases the theatre of the movement within the bar.

Stairs, being three-dimensional, can be given a sculptural quality. Stairs are sometimes the only vertical emphasis in a building, the only indication or reference to the three-dimensional qualities of the space. It is easy for them to become focal points and it is not uncommon for a lot of energy to be expended on their design and expression in contrast to the relative austerity of their surroundings. This is a tactic used to considerable effect by Eva Jiricna in a series of clothing shops for Joseph. The shops are deliberately simple and undecorated so that the focus of the space is placed upon the sculptural steel and glass staircase floating in the centre.

Stairs, lifts, escalators, ramps and bridges have the potential to bring expression and drama to a space. The purity of the escalator at the National Portrait Gallery adds to the serene experience of visiting the museum, as it slowly lifts the visitor towards the light and through a thousand years of history. Ian Ritchie designed some fun rib-like bridges across the Ecology Gallery at the Natural History Museum and the ridiculous staircase at the Küppersmühle Museum in Duisburg by Herzog and de Meuron provides a contrast with the simplicity of the building. The Imagination headquarters in London contains a large atrium and its dramatic qualities are exploited by the slinging of a number of bridges high up across the void. The silhouette of these powerful elements picked out against the top-lit space is symbolic of the ethos of the dynamic design practice.

Fig. 3. Bridges linking the display spaces in the Ecology gallery at the Natural History Museum reflect the nature of the exhibition

Joseph

Location: **Sloane Street, London**
Remodelled: **1989**
Architect: **Eva Jiricna**

Fig. 1. With its light skeletal structure, the glass and steel staircase rises through the austere building

One of the most celebrated exponents of the design of elaborate staircases is the architect Eva Jiricna. To guarantee that the strains and tensions within the staircase are safe, she works very closely on each project with a structural engineer. Although each staircase is the evolution of the last, in order to prevent the design being the product of the engineer rather than herself, the engineering practice is changed after each series of designs. Jiricna designed the interiors for a number of Joseph shops during the 1980s and 1990s. Her approach was to create a minimalist, colourless interior to contrast and enhance the sculptural qualities of the complex staircase. The stair combines utility, function, aesthetic consideration and structural articulation in one single element. For the design of the Joseph retail store in Sloane Street, London, Jiricna inserted a lightweight glass and stainless steel structure into the slot cut from the three floors of the shop space. The structure of the stair is a piece of sophisticated engineering that ensures that each member of the stair is reduced to its thinnest possible proportions. The stair is suspended from the second floor slab and then braced at each level. To achieve lateral support, the rods, struts, spars and wires of the structure are connected to the building by a series of connectors and bolts. The tension of the piece is such that when used, it actually shakes slightly.

The result is a stunningly powerful composition of light, reflection and movement running vertically through the centre of the shop.

Fig.1. The stair leading down into the old church looks as though it was carved from the very masonry of the building

Museum Sant Pere de Roda

Location: **Port de la Selva, Gerona, Spain**
Remodelled: **1991**
Architect: **Lapeña Torres**

The architects Lapeña and Torres restored the Monastery of Sant Pere de Roda, situated on the side of a hill overlooking the old town of Port de la Selva, near Gerona in Spain. It dates from the 9th century, but was abandoned in the 17th, hence its ruinous state.

The architects' approach was to repair and restore the buildings, then to remodel specific areas to house the new functions. This preserved the distinct character of the complex while ensuring that the new inserted elements did not detract from it. The typical facilities for a small museum were needed: ticket kiosk, bar, toilets and, of course, the gallery space, but really it was the building itself that was the main exhibit.

The installation of a contrasting circulation system was the key to creating a functioning museum. The most dynamic element of this was the walkway between the cloister and the church. The architects cut away the floor of the cloister and inserted an elevated bridge across the roof of the basement. The new bridge comes as a complete surprise to the visitor as they turn the corner of the cloister. The view prompts further exploration of the open basement, a journey made accessible by the solid new staircase positioned at the other side of the cloister.

Fig. 2. The steel and timber walkway in the cloister area fills the void left by the removal of the floor, allowing views into the basement and making the journey feel like a route of discovery

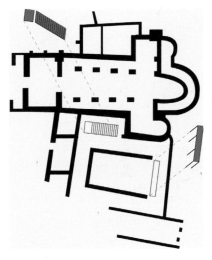

Fig. 3. Two key elements of circulation inserted into the monastery facilitate the movement of visitors around the ruins

Fig.1. The organic, sculptural
staircase seems to have been
carved from the terracotta
coloured concrete

Küppersmühle Museum

Location: **Duisburg, Germany**
Remodelled: **1999**
Architect: **Herzog and de Meuron**

Eva Jiricna created a vertical connection between different floors by constructing a lightweight skeleton of steel and glass that appears to float between the slabs. The opposite approach was adopted by Herzog and De Meuron for the Küppersmühle Museum when they constructed a solid sculptural mass that appears uneven, dense and cast as a single unbroken rock-like unit. This completely new stair tower is situated next to the front elevation of the building, adjacent to the main entrance.

From within, this strange staircase looks as if it is carved from the terracotta coloured concrete. The walls and the stairs are all thick and solid and seem to be a single element; even the lights are recessed so that the riven, unadorned walls are not interrupted. The only object occupying this vertical cave is the thin spidery steel handrail that appears to be only vaguely bent to shape and hardly fixed to the walls. It possesses a vulnerability that contrasts strongly with the massive solid nature of the staircase. The unevenness is further accentuated by the stair risers which become shallower as they rise through the building, ostensibly to slow the visitor down and prepare them for the gallery space, but certainly adding to the expressionist experience of ascending this outrageous staircase.

The staircase is, strangely, extremely ordered from the outside. It is orthogonal with a sloping roof to match the pitch of the existing building. Carved into it is a ground to roof vertical slot, not unlike those cut into the opposite façade, provides light to the space. The formwork board markings of the terracotta concrete are quite visible and this accentuates the appearance of structure and control.

**Fig.1. The long contrasting
gallery vaults over the steel
works, linking the different
areas together**

Landesausstellung

Location: **Huttenberg, Austria**
Remodelled: **1995**
Architect: **Günther Domenig**

Günther Domenig is a leading figure of Austrian architecture. He invested a great deal of physical and emotional energy in the conversion of the abandoned Carinthian steelworks in Huttenberg into the main exhibition building for the Landesausstellung – or regional exhibition – because Carinthia was his birthplace.

The old works, which had not been used since 1908, consisted of a set of workshops and a three-storey, u-shaped, stone building with two extremely robust and richly decorated blast furnaces attached to the central section. The buildings were relatively easy to occupy, but attempts to use the oddly shaped blast furnaces proved to be much too costly. The decision was therefore made for them to become the object of the exhibition and the generating principle was that they should be visible from as many viewpoints as possible.

Domenig defined a new axis based upon the geometry of the site and designed a long bridge or gallery that celebrated this and tied the whole group of buildings together. The materials and the language of this obviously modern and contrasting element speak of lift cages, winding gear and other mining equipment. It is of a sufficiently large scale not to be overwhelmed by the original buildings as it soars over the top of them. At its highest point it becomes an enclosed indoor gallery space with stunning views over the valley the mine occupies. Domenig draws the disparate set of buildings together into a coherent whole and the circulation allows people to move freely through the complex.

Fig.1. Aerial view
showing the
relationship of the old
museum to
the dynamic new
extension, the splayed
plan reflecting the
direction of the cities
where Nussbaum
lived and his forced
migration

Fig. 2. The Nussbaum
corridor represents
movement and
deportation, its
darkness evoking a
sense of the horrors
faced by Nussbaum

Location: **Osnabruck Germany**
Remodelled: **1998**
Architect: **Daniel Libeskind**

Fig. 3. Nussbaum's final painting before his deportation to Auschwitz is positioned in the last room of the museum, over a steel mesh floor, ensuring that the visitor remains slightly uneasy while viewing it

Felix Nussbaum, a Jew born in Osnabruck, recorded many of the important events of the period between the two world wars. The ironic and light-hearted qualities of his early paintings quickly disappeared with the rise of the Nazis and the beginning of his refugee existence. Nussbaum was persecuted and chased across Europe until his capture and deportation to Auschwitz in 1944. During all this time Nussbaum managed to paint and collect documents of his life, until his death in the camp.

Daniel Libeskind, a Polish Jew who emigrated to Israel in the 1950s and studied architecture in America, gained a reputation as an architect who can express emotion through the manipulation of light, space and movement. His masterpiece, the Jewish Museum in Berlin, is full of those dramatic and evocative qualities.

The Felix Nussbaum Museum is an extension of the Osnabruck Museum. The museum documents the life and works of the painter and is a symbolic chronological narrative of the time and place in which the work was produced. The building is a collection of long dramatic juxtaposed building forms, clad in materials of gradually increasing metaphorical coldness. It is the interior that really exposes the traumatic nature of Nussbaum's life; at the centre is a long dark inclined two-level corridor that breaks the narrative and is symbolic of Nussbaum's periods of forced exile. The journey through the upper level of the corridor represents Nussbaum's hiding place in an attic in Brussels. In this part of the building there are hardly any paintings and the floor is edged with metal grille so the visitors below are visible almost as though they are in the lower floors of his precarious hideout. The end of the corridor is marked by a steel door with a cross: the final departure.

Location: **London**
Remodelled: **1989**
Architect: **Ron Herron**

Fig.1. **The sculptural
steel and glass
walkways slung
between the
buildings accentuate
the height and
draw the eye to
the light**

The Imagination building is the London headquarters for a design company responsible for interiors, graphics, and communication media. It is housed in a space constructed from two townhouses and the yard area in between them. The architect Ron Herron, a founding member of the radical 1960s architects, Archigram, covered the interstitial space with a lightweight tensile structure turning it into a light-filled atrium. Within this space Herron built a series of steel and glass bridge walkways that allows the workers to commute between the rooms in the different buildings. Circulating high up in the space, the walkways have become social areas where workers can meet and chat.

Walkways and ramps are a method of moving people between spaces and floor levels in a way that can be slow and graceful. Less abrupt than a stair, a ramp allows the passenger to ascend or descend at a more leisurely pace.

Reichstag

Location: **Berlin**
Remodelled: **1998**
Architect: **Foster Associates**

In conjunction with the views it presents, a ramp can offer a most sensational ascent or descent within a space. On top of the Reichstag building, Foster Associates created a new glass and steel dome. The structure resembles the previous form of the building but, rather than imitate the old masonry tower, a politically insensitive gesture, the new dome is transparent and light to symbolise democracy and unity. In contrast with the existing building the new tower is a beacon, a public space above the new German Chancellery building.

The new glass dome offers a fabulous view across Berlin. It is constructed above the main debating chamber and at the very top level visitors are afforded views down into the space. The transparency of democracy should be there for all of the visitors to see. In reality this does not actually happen; the reflective qualities of the glass distort and interfere with the image but the views from the ramp over the city more than compensate for this shortcoming.

**Fig.1. The ramp
spirals up
within the dome**

Chapter Four
Case Studies

Previous pages:
The Castlevecchio
Museum, Verona.
Carlo Scarpa

Case Study
Irish Film Centre

Location: **Temple Bar, Dublin**
Former Function: **Quaker Meeting House**
Built: **17th century**
New Function: **Two cinemas with bar, café, bookshop, foyer and archive**
Remodelled: **1992**
Architect: **O'Donnell and Tuomey**

Temple Bar in the centre of Dublin was an area of the city that had suffered from depopulation and neglect. Situated next to the river Liffey and not too far from the main shopping streets, the place was the subject of a competition to revive and rejuvenate it. The concept of the winning entry was to regenerate through the introduction of public space and key cultural buildings. These would generate interest and activity and encourage other smaller supporting activities to follow. Group 91, the collective of architects involved in the whole area, advocated this patient, sensitive approach of reuse rather than brutal slaughter and new build. Although not actually part of the proposed Temple Bar regeneration, the Film Centre, which was the first building in the area to be completed, had a strong affinity with the ethos of this approach, and indeed coincidentally the architects were involved in both projects.

Fig.1. The covered internal courtyard has the feel and appearance of an outside space

Fig. 2. A long curving
ochre wall links the
different buildings
and spaces

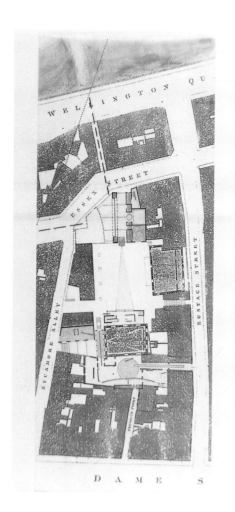

**Fig. 3. Block plan showing
how the building is
completely enclosed
within its context,
with no façade onto
the street**

Analysis

The Quaker Meeting House Headquarters
was a remarkable assemblage of buildings
gradually collected together since 1692.
It was situated in the heart of Temple Bar, at
the centre of a city block with no significant
street frontage, but with narrow routes of
access from three streets. The extraordinary
position was as a result of the law that
forbade non-established churches from
having a frontage on the street.

The recording of the existing building
was meticulous: the architects completed an
extensive and detailed survey and
discovered that the site contained nine
separate buildings. These were in varying
degrees of age, condition, relevance to the
project and appropriate or inappropriate
positions. It was also important to discover
whether there were spaces within the
complex of sufficient size to accommodate
the two cinemas.

The architects see an analogy between
archaeology and architecture. They
regarded the process of discovering,
understanding and recording the site as one
that provides the basis for the architectural
intervention. Buildings are always changing
and the architects' contribution is but
another layer in the evolution.

Fig. 4. Within the cinema
the original openings
were retained and
highlighted. The screen
is placed as a free-
standing object

Intervention

Intervention is a process of reactivating
a building or collection of buildings with
a series of small moves. The process is both
destructive and constructive, with elements
being removed and others added to produce
a coherent whole.

The architects' reading of the site quickly
established that the main meeting room and
the smaller ladies' meeting room were
the only possible positions for the cinemas
themselves. For the project to be
economically viable they had to share a
projection room and thus its position and the
orientation of the two screening rooms was
quickly established; the firm positioning
of these elements dictated the arrangement
of the other activities in the centre.

They then employed a process of
selective demolition. They stripped the
existing complex to its essential fundamental
elements, which created the tabula rasa for
the subsequent remodelling interventions.
Thus an essential order was created.
The architects did not intend to obliterate the
history of the place, but to create a sense
of equilibrium between the old and the new.

A series of new elements was introduced
into the complex. These are obviously of the
late 20th century and yet they provide a
balance because their language is
appropriate to the existing building and their
newness does not seem out of place. This
process is virtually self-directing. The
courtyard in front of the meeting room has
become the public foyer space and the
supporting activities occupy the opened up
spaces around it.

The block has been turned inside out; the primary public space instead of being by the street is situated right at the centre, accessed through long pedestrian paths. Three alleys were created, each of a different character and each with a small neon sign at the junction with the street.

On the floor of the courtyard, a circular pattern made of limestone with steel rods, served to tie the different geometries of the disparate buildings together. The courtyard is completely covered with a simple folding glazed roof, which is supported by plain I beams; this allows daylight to penetrate into the whole space. These plain materials combine with the natural light and the repaired brick walls of the original buildings to give the space an outdoor quality.

It was important for no natural light to enter the cinema, so the windows to these spaces were blocked up. Although the windows are filled in with reclaimed bricks, their recess and frame details are still apparent from the inside. From the covered foyer, the walls are flush but the cills, arches and slightly different colour of the bricks make the intervention apparent. The characteristic elements of the existing building are restored and emphasise the counterpoint between the original and the interventions.

Fig. 5. The main corridor entrance is made from two spaces of different proportions, each treated in the same way and unified by the under-lit glass floor

Fig. 6. The rear entrance: a narrow intervention guiding the visitor to the cinema spaces and holding the projection box above

Tactics

It was important to address the movement in an inside-out building like this, to link the centre and focus of the building with the surrounding streets. This was complemented by the careful positioning of objects and planes.

Movement

Visitors are led from the main entrance through two long connected but different spaces to the heart of the building. Although the width of this, the longest corridor, changes, as does the ceiling height, the space is unified by the under-lit glass floor. This is a simple device of frosted glass laid over a channel containing fluorescent lights that is set into the centre of the long limestone floor. It is the only consistent element and so ties the street entrance to the foyer courtyard.

Plane

To connect the central activities and spaces together, a huge curving screen was placed at the heart of the building, which acts to contain and to link the bookshop, ticket office and bar. This perforated three-storey ochre wall is an organising element that controls the rhythm of the roof and the curve acts as a foil to the surrounding existing walls.

Object

Opposite this, an intense blue screen shields the entrance to the main cinema. It is constructed from layers and layers of polished pigmented plaster held in a number of steel frames. The layering and polishing of the material creates the depth of colour. A single line of blue neon, similar to that used to guide people through the entrances, focuses attention upon the cinema advertising displayed on a panel in the middle of the screen.

The attitude of the architects is that buildings are always evolving. The work that they conducted at the Film Centre is just part of a process, another layer in time. They aimed not to erase the history of the complex but to create a balance between old and new. The architects selectively removed elements to carve a public space from the centre of a complex block of many different buildings and then carefully added new elements that tied the different parts together. Inevitably changes will be, and have been made, but the organising strength of the strategy will allow the basic nature of the Film Centre and the site to continue.

Case Study
Castelvecchio Museum

Location: **Verona Italy**
Former function: **Castle, Barracks, Museum**
Built: **1st to 18th century**
New Function: **Museum**
Remodelled: **1957-1964**
Architect: **Carlo Scarpa**

Carlo Scarpa's approach to remodelling was based upon an interpretation of the meaning of the original building. He endeavoured to understand the historical and contextual qualities of the place and then to apply a new contemporary layer of value and consequence to the building. This attitude, in the midst of modernism, was revolutionary and even today he is probably regarded as the greatest exponent of the art of remodelling. The Castelvecchio museum is possibly Scarpa's greatest work but his contribution to the history of architecture is an even greater legacy than the building itself.

The Castelvecchio museum in Verona is composed of the complex of buildings, courtyards, gardens and towers of the Scaliger castle. It is situated next to a bridge over the river Adige, which runs through the centre of Verona. The bridge marks the line of the old wall that surrounded the city and divided the castle in two; on the eastern, city side was the fortified garrison and on the other, the residential palace.

The museum was designed to house a collection of sculptures, paintings and artefacts about the city and the surrounding area from the 12th to the 18th century. The most important piece was a sculpture that had acquired an important symbolic value for the city, a statue of one of the original members of the family, seated upon a horse: Cangrande I.

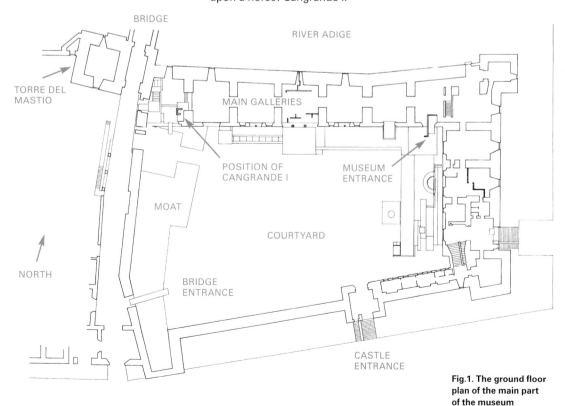

Fig.1. The ground floor plan of the main part of the museum

Fig. 2. The light in the
space is very restrained
yet is sufficient to
illuminate the rough
textures of the existing
walls

Analysis

The Castelvecchio museum was originally constructed as a fortified castle for the della Scala dynasty in the 14th century. It incorporated several existing structures dating from Roman and medieval times, including the 8th century church of San Martino in Aquaro and part of the 12th century city wall. Its position was strategically important; it assured the family's control of Verona while also providing them with an escape route to the north via the fortified bridge. The original building was enclosed on three sides by a strong sheer wall with battlements and corner towers, with the open side protected by the river.

The buildings were transformed into a military garrison during Napoleon's occupation of the city. Two large barracks were constructed in the period 1802–6 along the north and east sides of the main courtyard. The castle was first converted into a museum in the 1920s in a Romantic Italian style by Arnaldo Forlati with Antonio Avena. Gothic doorways and window surrounds removed from local buildings were inserted into the courtyard façades of the barracks and the interiors were remodelled in the manner of an early Renaissance palace. In 1923, five centuries of exclusive use of the bridge by the residents of the castle was ended by the opening of a new road. The result of this was to cut the complex in two along the axis of the ancient city walls.

Scarpa greatly benefited from the close relationship that he developed with Licisco Magagnato, the museum director. Their understanding enabled the design to evolve even as the works were progressing. As unexpected elements were exposed or if Scarpa felt that the proposal was not quite right, then changes could be made. Both Scarpa and the director developed an in-depth knowledge of the place during the eight years that the work took to complete and this meant that they were able to make informed decisions about which elements were to be conserved from the historical structure of the building and which could be demolished.

Intervention

Any intervention has to be designed and thought out in a new way. You can't say: 'I'm modern – I'm going to use metal and plate glass.' Timber might be more suitable, or something more modest. How can one make certain statements if one isn't educated, educated to histories.[1]

The work was completed in three phases. Scarpa was first approached in 1957 to remodel the Reggia or west wing of the residential palace, to hold the exhibition 'From Altichiero to Pisanello'. The second and most important phase was the design and construction of the main museum, and the final stage, which occurred two years after the museum was opened, was the transformation of the northwest corner of the castle into the library and Sala Avena. In August 1958 the exhibition opened, and it confirmed Scarpa's sensitivity and skill as an architect to the Verona City Council, who then agreed that he should remodel the whole museum.

Scarpa approached the initial design project as he tackled the others, by studying the existing, then stripping it to the essential elements before adding a contemporary layer of facilitating design. The first excavations in the west Reggia wing revealed the Porta del Morbio, an underground passageway that link the castle to the bridge. This was excavated and above it, the Torre del Mastio or Keep, was joined to the Reggia by a hanging bridge and thus a double connection, above and below ground, was made. The Reggia was restored in a fairly understated manner: the 14th century masonry was preserved and the original frescoes were exposed. A new simple timber and steel staircase links the floors. It was in this part of the castle that Scarpa first introduced the modest approach and simple appropriate detailing that was to be used throughout the whole design. The sculptures are supported by austere limestone blocks and planes, and special frames were constructed to hold the paintings.

Scarpa felt that the false Gothic symmetry of the Napoleonic barracks, or north wing, had to be broken and to achieve this he made it appear as if the façade was an attached stage screen. The windows were recessed and appear to belong to another wall behind, the grid or rhythm of which was not synchronised with that of the façade. The Napoleonic staircase at the west end is demolished. The entrance was moved from the centre to the northeast corner and a number of elements now project through existing openings to create a dialogue with the courtyard.

The interior of this wing was treated in the same understated manner as the Reggia. It was originally arranged as an enfilade of rooms, an arrangement that was kept in the final design. The floor of the first level was replaced with reinforced concrete supported by a series of steel cross beams which in turn were carried by a single long steel beam stretching the whole length of the wing. This not only provides the physical support, but also visually links the series of spaces on the ground floor. The natural light of the day and of the seasons within this gallery space was intensely studied, followed and mapped.

The exact positions of the permanent exhibits was determined by placing them on temporary plinths and observing the effect of the changing light.

The Cangrande statue held high emotional importance and its position is the denouement of the museum. When the Napoleonic rooms and staircase were demolished, a pivotal space was created between the city walls and the north wing, or barracks building. The gap allowed the previously interlocked parts to be read as individual elements. The connection between the city wall and the bridge over the Adige became apparent. The Torre del Mastio (tower) assumed it's fortified position at the junction of the two and the nineteenth century façade of the north wing appeared to have been slid back. In the midst of these dramatic frames and theatrical backdrops the statue was placed high up as a single highlighted enigmatic object. The roof of the north wing was extended in an irregular fashion to provide the statue with a degree of shelter. The plinth that supports the Cangrande statue, a suspended concrete platform connected back to the first floor gallery space, is radically different from its surroundings. The statue is seen many times as the visitor walks around the museum. When entering the castle grounds, it can be observed from a distance, almost in silhouette, in its framed and sheltered position. The final time it is seen, this time much more intimately, is as part of the journey through the museum. The visitor moves from the relative darkness of the gallery space into the bright light of the link between the north wing and the Reggia, and there is the statue, his face turned towards the viewer with a conspiratorial grin.

Fig. 3. View across the courtyard towards the main façade

Fig. 4. The statue of Cangrande. The final bay of the building was demolished, but the roof was retained to provide a sheltered yet prominent position for this pivotal element

Two orthogonal elements were designed to control movement through the courtyard. A passage between two parallel hedges leads across the space, and joins a paved path that leads to the entrance. The tops of the hedges are absolutely level, while the courtyard contains a slight gradient, so that as the visitor travels upwards between the hedges, the entrance gradually appears.

As we have seen, intervention is a strategy that activates the potential within a building, and is based upon a close reading of the attributes of the host and then making informed decisions about how to change it. Intervention is usually characterised by a series of small interconnected alterations throughout the building, rather than a single large move. It always irretrievably alters the original building, any additions or subtractions made being permanent.

It was the strategy of intervention that was used to unlock the hidden meaning of the building in the remodelling of the Castelvecchio. Scarpa's approach was almost surgical in his determination to expose the junctions of the building where the accumulated history of the building is most obvious. Scarpa removes as much as he adds to the Castelvecchio. In response to the three main periods of the building's history, the layers were scraped away or exposed until clarity was achieved. The intervention led to a new layer of small beautifully composed additions imposed upon the building, a layer that expressed the contemporary nature of its design but which was totally appropriate and sympathetic to the original building.

Tactics

The manipulative qualities of key elements within the museum was of great concern to Scarpa. He took care in the choice of materials as these emphasized the nature of the exhibits, the movement between them and the perception of the building.

In the words of Ignasi de Sola Morales:

… the analogical procedure is not based on the visible synchronism of interdependent orders of form, but on the association made by the observer over the course of time. By this means situations of affinity are produced and, thanks to the connotative capacity of the languages evoked in the intervention, relations or links are established between the historic building – real and/or imaginary – and the elements of design that serve to make the building effectively dependent.[2]

Fig. 5. The entrance screen penetrates the opening, beckoning visitors into the museum

Plane

Scarpa consolidated the museum access and exit with a plane that dissects the Gothic arched doorway. The threshold is split by the screen wall which returns at both ends to define the movement. From the outside it appears to beckon the visitor in, and from the interior, it points to the way out. The screen is constructed, like the others within the gallery, from a steel frame with a polished plaster infill. Throughout the museum, the same type of screen is used to create individual backdrops for specific works of art. The plaster is at times coloured to emphasise the particular piece and sometimes a clearly articulated steel arm is cantilevered from the frame to support a sculpture.

The floor plane is treated as an important point of articulation in the dialogue between old and new. Both on the exterior and the interior of the museum the floor is used to illustrate narrative and to facilitate movement. Outside, the visitor moves towards the new corner entrance on a path of irregular stones and paving, the original and the new elements being juxtaposed. Inside the gallery spaces of the main wing, the new floors are quite separate from the walls and the square plan of each room is emphasised, with the dark plane of polished concrete bordered with white Prun stone. The sculptures are raised on horizontal plinths, elevated so as not to compromise the floor's geometry; they appear to hover above the floor with an independent importance.

Object and Movement
In the Castelvecchio museum object and movement are inseparable. Scarpa uses one to reinforce the other. The paintings and sculptures are used to orientate and direct movement and views. Objects are used to illustrate narrative breaks in the building's history, their placement often emphasising an important junction. The Cangrande statue, probably the most important piece within the museum's collection, is positioned at a significant point in the building. The narrative through the museum culminates at this main point. As Liscisco Magagnato, the museum director, points out:

> … this splendid statue, which keeps recurring to the visitor's gaze, becomes a central and recurrent point in (the museum) experience. It is the pivot of the museum circuit, its centre of gravity, virtually the lynchpin of the whole castle complex.[3]

In the ground floor room of 12th to 15th century work, the statues are placed facing away from the point of entry to the room. The visitor is required to focus firstly on the back or side of the statue and then move around the room to view the face, the front.

This extraordinarily clever manoeuvre then places the visitor in a position to see the next piece and controls their subsequent movement.

Fig. 6. In the main museum space Scarpa uses the statues to facilitate movement and views. The flat plinth raises the statue above the floor but its back is most prominent and the visitor has to move around to see the face

Surface
Scarpa uses surfaces to open the dialogue between old and new in a variety of spaces. On the exterior of the façade a small room slides out of one of the openings into the courtyard. The Sacellum is a small top-lit space accessed from inside the first room of the sculpture gallery. Its exterior is decorated with little blocks of flamed Prun stone. These range in texture from smooth to rough, from white through to pale pinks and reds. The surface pattern of the wall is not unlike an abstract geometrical painting. The rough and smooth surfaces are a miniature version of the contrast between textures on the interior of the space.

The richness of this scheme is born from the careful reading of the original building and this understanding leads the architect to a courageous, brutal and yet extraordinarily sensitive series of manoeuvres. The perceptive remodelling of the building guides the visitor to an understanding of the truth of its history and growth. They are made aware not only of the objects that the museum holds but also of the life of the space they inhabit.

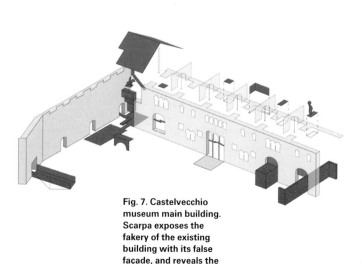

Fig. 7. Castelvecchio museum main building. Scarpa exposes the fakery of the existing building with its false façade, and reveals the layers built up over time

Case Study
Marienkirche and Library

Location: **Muncheberg, Germany**
Former Function: **Church**
Built: **13th century,**
remodelled 19th century
Architect: **Karl Freiderich Schinkel**
New Function: **Library and Church**
Remodelled: **1994**
Architect: **Klaus Block**

The small town of Muncheberg in Germany, near the border with Poland, has had a church at the centre of its community since the 13th century. In the early 19th century the church was remodelled and extended by Karl Freiderich Schinkel. This relatively unknown project in Schinkel's collection was the addition of the Campanile and imposition of several Gothic details such as the porches and remodelling the windows. Muncheberg was of strategic importance during the ravages of the Second World War and both the Allies and the Germans inflicted great damage. The church was ruined and remained in this sad and roofless state until the early 1990s.

After German reunification, it was important for the church to be restored and repaired and once again for it to be at the centre of the community. The local parish was not large enough to support the complete building and therefore a temporal and religious partnership was formed to develop new functions alongside the existing. A true community building was planned with the addition of a library, council chamber, community office and services such as toilets and storage.

The church itself contained one huge space, although this easily and obviously divided into the larger rectangular nave and smaller, brighter, pointed chancel. The German architect Klaus Block won the competition to redesign the building and resolved the sensitive problem of secular and spiritual activities happening within the same building by inserting a free-standing, self-contained structure to hold the library and meeting rooms in the much taller nave, thus leaving the open chancel for religious worship.

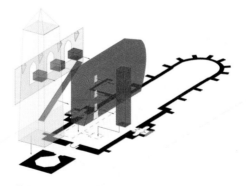

**Fig.1. Axonometric
shows how the small
footprint of the new
vessel is tucked into the
nave of the church**

**Fig. 2. Viewed from
the altar, the pointed
arch of the church
frames the new library**

Analysis

The interior of the building was essentially one open space, in two parts, the nave and the chancel. The tall nave of the church, unbroken and without any internal structure, offered Block the opportunity to utilise its height. The reduction of the parish of Muncheberg meant that the ground floor space was far too large to be regularly filled with worshippers and therefore the building quite clearly divided. The chancel would always be the focus for the worshippers' attention; therefore the congregation could remain in this part of the church, directed toward the altar. This left space free for reuse and at the same time it allowed a distinction between the congregation and the library, although a degree of flexibility was important to allow for processions or special religious gatherings.

This situation was complicated, however, because all the entrances to the space were situated in the nave end of the church. The west wall door leading to the Campanile was only opened on ceremonial occasions, but the two new porches added by Schinkel on the north and south sides provided the main routes into the building and therefore anything occupying this space would need to facilitate movement and allow circulation.

The requirements of the proposed library were book stacks, reading spaces, circulation and reception plus storage and toilets, and the added requirement of the community meeting room. The church needed space for worship and some circulation.

Insertion

The strategic approach taken by the architect can be classified as one of insertion.

The library is treated as a vessel within the church: a tall, elegant, steel-framed object built into the nave. The main body of the four-storey building is glazed and then secondarily clad with ash slats to give the building a semi-transparent quality.

The rhythm of these slats changes with the different functions of each level. This structure is separated from the walls of the church by the stairs and the horizontal circulation; these elements ensure an exact fit to the original building. Separated from the inserted structure and protruding into the body of the nave is the tall vertical black tower of the lift. This is connected back to the library by a series of bridges. The insertion corresponds to the wall of the church that it is attached to. Although it appears to exist freely within the space, the proportions and the rhythm are derived from those of the original building. The insertion is built to fit.

The timber-clad structure rises from the floor and soars up into the heights of the roof space. Its elegant curved form is derivative of two things. The most striking one is of a moored boat. The necessity for movement and flexibility of use at the ground level of the building requires that at this place the object is at its thinnest. The architect's use of the height of the nave to allow each floor plate to have extra width results in a bulging profile. The other impression of the new element's form is as an abstraction of the silhouette of the church and the campanile. The tenuous connection between tower and church is expressed in the relationship of the lift tower to the library. The walkways connect to the vessel as the campanile connects to the church.

The inserted object is a powerful addition to the existing space. Because the library function is contained within the new insertion, the religious and the secular activities are kept apart. The church occupies almost all of the ground floor of the whole building, while the library claims the vertical space of the nave. The scale and form of the insertion ensures that it is not dwarfed by the space yet it does not dominate the building. The library appears to peer around the corner of the nave rather than charge into the church.

Fig. 3. The narrow gap between the church and inserted library holds the stairs and also serves to accommodate any variations or movement within the original walls

Tactics

Object and movement are key tactics used with insertions because they promote independence and autonomy. They also signify a dialogue between a host and the remodelling

Object

The building is designed to be read as a large continuous timbered object with a detached slender attachment rising up through the space of the church. Sufficient space is left around the insertion to allow it to be read as autonomous and the abundant natural light falling from the tall south-facing lancet windows highlights the extreme contrast between old and new.

Movement

Visitors normally enter the building through the north porch and then through an aperture in the library structure. They then encounter the full height of the nave from the enclosure of the library undercroft. From the south side, the front wall of the four-storey library is exposed as the visitor enters the porch. The inner porch doors are glazed, ensuring that the towering façade is presented from within the confines of the porches. Incidentally, on both interior porch doors Block designed new timber handles with the same profile and shape as the library structure. The play on scale gives the visitor an early tactile impression of the object in the space. This sequence ensures that the library is read from both sides in a different way, reminding the viewer that there are two sides to this library.

The circulation in the library is placed outside the confines of the new structure, in the gap between it and the church. The staircases and horizontal walkways connect the various levels. They are constructed from stainless steel and glass with the treads from ash and the floor a plastic vinyl. The brick of the window mullions is protected with semi-circular stainless steel pivoting devices. The gap between the handrail and the church absorbs any variation or movement in the walls. Carefully positioned within this slot of circulation are special alcoves of space connecting the windows to the main floor levels. These provide little reading spaces or places for private conversation.

The lift tower is placed off-centre in the nave. It is clad in grey steel mesh and lightly connects to each floor with a steel and timber walkway. The leaning library façade appears to be steadied by the tower. The vertical supports of the balustrade are deliberately positioned towards the lift tower, which gives the appearance of the lightest of touches between walkway and library.

Fig. 4. Seen from the top of the library, the piers of the ribbed arches are the only reminder of the old roof

Surface

The restoration of the fabric of the church led to an unusual patchwork quality of the surface of the host. On both the exterior and the interior, building repairs were made with no attempt to conceal their difference. This unusual patchwork quality is also discernible in the upper levels of the building where Block makes use of its qualities. Before reuse the church was ruined and without a roof and thus before work could commence the building had to be re-roofed. Originally, the church had had an elegant ribbed vaulted brick roof. This kind of structure proved to be too expensive and time-consuming to replicate. Instead it was replaced with a timber and slate structure. The springing points of the original ribs were retained and became sculptural fragments of the old structure. In the upper level meeting room, Block had them illuminated and framed.

Block operates with a distinctly light touch on other parts of the building surface. The new reading rooms use the upper parts of the arched windows as picture windows for light and air. In order to be able to open these and to ventilate the glass boxes, the delicate stone mullions are left untouched by making new unobtrusive stainless steel window frames connected to the inside of the box. This allows the new openings to hinge without touching the stone.

The power of this scheme is derived from the contrast between the new inserted object and the original building. The relationship between the simple space for gathering and worshipping and the space for reading books in light, airy rooms is elegantly expressed. The rough surface of the repaired church stonework provides a contrasting backdrop to the crisp detailing of the timber and steel structure. The insertion of the dynamic new structure offers a counterpoint to the heavy masonry composition of the church, resulting in an exceptional conversation between old and new.

Case Study
The Archbishopric Museum
of Hamar

Location: **Hamar, Norway**
Former Function:
Barn built upon medieval settlement
Built: **Medieval fortress settlement 1250-1567**
Storhamar barn early 19th century
New Function: **Museum**
Remodelled: **1967-1979**
Architect: **Sverre Fehn**

The Museum of Hamar was designed to disclose the strata of time, to expose the important layers of history and pre-history of a place. The museum is but another layer within that sequence, an insertion floating over the remains of the past. The insertion at the museum is almost as brutal as the Norwegian weather itself, an uncompromising concrete structure designed to protect and reveal the important remains. The architect Sverre Fehn describes it:

> The concept has been developed of a 'suspended museum' which will make it possible to get a grasp on history, not by means of pages in a book written with ink – but as it emerges in the world of archaeology.[4]

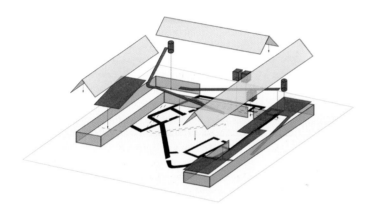

Fig.1. The new museum is inserted over the ruins of the old fortress

Analysis

The Archbishopric Museum, sometimes known as the Hedmark Cathedral Museum, is situated in the small Norwegian town of Hamar, just north of Oslo and the site is particularly important because it lies on the Kaupang Trail, along which the Bishop of Hamar made his way to Rome in 1302. The site is surrounded by a thick masonry wall and was originally a medieval fortress, which consisted of a tower, bakery, grill house and also a prison. It was demolished in the latter part of the 16th century and a barn was built on top of the remains, incorporating some of the parts of the old fortress walls into its fabric. This building was a fairly typical rural type and was of a simple construction and detail. The barn was u-shaped in plan with a central, west-facing, middle wing where most of the archaeology excavations have taken place. The north wing was the old cowshed and the south wing was actually outside the old wall of the settlement. The buildings were in a particularly ruinous state.

Fehn was commissioned in the mid-1960s to design the new museum in which artefacts that had been recovered from the excavations of the site could be displayed. The new museum was also intended to allow the dig to continue and this became part of the exhibition. The requirements for the museum were exhibition rooms for a series of displays on peasant life (ethnography), a temporary exhibition gallery, a large auditorium and administration offices as well as showing the finds from the site.

Insertion

The strategy that Fenn employed was to restore and reveal as much of the original building as possible, then to protect it and lastly to insert the new modern layer of the museum.

The function of the museum was split into three parts in accordance with the nature of the site. The central wing, the medieval gallery, was dedicated to displaying the finds excavated from the digs. The north wing, the old cow shed, was the ethnographic museum and the south wing, outside the old wall of the settlement, was the temporary exhibition space, the auditorium, and the offices. The understanding of the context stressed the importance of the ground plane of the barn. The existing buildings were protected firstly with a simple timber and tiled roof and then the windows and other uneven openings were covered with sheets of reinforced glass attached quite crudely to the exterior of the wall. A huge varying museum and walkway element was then inserted into and around and above the existing structure. The museum was designed to hang as though floating in the space, never interfering with

the ancient ruins. Its display rooms were suspended above the floor to stand clear of the relics below. The floating museum allowed the archaeological dig to carry on beneath it while allowing visitors an aerial view of the progress.

It is important to distinguish between the elements of environmental control and the inserted museum elements. The ruinous state of the buildings meant that early on in the project Fehn had to build the roof for the barn. The new pitched roof was supported by substantial laminated timber trusses. In the old cowshed these were supported by columns placed on the interior of the building next to the thick outer masonry walls. In the central medieval wing the trusses took their support from the original walls of the fortress. The new trusses and columns give the interior space a new structural rhythm. The roof combined with the simple glass sheets placed over the openings to offer shelter from the wind and the rain, but little thermal protection as the museum is only open in the summer.

Fig. 2. The museum walkway soars over the old settlement and flies through an existing opening

The series of elements of the museum begin in the courtyard. A brutal concrete ramp veers away from the site before performing a u-turn and gliding into the building high up at the junction between the south and central wings. No more than three big columns support this board-marked, uncompromising element as it powers through the open air. Once inside the building, it becomes a platform, which is actually the roof of the auditorium, that almost fills the south wing. A spiral staircase in the corner of the platform leads to a lower bridge which is constructed exactly as the ramp. This element cuts through the middle of the contained space of the central wing. The huge shuttered concrete elevated boxes of the Medieval Galleries are accessed from this dynamic structure. It flies precisely through an original opening in the end wall of the vast open space and into the north wing where, much less stridently, it connects to the much larger, built-to-fit insertion of the ethnographic museum. The different qualities of natural light within each space are accentuated and delicate. The suspended museum touches the ground as little as possible and when it does its weight is channelled into pilotis that connect to the ground at certain strategic moments in the building.

The ramp/bridge responds to the structure of the existing building; it is designed to fit exactly into and around the spaces. The dimensions and position are based upon the available room, the height of the existing opening, the amount of space necessary to conduct the archaeological investigations and the position of the historical remains. It was built to fit, and was designed as a single huge object that traversed and chronologically examined the relics of a former age.

Fig. 3. The museum boxes hang over the ruins and are raised on a single column

Tactics

The main tactics employed in the design reflect the nature of the museum. The circulation is a series of magnificent gestures; these and the positions of the floating galleries are influenced by the existing openings.

Movement

The most obvious tactic used is movement: the ramp/bridge directs and controls the circulation of visitors around the complex. It serves to protect the valuable remains and to allow complete visual interaction with them. It links the exterior with the interior and the three parts of the original building. The ramp/bridge is honestly brutal, but then so is the language of the original building and probably the lives of those who occupied it.

Opening

Fehn explores the close connection between the exterior of the site and the interior spaces of the barn. This connection is complex and unsure. The ruins of the medieval settlement extend from beneath the barn and out into the courtyard. The barn was unceremoniously built on top of the site. The exposure of this archaeology makes indistinct what is actually contained within the museum. Fehn attempts to clarify this by preserving the ruinous qualities of the west wing courtyard wall. The openings and ragged appearance offer views from the interior to the outer courtyard. Fehn covers the openings with large loose fitting panels of clear glazing which also allows views into the building from the court, thus connecting the outside to within. He also uses the same detailing method for the entrance doorway. The delicacy of the existing building and the layers of history are exposed.

Fig. 4. The new roof protects the ruins while admitting plenty of natural light

Fig. 5. The long concrete walkway swings away from the building before turning and ruthlessly entering at high level

Object

Three elevated shuttered concrete display rooms, suspended in the air, dominate the central museum hall. These object-like rooms hang above the ruins and are the only new elements other than the bridge to occupy the space. They are used to house the artefacts excavated from the dig below. The transition from the ruins below to the museum display space above is symbolic of the process of finding, excavating and finally bringing to light.

Fehn in a sensitive and daring manner interpreted the site and uncompromisingly created the next layer of history upon it. As he said when he accepted his Pritzker prize for architecture: 'Only by manifestations of the present, you can make the past speak'.[5]

The analysis of the site led to a natural distribution of activities around the different buildings. The original structures were repaired and the simple environmental controlling devices of a new roof and uncomplicated glazed coverings to the openings were fitted to protect them. A dynamic structure was inserted to control the movements of the visitors and tie the different parts of the building together. The integrity of the original building was retained and a new contrasting yet balanced element had been added.

Case Study
The Brasserie

Location:
Seagram Building, Manhattan, New York
Former Function: **Restaurant**
Built: **1959**
Previous Architect:
Ludwig Mies van der Rohe and Philip Johnson
New Function: **Restaurant**
Remodelled: **2000**
Architects: **Diller and Scofidio**

The restaurant is situated in the basement of the famous Seagram building in mid-town Manhattan. Ludwig Mies van der Rohe designed the 38-storey tower in the 1950s for the Seagram distillers and it occupies a unique place in architectural history. The bronze and smoked glass tower is regarded as one of the seminal architectural moments of modernism and it defined the image of the prestigious office block for a generation.

The building occupies only half of the block and a large public area or plaza – a move at the time regarded as daringly contextual – occupies the remainder. Set into this plinth, in the basement of the building, was the Four Seasons Restaurant designed by Philip Johnson in 1959. This opulent walnut-panelled dining room was planned around a square pool. Every little detail was considered and designed down to the napkins and even the seasonally changing suits of the doormen.

The Four Seasons restaurant was damaged by fire and closed in 1995. Phyllis Lambert, the daughter of the Seagram President who originally commissioned Mies van der Rohe and Johnson, appointed Diller and Scofidio to remodel the space. The restaurant was one of the most sought-after venues in the city and the Seagram committee was anxious that the pedigree of the building be maintained. Therefore the restaurant needed to retain its fashionable appeal.

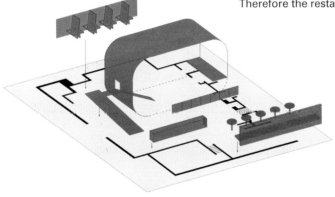

Fig.1. Controlling elements are installed within the space to define the restaurant. The main dining space is formed by a huge wrapped tube, with an entrance stair cut through it and intimate booth dining areas placed either side. The bar is an illuminated plane

Analysis

The Seagram tower is a symbol of modernity's fascination with transparency, glazing and view and the obsession with things taller, bigger and lighter. The location of the restaurant in the basement, however, meant that it had no view to the outside city at all and there was no natural light. This contradiction was not lost on the designers and the irony prompted a series of contemplations about glass and transparency in the formulation of their strategy and tactics for remodelling.

The substantial structure of the building caused the restaurant to be divided into two parts: the major area, which naturally became the main dining space, and a side gallery, the private dining room. The entrance, to the side of the Seagram Building, was about a metre or so higher than the floor level of the restaurant.

Installation

A number of huge elements were placed in the restaurant to define and control the space. The room and the elements that populated it were designed and positioned to give maximum impact to both them and to the building. A deliberate juxtaposition or contrast with original building was created. The restaurant can be likened to a theatre set: the space is the stage, the elements are the backdrop and the diners are the actors. This strategic approach can be categorised as that of installation.

The installations can be considered as events, each with a slightly different character or atmosphere, but ultimately they are designed to stage the performances of eating, drinking, and socialising.

The most dominant installation is the enormous timber wrapper around the dining space. This pear-veneered plywood tube is is folded at the base to form bench seating and articulated in the horizontal plane of the soffit to conceal lighting. A glass staircase supported on stainless steel stringers slices through this element to link the entrance with the sunken dining area. The highly illuminated bar is recessed into a sidewall and throws light into the dimly lit tube. The seats at the bar are filled with medical gel that mould to the sitter's profile. Private booths, which are separated from each other by tilting panels of green vinyl, are installed into the opposite wall. As Nicola Turner says: 'This is the New York restaurant to see and to be seen in.'[6]

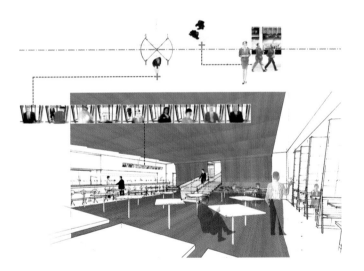

Fig. 2. Concept sketch
by the architects
showing the elements
of the design

Fig. 3. The articulated
tube controls and
contains the diners

Tactics

The architects used appropriately dramatic tactics to re-inforce the theatrical qualities of the installation.

Plane

The most dominant and obvious tactic to be used is that of plane. A huge timber surface wraps around the main dining area. Upon closer inspection, it is not a single continuous sheet, but a series of connected overlapping segmented sheets that run horizontally across the complete element. The basic nature of the loop is consistent, but the detail changes to conform to different specific functions as it moves through the space. It is folded at the base to provide bench seating and supported upon a steel frame at the sides. The sheet above this one is positioned slightly behind it, to conceal the lighting, before it curves

upwards to be supported by the ceiling of the building. The soffit is a succession of scrolling layers that again conceals lighting and is attached to the original building. The floor of the element appears to be continuous, while the edges curl up to join the folded seating and thus continues the movement of the loop.

The bar back area is a very long wide vertical plane. Its brightness is achieved by backlighting the cupboards containing the bottles. It is bright compared to the subdued light of the rest of the space and throws light into the inadequately lit dining area.

Fig. 4. The booth seating provides intimacy

Fig. 5. Corner detail of the layers of timber forming the wrapped screen with the booth seating framed beyond

Fig. 6. The act of
entering the dining
area can be quite
intimidating

Opening

The location of the restaurant prompted the designers to reflect on the preoccupations of the architects of the original building. The basement of the Seagram is entirely without a view to the outside and is also devoid of natural light. Ironically, this is completely the opposite characteristic of the glass tower above. Diller and Scofidio highlighted this contradiction with a video installation. This was a development of The Para-site Installation that they made at the Museum of Modern Art in New York in 1989. Visitors are filmed as they enter the building. The act of 'making an entrance' is caught on a camera placed within the revolving door. The image is then relayed to one of a line of 15 monitors positioned above the bar. As each new guest arrives, so the pictures of the previous guests move along the monitors, until upon leaving the fifteenth, they disappear. The entrance and the long theatrical catwalk staircase into the restaurant are not in line, so that, upon entering the space the diner cannot physically see the space. The shock of the restaurant is not a complete surprise, however, because to balance the video installation in the bar, a monitor relays images of the activity within the space to those just arriving.

The long shallow staircase that cuts through the opening in the plywood wrapping creates a dramatic physical entry for the guest. They are aware that their arrival has already been observed on the monitors, so this 'real' entrance has greater impact; the performer enters the stage.

The analysis of the original building does not necessarily rely only on the physical attributes of the host. It can consider its reputation and history as a starting point for reuse. The nature of the deployment of elements in the Brasserie is based upon the critique of the meaning of the host building. Installation is used to contrast with the seriousness of the reputation of the Seagram. The exaggerated nature and illusory qualities of installation are an apposite gesture by the designers, while opening and plane are suitably theatrical tactics.

Case Study
Galleria Nazionale

Location: **Parma, Italy**
Former Function:
Palazzo Della Pilotta, Farnese Theatre
Built: **1583 to 18th century**
Previous Architect:
Ranuccio 1, Giovanni Battista Aleotti
Remodelled: **1987**
Architect: **Guido Canali**

Italy is renowned not just for its fabulous art treasures but also for the sophistication of the galleries designed to hold them. Many of the museums are in remodelled castles, palaces and monasteries, and the best exploit the power of the building to house treasures combined with drawing out the building's own treasure-like qualities. Guido Canali's remodelling of the Farnese Palace is a great example of this delicate balance.

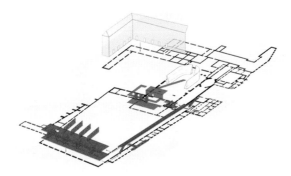

Fig.1. The museum is installed in the rambling palace complex

Analysis

The existing Palazzo della Pilotta buildings were extraordinarily complicated, being an amalgamation of different buildings, spaces, forms, styles, functions and eras. Ranuccio 1 constructed the first palace, situated by the river and in centre of the city, to house the Farnese family in1583 and the complex was altered and extended over hundreds of years until it also contained the small National Art Gallery of Parma, the Bodoni Museum of Printing, the National Museum of Antiquities, the Palatine Library and its most famous building, the fabulous Farnese Theatre. This magnificent Renaissance theatre was designed by Giovanni Battista Aleotti in the early 17th century and was constructed entirely of timber. The Palazzo was extensively damaged in the Second World War but was subsequently completely restored. The military occupied the north wing of the palace from 1843 until 1960.

The palace was composed of a number of different buildings or parts, each with their own particular characteristics. The theatre derived its plan from the classical world, a semi-circular rake of seating wrapped around the edge of the generous floor space, to leave an area in the centre where large performances could take place. The raised stage area was next to this and framed by a timber proscenium arch decorated with statues of the Farnese family. The stage contained a wonderfully carved fixed scene, and was enclosed by a tall tower that housed one of the first ever mechanical scene-shifting devices. This unusual space was a precursor to the flytower prevalent in many latter day theatres. The back stage area was a generously proportioned hall space with views out into the courtyard.

These were the largest covered areas in the palace but the rest of the building

Fig. 2. Using the Teatro Farnese as a starting point, the remodelling ingeniously directs the visitor through a succession of spectacular spaces, ultimately traversing the whole length of the building before finally bringing them back to the theatre again

allocated to the remodelling was of a very different character. On the west side of the Palazzo courtyard, an extremely long corridor, 8 m wide and over 100 m long, linked the theatre to the north wing. Its north–south axis ensured that it received sunlight most of the day. Originally designed as stables, the double height, very bright, north wing was where the military had been billeted. It was in a ruinous condition and in danger of collapsing at the beginning of the project. So the form of the original building was made up of a series of contrasting spaces. The ornate theatre, with its raked seating and curved stage scenery, the hall-like backstae area, the exceptionally long west wing and the bright high stable block or north wing. Other areas in the palace were not included as part of the project.

Fig. 3. The sculptures at the end of the long corridor signal the change in atmosphere from a dark enclosed space to an open bright one

Fig. 4. The long corridor linking the theatre with the old stable block has no natural light and the space is given rhythm by spotlights picking out the individual exhibits.

Installation

The strategic approach taken by Canali was to strip the building to its bare form, to remove any discordant additions and repair any damage caused by both the ravages of time and by the military. Wherever possible, original elements were preserved or revealed. He then installed a simple method of exhibiting the works of art and linking the disparate parts of the building together. This process took over ten years, allowing Canali time for an archaeological investigation of the buildings' structures and forms, and room to design the sensitive additions.

The long corridor was the key element in the remodelling and it served to link the theatre at the south end of the palace with the stable block at the north. Canali introduced a raised circulation system through this area and the uniformity of this connected the three disconnected spaces. A temporary exhibition was installed in the north wing, although it proved to be not that temporary as it is still there, and the theatre itself needed no attention as it was considered to be the exhibition.

Circulation was the controlling device throughout the building and all the exhibits are either seen from the imposed route or are attached to it. The journey begins at the main entrance to both the theatre and the museum. The visitor arrives at the grand staircase at the rear of the theatre and moves through the raked seating on an axis with the centre of the stage. The great space of the theatre, with the open trussed roof and the elaborately carved walls and stage, is extremely impressive and dramatic. A huge ramp protrudes into the open area in the centre of the great hall and invites the visitor up onto the stage. An ornate screen placed on axis at the back of the stage encourages the visitor to turn around and look again at the space from a different perspective.

Behind the screen the journey continues: a lightweight steel structure supports the rough wooden floor of a continuous walkway. This construction is held away from the original building and dictates the visitor's exact route. It glides through the back stage area and then bridges the gap to the west wing corridor. The length of the huge corridor is both accentuated and made less daunting by carefully positioned exhibits and the rhythm of the raised structure. An elevated collection of statues greets the visitor at the junction of the west and north wings, signalling the change of both direction and height. Huge screens hang from a complex grid of scaffolding filling the ceiling, but these are dwarfed by the enormous size of this hall. The system also holds the lights and other equipment, and natural light filters through it from skylights cut into the perimeter of the walls. The modern lightweight steel connecting walkway is quite different to the crumbling existing building. It is deliberately separated from the building, as are all the newly installed elements.

The installed walkway is not without a relationship to the existing building, because the size and shape of the structure changes depending upon which part of the building it is occupying. The steel footbridges have an ephemeral quality; they are not built to fit the space exactly but rather are liberally placed within it. It is almost as if the new elements could quite easily be removed without damaging or affecting the original building and this sense is reinforced by the fact that the system installed in the north wing is indeed temporary. Statues and other sculptures are displayed in packing cases, again a signal of impermanence. There is abundant space between the structure of the original building and the structure of the installation, and the contrast helps to heighten the awareness and appreciation of both.

Tactics

Movement is the most dominant characteristic of this installation. It connects the distant and different spaces together and establishes order in the complicated set of buildings, rooms and spaces. Objects provide key moments or reference points in this journey.

Movement

The whole of the museum is on or above the first floor level of the Palazzo and the sequence throughout the space is a journey of substantial intrigue and enjoyment. Canali strings together the series of disparate spaces and events to make a wonderful circulation sequence.

The raised footbridge is a refined steel structure whose dimensions alter depending upon the exact space that it occupies. The ramp placed on axis from the theatre floor to the stage is plain, with an open balustrade and panelled floor. Within the backstage area, Canali alludes to the lost machinery of the old fly tower. The structure is much more complex: long vertical double columns support a tensile structure, which in turn support the rough wide oak planks of the floor. Substantial vertical panels define the positions of the sculptures, which are actually displayed in crates.

A large triangular truss supports the bridge between this space and the west wing, where the structure is slightly different again. The double handrail accentuates the length and the divide or gap between it and the walls of the building. The atmosphere is very different to the main hall and theatre space, being dark and lit only with artificial light. No natural light is allowed into the corridor as the solar gain would make the space unbearable and damage the displayed art works. The walkway opens up to encompass almost the whole width of the floor in the north wing, although it is still raised from the ground. The visitor is returned to the entrance via the same route but at a different level, the west wing corridor being double height.

The walkway, while imposing order, offers the contradiction of restricting movement while exposing a huge space; exactly where visitors go and what they see is very prescribed.

Fig. 5 The elevated
corridor behind the
stage has a rhythm and
nature that is unrelated
to the host building

Object

Carefully placed objects can provide
reference points from which the visitors can
orientate themselves. Strategically
positioned sculptures offer both beauty and
surprise. A row of four big statues sit on
a steel beam at the junction of the long
corridor and the north wing. They are highly
illuminated by the strong natural sidelight
and act as a denouement to the story of the
long artificially-lit corridor space. The statues
signal the change from one condition to
another, and the surprise is upon actually
encountering them.

The sculptures are gradually revealed
during the journey along the corridor and
appear to be at the same level as the visitor,
but as they are approached, it becomes clear
that they are floating high up in the space of
the old stable block, precariously balanced
on a thin steel beam with an enormous void
below. The eye moves from the statues to
the vastness of the space. The position acts
a pivot, signalling the change from one
space to another.

Canali carefully and devotedly restored the
existing building and then installed a series
of elevated walkways and display systems
that are completely detached from the
original. The modern and the ancient exist
together in great harmony; the language of
each is radically different yet neither
overpowers the other.

Introduction

1 Benedict Zucchi,
Giancarlo de Carlo,
(interview), pp. 167.

2 Christine Boyer, *The City
of Collective
Memory,* pp. 322.

Analysis

1 Rodolfo Machado,
'Old Buildings
as Palimpsest',
Progressive Architecture,
Nov 1976.

2 Robert Bevan,
'Slim Volume',
Building Design,
4 June 1999.

3 Max Risselada,
*Raumplan versus Plan
Libre*, 1988, pp. 145.

4 Rosamund Diamond
and Wilfred Wang,
'9H: No 9 On Continuity',
1985, pp. 61.

5 Nigel Hetherington,
Architecture Today,
119, pp. 25.

6 *ibid.*, pp. 26.

7 Brendan Macfarlane,
Architectural Record,
Sept 2000, pp. 128.

8 Peter Blundell Jones,
'Masters of Building,
Eric Gunnar Asplund',
Architects' Journal,
pp. 96.

9 Lance Routh, Union
North, *Architects'
Journal,* 7 March 2002,
pp. 22.

10 Walter Benjamin, quoted
in Beatriz Colomina,
Privacy and Publicity,
pp. 233.

11 Sergio Los, *Carlo
Scarpa, An Architectural
Guide*, 1995, pp. 54.

12 AA Files 32.

13 Mohson Mostafavi and
David Leatherbarrow,
*On Weathering:
the Life of Buildings in
Time,* 1993, pp. 6.

14 Henri Ciriani, quoted in
Architectural Review,
Jan 1993 No 1151, pp.65.

15 Dominic Williams,
Architecture Today,
Oct. 2002 No 132,
pp. 68.

16 Rita Cappezutto,
'Confronting the
Architecture
of Evil', *Domus* 847,
April 2002.

17 Joshua Wright, Shed 54,
Building Design,
20 Oct 2000.

18 Gordon Cullen, *Concise
Townscape,* 1961, pp.10.

19 *Ibid.*

20 Colin Rowe and Fred
Koetter, *Collage City,*
1978, pp. 121.

21 Robert Irwin, 'Being and
Circumstance:
Notes Towards a
Confidential Art', in
Kritstine Stiles and Peter
Sels (eds.), *Theories and
Documents of
Contemporary Art,* 1996.

22 *ibid.*

23 Gilberto Botti, 'The
Bishop's Architect:
Karl-Josef Schattner at
Eichstatt', *Lotus* 46, 1985.

24 Peter Buchanan,
Architectural Review,
Nov 1985, pp.43.

25 *Giancarlo De Carlo –
Urbino. The History of a
City and Plans for its
Development*, 1970.
Cited in Bendict Zucchi,
Giancarlo De Carlo,
pp. 45.

26 Interview with Pierluigi
Nicolin, *Lotus,* 1978,
pp.10. Cited in Zucchi,
Giancarlo De Carlo,
pp. 47.

27 Sheila O'Donnell:
conversation with Sally
Stone, April 2003.

28 Machado, *op. cit.,* 1976.

29 Roger Mann, *Frame,*
Mar/April 2001, pp. 68.

Strategy

1 John Kurtich and Garret
Eakin, *Interior
Architecture,* 1993,
pp. 26.

2 Rowan Moore and
Raymond Ryan, *Building
the Tate Modern,* 2000,
pp. 125.

3 Kenneth Powell,
Architecture Reborn.

4 'Installation Art',
Art and Design no 30,
1993, pp. 41.

5 *ibid.*

6 Frederick Fisher,
Blueprint, Dec 1997,
pp. 30.

7 Francine Houben,
Composition, C*ontrast,
Complexity,* 2001,
pp. 104.

8 Tomáš Valena, *Jože
Plečnik, an Architect of
Prague Castle*,
pp. 270.

9 John Hejduk, in Kim
Shkapich (ed.) *Josef P.
Kleihues, The Museum
Projects*, pp. 37.

10 *ibid.*

11 *ibid.*

12 Martin Pawley, 'Bridging
the gap (Sackler
Galleries, London)'
*Perspectives on
Architecture*, June 1994,
pp. 19.

13 Rowan Moore, 'Sackler
Galleries Royal
Academy London
Architects Foster
Associates', *Blueprint
Extra,* April 1992, pp. 9.

14 Joseph Fuses and Maria
Viader, 'The Strength of
Simplicity', *Architecture
and Urbanism,*
Feb 1997.

15 *ibid.*

16 Amanda Birch, *Building
Design,*
5 May 2000, pp. 20.

17 Dennis L. Dollens,
El Croquis 47, 1991,
pp. 85.

18 Ada Toller, *Blueprint,*
May 2002, pp. 96.

Tactics

1 Marco Frascari, 'The
Tell-the-Tale-Detail', in
Kate Nesbitt (ed.),
*Theorizing a New
Agenda for
Architecture*, 1996,
pp. 450.

2 Umberto Riva, *Abitare,*
Sept 1993, pp. 236.

3 Rob Krier, *Architectural
Composition*, 1988.

4 Eric van Egeraat,
'Architecture of
Contemptation and
Solace', *Architecture
and Urbanism,* 325 No
10, Oct 1997, pp. 48.

5 David Watkin,
*A History of Western
Architecture,* 2000,
pp. 391.

6 Jan Tabor,
'The Propeller Image',
Frame,
Jan/Feb 2003.

7 Mackay Hugh Baillie
Scott, in Kurtich and
Eakin, *Interior
Architecture,* 1993,
pp. 305.

8 Kevin Lynch, *The Image
of the City,* 1960.

9 Stanley Abercrombie,
*A Philosophy
of Interior Design,* 1990.

10 Frederick Hart, *History
of Italian Renaissance
Art,* pp. 397.

11 Robert Mugerauer.
'Derrida and Beyond',
in Kate Nesbitt (ed.)
*Theorizing a New
Agenda for
Architecture,* 1996,
pp. 190.

12 James Turrell,
'Installation Art', *Art and
Design
No 30*, 1993, pp. 43.

13 James Turrell, *Mapping
Spaces,* 1987.
Reproduced in *Theories
and Documents
of Contemporary Art*,
pp. 574.

14 Rogier Van Der Heide,
Architectural Record,
Jan 2001, pp. 66.

15 Matthias Sauerbruch,
Architectural Record,
Sept 2000.

16 Louisa Hutton, in *Frame*
18, 2000,
pp. 52.

17 John Kurtich and Garret
Eakin,
Interior Architecture,
pp. 171.

18 Layla Dawson,
Architectural Review,
April 1994,
pp. 25.

19 Marcus Field,
'A dramatically different
theatre', *Independent on
Sunday,* 13 Feb 2000,
Sunday Review,
pp. 12.

20 Steve Tompkins,
Blueprint, March 2000,
pp. 46.

21 Beatriz Colomina,
Privacy and Publicity,
pp. 28.

22 Adolf Loos, quoted in
ibid., pp. 297.

23 *El Croquis* 78, 'Steven
Holl 1986-1996', pp. 132.

24 Elizabeth Diller and
Ricardo Scofidio, *Flesh,*
1994 pp. 163.

25 Robin Evans, 'Figures,
Doors and Passages.'
*Translation from
Drawing to Building and
Other Essays,*
pp. 78.

26 Geoffrey H. Baker,
*Le Corbusier:
an Analysis of Form,*
1984, pp. 260.

Case Studies

1 Francesco Dal Co and
Giuseppe Mazzariol,
Carlo Scarpa,
pp. 287.

2 Ignase De Sola Morales,
'From Contrast to
Analogy', *Lotus* 46, 1985,
pp. 42.

3 *Op. cit.,* Francesco
Dal Co, pp. 198.

4 Sverre Fehn, quoted in
Leif Knutsen,
The Museum Guide, 16
July 1986.

5 www.pritzkerprize.com

6 Nicola Turner,
'Gin Palace', *World
Architecture* 88,
July/Aug 2000.

Books

Aben, Rob and
de Wit, Saskia,
The Enclosed Garden,
010 Publishers (1999).
ISBN 9 06450 349 4

Abercrombie, Stanley,
*A Philosophy of Interior
Design*,
Harper & Row (1990).
ISBN 0 06430 296 2

Atlee, James and
Le Feuvre, Lisa,
Gordon Matta-Clark:
The Space Between,
Nazraeli Press (2003).
ISBN 1 59005 049 5

Baal-Teshuva, Jacob,
*Christo and Jeanne-Claude
/ Wrapped Reichstag
Berlin 1971-1995*, Taschen.
ISBN 3 82289 268 8

Baker, Geoffrey H.,
*Le Corbusier:
an Analysis of Form*,
Van Nostrand Reinhold
(UK) (1984).
ISBN 0 44230 556 7

Bezombes, Dominique,
*La Grande Galerie Du
Museum – National
d'Histoire Naturelle*:
*Conserver C'est
Transformer*,
Le Moniteur Publications
(1994).
ISBN 2 28119 082 X

Blundell Jones, Peter,
Dialogues in Time: *New
Graz Architecture*, Haus
Der Architektur (1998).
ISBN. 3 90117 436 2

Boucher, Bruce, *Andrea
Palladio*: *The Architect
In His Time*,
Abbeville Press (1998).
ISBN 0 78920 416 9

Boyer, M Christine, *The
City of Collective Memory*:
*Its Historical Imagery and
Architectural
Entertainments*,
MIT Press(1994).
ISBN 0 26252 211 X

Brace-Taylor, Brian,
Pierre Chareau,
Taschen (1998).
ISBN 3 82287 887 1

Buzas, Stefan and
Menges, Axel (eds.),
*Sir John Soane's
Museum*, *London*,
Wasmuth (1994).
ISBN 3 80302 714 4

Buzas, Stefan and Carmel-
Arthur, Judith,
*Carlo Scarpa, Museo
Cannoviano*, *Possagno*,
Edition Axel Menges
(2002).
ISBN 3 93069 822 6

Caldenby, Claes and
Hultin, Olof, *Asplund*,
Gingko Press Inc. (1997).
ISBN 3 92725 851 2

Catacuzino, Sherban,
*ReArchitecture – Old
Buildings New Uses*,
Thames and Hudson
(1989).
ISBN 0 50034 108 7

Colomina, Beatriz, *Privacy
and Publicity: Modern
Architecture as Mass
Media*, MIT Press (1996).
ISBN 0 26253 139 9

Cook, Peter and Rand,
George, *Morphosis*:
Buildings & Projects,
Rizzoli (1989).
ISBN 0 84781 030 5

Cullen, Gordon, *Concise
Townscape*,
Architectural Press (1961).
ISBN 0 75062 018 8

Curtis, William, J. R.
*Modern Architecture
since 1900*,
Phaidon, 3rd edn (1996).
ISBN 0 71483 524 2

Dal Co, Francesco and
Mazzariol, Giuseppe,
*Carlo Scarpa:
The Complete Works*,
Electa Editrice/Rizzolli
(1984)
ISBN 0 84780 686 3

Diamond, Rosamund and
Wang, Wilfried, *9H: No 9
On Continuity*,
Chronicle Books (1995).
ISBN 1 56898 028 0

Diller, Elizabeth and
Scofidio, Ricardo, *Flesh –
architectural probes*,
Triangle Architectural
Publishing (1994).
ISBN 1 87182 504 0

Evans, Robin, *Translation
from Drawing to Building
and Other Essays*,
Architectural Association
London (1997).

Ferguson, Russell,
Robert Irwin,
Rizzoli (1993).
ISBN 0 84781 770 9

Fisher, Frederick, *Frederick
Fisher Architects*,
Rizzoli (1995).
ISBN 0 84781 864 0

Gregotti, Vittorio, *Inside
Architecture*,
MIT Press (1996).
ISBN 0 26257 115 3

Harvey, David,
*The Condition of
Postmodernity*,
Blackwell (1990).
ISBN 0 63162 294 1

Hausler, Wolfgang (ed.),
*James Turrell: Lighting
a Planet*,
Hatje Cantz Verlag (2000).
ISBN 3 77579 052 7

Honnef, Klaus, (ed.),
*Bunker – Erasmus
Schroter Photography*,
Ubs Verlag Der Kunst
(1996).
ISBN 9 05705 025 0

Houben,
Francine / Mecanoo
Architects, *Composition,
Contrast, Complexity*,
Birkhauser (2001).
ISBN 3 76436 452 1

Johnston, Pamela (ed.),
Off the Shelf,
AA publications (2001).
ISBN 1 90290 221 1

Joselit, David, Simon,
Joan and Salecl, Renata,
Jenny Holzer,
Phaidon (1998).
ISBN 0 71483 754 7

Krečic, Pĕter, *Plečnik
The Complete Works*,
Academy Editions (1993).
ISBN 1 85490 290 3

Krier, Rob, *Architectural
Composition*,
Academy Editions (1988).
ISBN 0 85670 803 8

Kurtich, John and
Eakin, Garret,
Interior Architecture,
Van Nostrand Reinhold
(1993).
ISBN 0 44224 669 2

Lambot, Ian (ed.),
*Norman Foster
– Foster Associates*:
*Buildings and Projects
Volume 4 1982-1989*,
Birkhauser/Watermark
(1989).
ISBN 3 76435 428 3

Lingwood, James (ed.),
Rachel Whiteread: House,
Phaidon (1995).
ISBN 0 71483 459 9

Los, Sergio, *Carlo Scarpa:
an Architectural Guide*,
Arsenale Editrice srl
(1995).
ISBN 8 87743 144 X

LOT/EK, *Urban Scan*,
Laurence King (2002).
ISBN 1 85669 307 4

Lyall, Sutherland,
*Imagination Headquarters
– Herron Associates*,
Phaidon Press Ltd (1992).
ISBN 0 71482 764 9

Lynch, Kevin, *The Image
of the City*, Harvard
University Press (1960).
ISBN 0 26212 004 6

Mastropietro, Mario (ed),
*Restoration and Beyond
Architecture from
conservation to
conversion. Projects and
Works by Andrea Bruno
(1960-1995)*,
Edizioni Lybra
Immagine(1996).

Moore, Rowan (ed.),
*Vertigo: The Strange
New World of the
Contemporary City*,
Laurence King (1999).
ISBN 1 85669 153 5

Moore, Rowan and Ryan,
Raymund, *Building the
Tate Modern*,
Tate Publishing (2000).
ISBN 1 8437 331 5

Mostafavi, Mohson and
Leatherbarrow, David,
*On Weathering: the Life of
Buildings in Time*,
MIT Press (1993).
ISBN 0 26263 144 X

Nesbitt, Kate (ed.),
*Theorizing a New Agenda
for Architecture: An
Anthology of Architectural
Theory 1965-1995*,
Princeton Architectural
Press (1996).
ISBN 1 56898 054 X

Newhouse, Victoria,
Towards a new Museum,
The Monacelli Press(1998).
ISBN 1 88525 460 1

Norri, Marja-Riitta and
Karkkainen, Maija (eds.),
*Sverre Fehn: The Poetry of
the Straight Line*,
published in conjunction
with the exhibition
'5 Masters of the North'
(1992).
ISBN 9 51922 973 6

O'Donnell and Tuomey,
*Buildings and Projects
1981-1988*,
Gandon Editions (1988).
ISBN 0 94664 104 8

O'Regan, John (ed.),
O'Donnell + Tuomey,
Gandon Editions (1997).
ISBN 0 94664 198 6

Olsberg, Nicholas (ed.)
Carlo Scarpa Intervening with History, Canadian Centre for Architecture and Monacelli Press in conjunction with the exhibition (1999).
ISBN 0 92078 561 1 (CCA)
ISBN 1 58093 035 2 (Monacelli)

Pellegrini, Di Pietro Carlo,
Il Museo della Cattedrale di Lucca, Umberto Allemandi (1995).
ISBN 8 84220 570 2

Powell, Kenneth,
Architecture Reborn,
Laurence King (1999).
ISBN 1 85669 129 2

Rajchman, John,
Constructions,
MIT Press (1998).
ISBN 0 26268 096 3

Ranalli, George,
George Ranalli Buildings and Projects,
Princeton Architectural Press (1988).
ISBN 0 91041 342 8

Risselada, Max (ed.),
Raumplan versus Plan Libre.
Rizzoli (1988).
ISBN 0 84781 000 3

Robert, Philippe,
Adaptations: New Uses for Old Buildings,
Princeton Architectural Press (1989).
ISBN 0 91041 373 8

Rodermond, Janny (ed.),
Fresh Facts: The Best Buildings By Young Architects in the Netherlands,
NAI Publishers (2002).
ISBN 9 05662 277 3

Rowe, Colin and Koetter, Fred, *Collage City*,
MIT Press (1978).
ISBN 0 26218 086 3

Schittich, Christian (ed.),
In Detail. Interior Spaces. Space. Light. Materials,
Birkhauser in co-operation with *Detail Magazine* (2002).
ISBN 3 76436 630 3

Shkapich, Kim (ed.),
Josef P. Klelhues,
The Museum Projects,
Rizzoli Publications (1989).
ISBN 0 84781 151 4

Stiles, Kristine and Selz, Peter, *Theories and Documents of Contemporary Art*,
University of California Press (1996).
ISBN 0 52020 253 8

Sussman, Elizabeth (ed.),
On the passage of a few people through a rather brief moment in time: The Situationist International 1957-1972,
MIT Press.
ISBN 0 26223 146 8

Various Contributors,
Old and New Architecture: Design Relationship,
The Preservation Press (1980).
ISBN 0 89133 076 3

Watkin, David, *A History of Western Architecture*,
Laurence King (2000).
ISBN 1 85669 223 X

Zdeněk Lukeš, Damjan Prelovšek, Miroslav Řepa, Tomáš Valena (eds.), *Josip Plečnik – An Architect of Prague Castle*, Prague Castle Administration.
ISBN 8 09020 515 1

Zucchi, Benedict,
Giancarlo De Carlo,
Butterworth Architecture (1992).
ISBN 0 75061 275 4

Periodicals

Art and Design Profile no 30, (ed. Andrew Benjamin) 'Installation Art' (1993).
ISBN 1 85490 213 X

Art and Design Profile no 20, (ed. Dr Andreas C. Papadakis), 'Art and the Tectonic' (1990).
ISBN 0 31205 563 3

El Croquis 47,
Architekturburo
Bolles I Wilson.
ISSN 0212 5683

El Croquis 62/63, 'Spanish Architecture 1993'.
ISSN 0212 5683

El Croquis 67,
Bolles+Wilson 1990-1994.
ISSN 0212 5683

El Croquis 78, 'Steven Holl 1986-1996'.
ISSN 0212 5683

Prototype 006, Dec 2001, stereomatrix, Lisbon.
ISSN 0874 4513

Articles

Bellosillo, Javier,
'Restoration and Conversion of the Monastery of Santa Maria La Real, Najera',
Domus 697,
Septr 1988.

Botti, Gillberto, 'The Bishop's Architect – Karl-Josef Schattner at Eichstatt', *Lotus* 46 (1985).

Brace-Taylor, Brian,
'The House of the Century',
Blueprint Magazine,
Nov 1993.

Buxton, Pamela,
'Court in the Act',
Blueprint Magazine,
March 2000.

Cappezzutto, Rita,
'Confronting the Architecture of Evil',
Domus 847, April 2002.

De Sola-Morales, Ignasi,
'From Contrast To Analogy – Developments in the Concept of Architectural Intervention',
Lotus 46 (1985).

Downey, Clare,
'Reinventing the Pompidou Centre,
Architectural Record,
Septr 2000.

Egeraat, Eric van,
'Architecture of Temptation and Solace',
Architecture and Urbanism 325, No 10,
Oct 1997.

Field, Marcus,
'A Dramatically Different Theatre', *Independent on Sunday*, Sunday Review,
p.12, 13 Feb 2000.

Fuses, Josep and Viader, Joan Maria, 'The Strength of Simplicity', *Architecture and Urbanism* 317,
Feb 1997.

Hart, Sara, 'Lighting & Building Technology combine to make a perfect match', *Architectural Record,* Jan 2001.

Long, Kieran, 'A bit of Rough', *Building Design*,
20 Octr 2000.

Machado, Rodolfo, 'Old Buildings as Palimpsest – Toward a Theory of Remodelling', *Progressive Architecture*, Novr 1976.

McKean, John, 'Space and Society', *Architects' Journal* no 6 vol217,
13 Feb 2003.

Meade, Martin, 'War Memorial', *Architectural Review* No 1151, Jan 1993.

Mecozzi, Daniela,
'Fear of the Future', *Frame*,
19 Mar/April 2001.

Moore, Rowan, 'Sackler Galleries Royal Academy London Architects Foster Associates',
Blueprint Extra 04,
1992.
ISBN 1 87423 504 X

Mulhearn, Deborah, 'Club Class', *Architects' Journal*,
7 Mar 2002.

Pendleton, Kate,
'Free Forms in Faversham',
Architecture Today 119,
June 2001.

Philips, Alan,
'Tyneside Renaissance: The Baltic Art Factory',
Architecture Today 132,
Oct 2002.

Raggi, Franco,
'From Space to Décor',
Abitare 318, May 1993.

Riva, Umberto,
'On Interior Design',
Abitare,
Septr 1993.

Romanelli, Marco,
'On Interior Design',
Abitare, April 1995.

Ryan, Zoe. 'Container Culture', *Blueprint* 195,
May 2002.

Scott, Chris,
'Colour the World',
Frame 18,
Jan/Feb 2001.

Turner, Nicola,
'Gin Palace', *World Architecture* 88,
July/Augt 2000.

Weathersby Jr., William,
'Zumtobel Staff Showroom', *Architectural Record,* Sept 2000.

Picture Credits